MW01633653

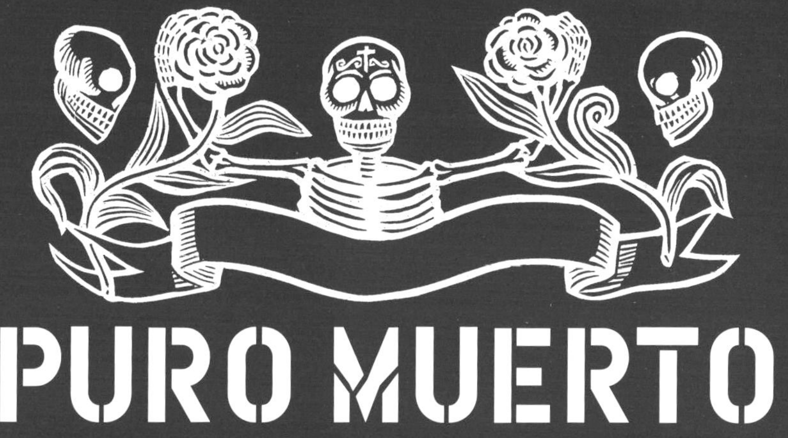

PURO MUERTO

◆ Artemio Rodriguez *Life is Fragil*
◆◆ Jorge Orozco *Esai*

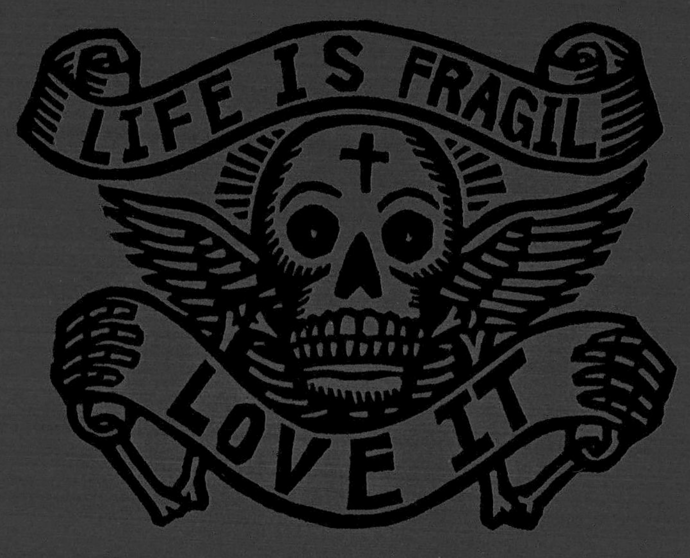
LIFE IS FRAGIL
LOVE IT

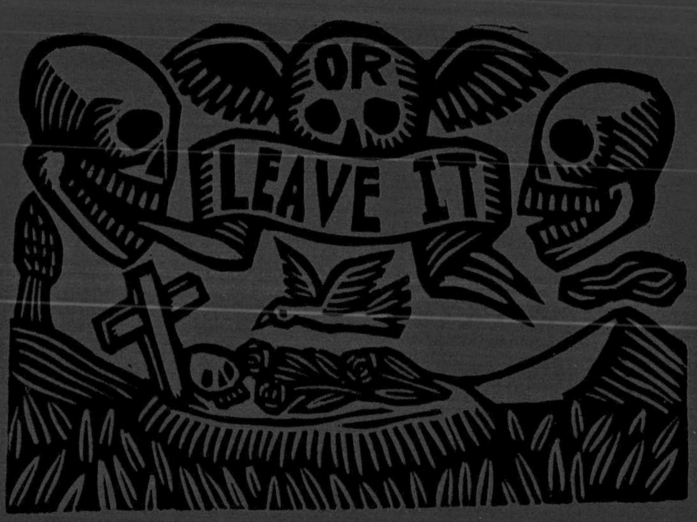
OR
LEAVE IT

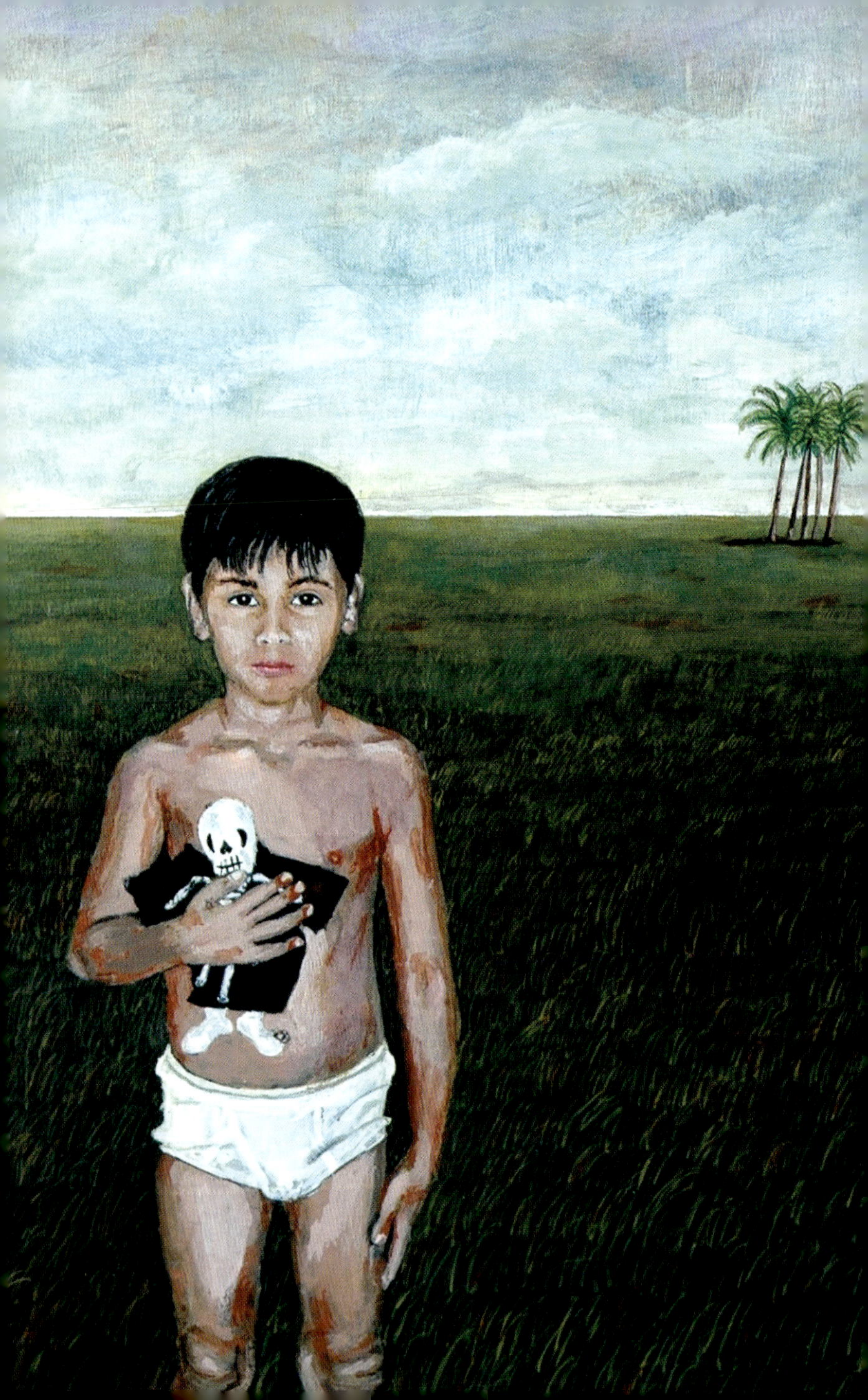

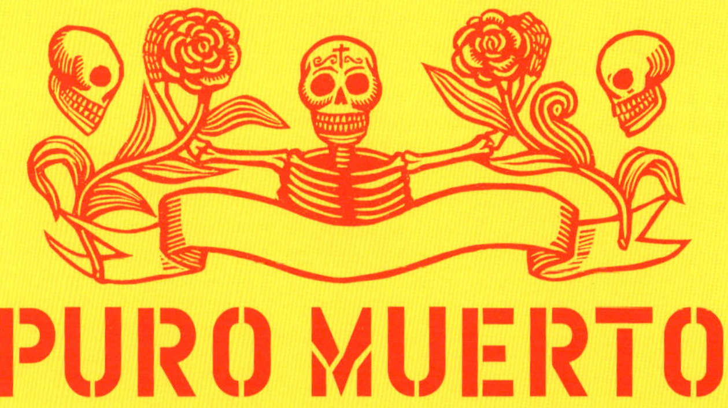

PURO MUERTO

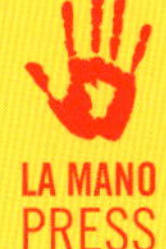

LA MANO
PRESS

LOVE

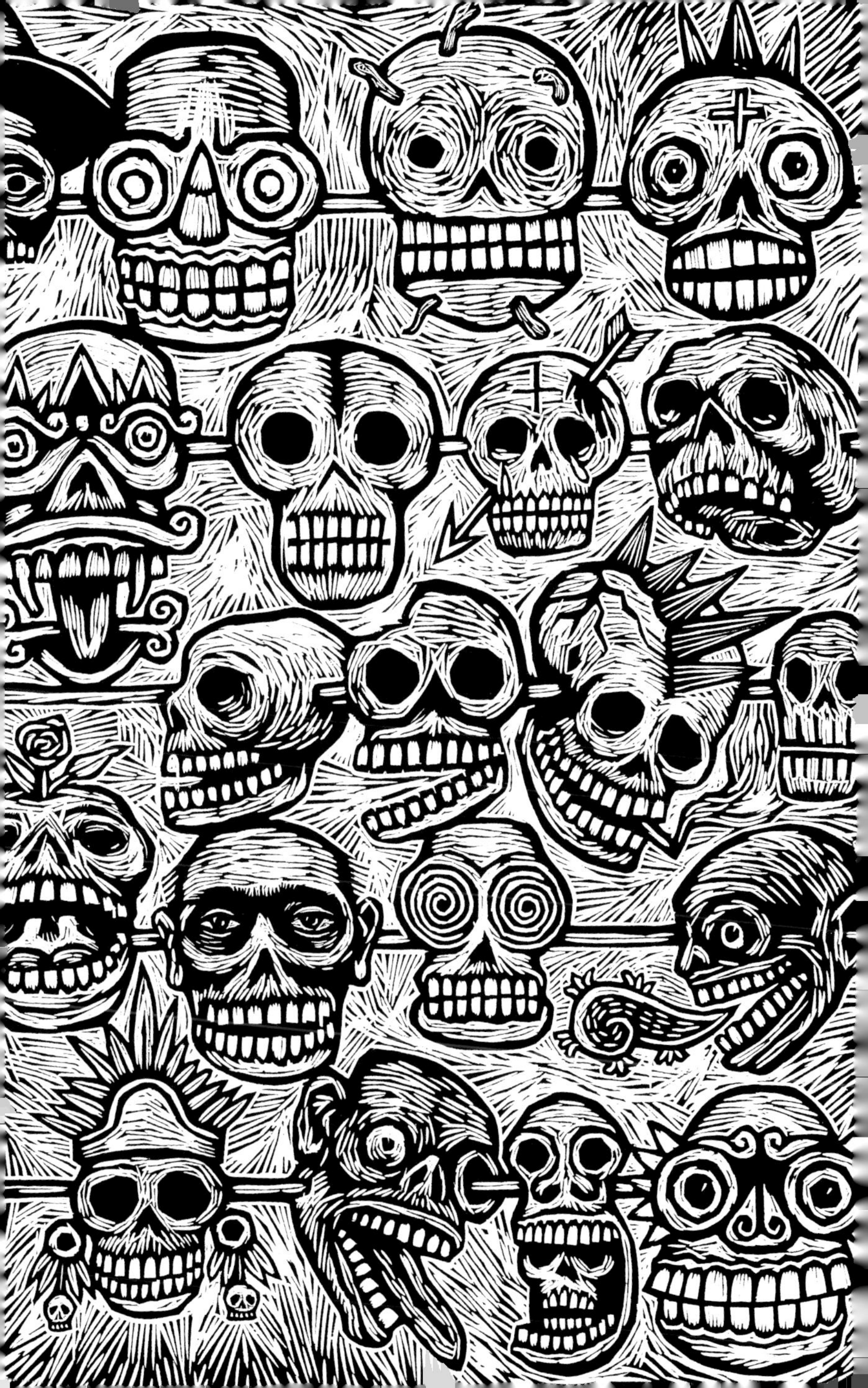

Cover & backcover: **Artemio Rodríguez**

Puro Muerto
First edition

Printed in China

ISBN 0-9724735-2-1

Acknowledgements & Credits
The publishers wish to thank the copyright holders who greatly assisted in this publication. Every effort was made to identify and contact individual copyright holders; omissions are unintentional.

Graphic Design
Silvia Capistrán
Artemio Rodríguez

Inquire about the art in this book and upcoming publications at **www.lamanopress.com**

◆◆ Artemio Rodríguez *Zompantli*
◆ Norma Pons *La muerte paseando*

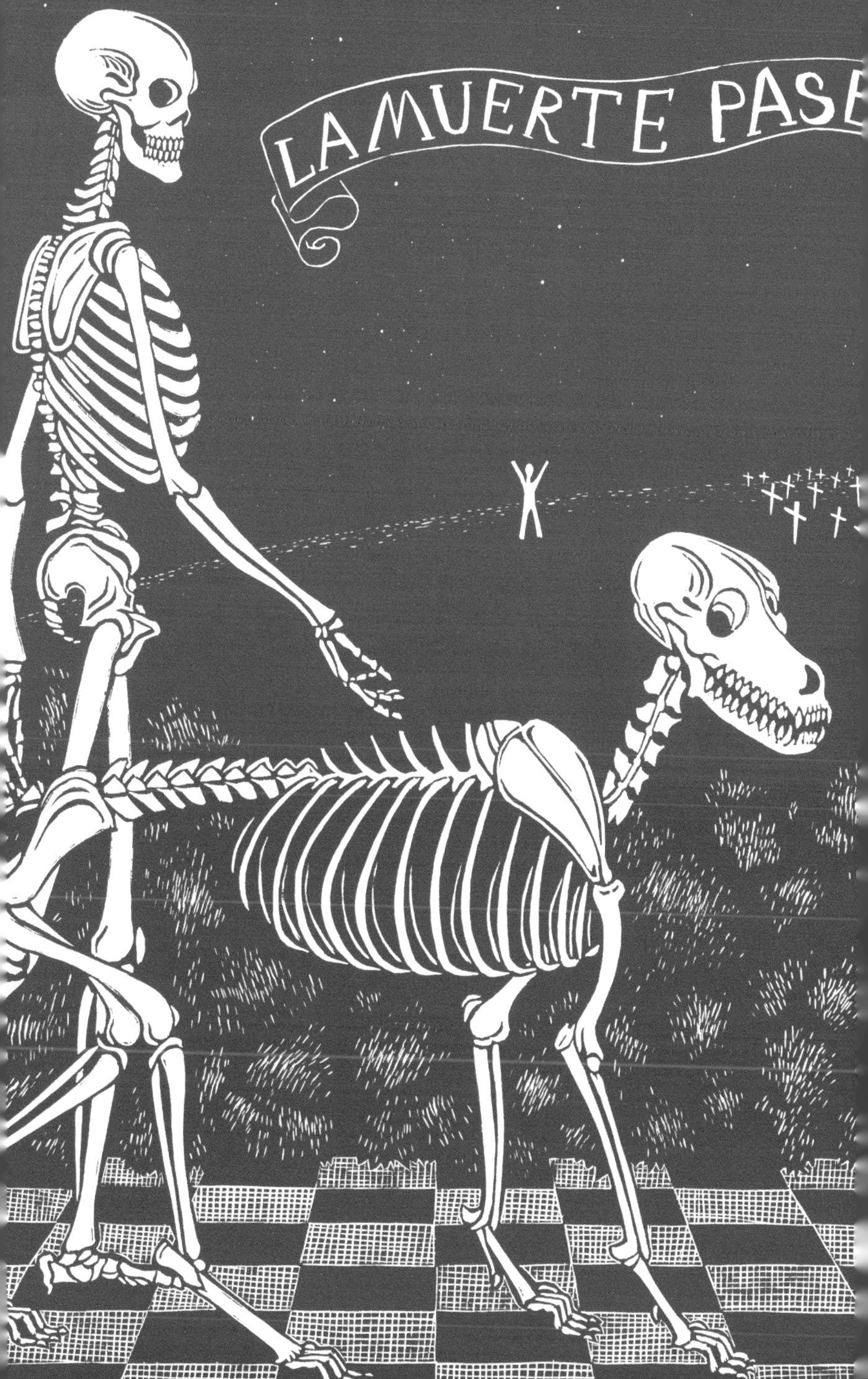
LA MUERTE PASE

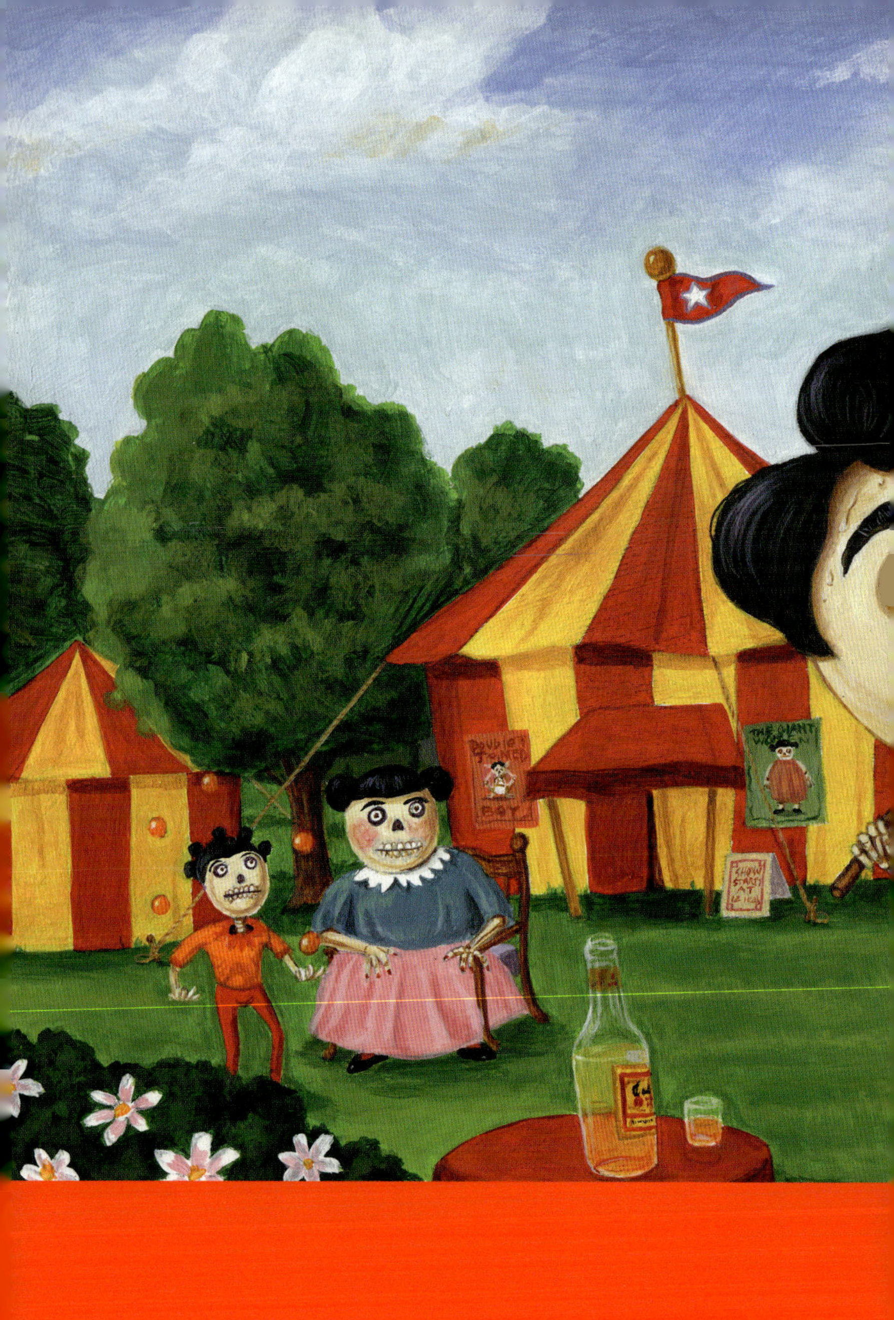
BOY
SHOW STARTS AT

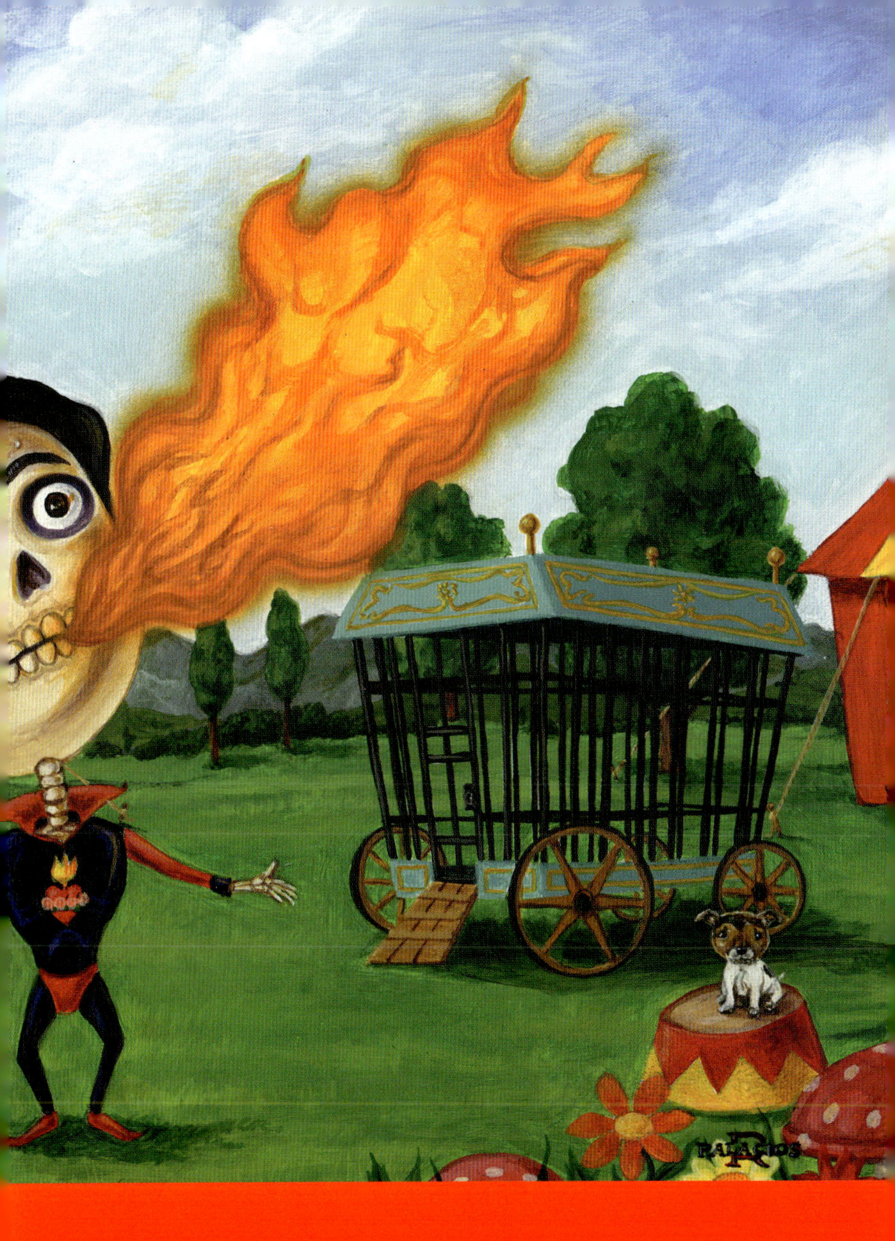

◆ Robert Palacios *El circo*

◆◆ José Guadalupe Posada *Vendedores de periódicos*

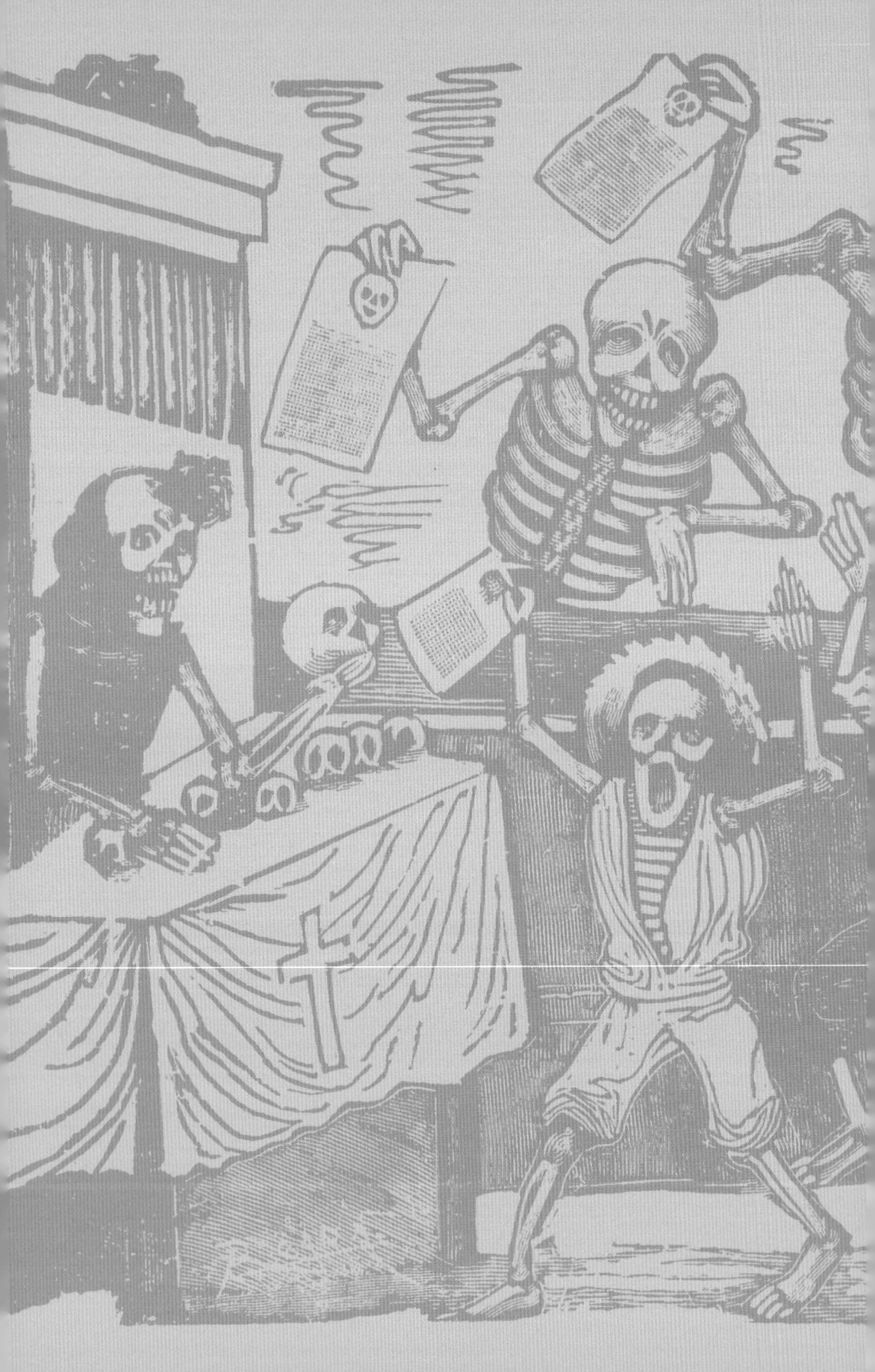

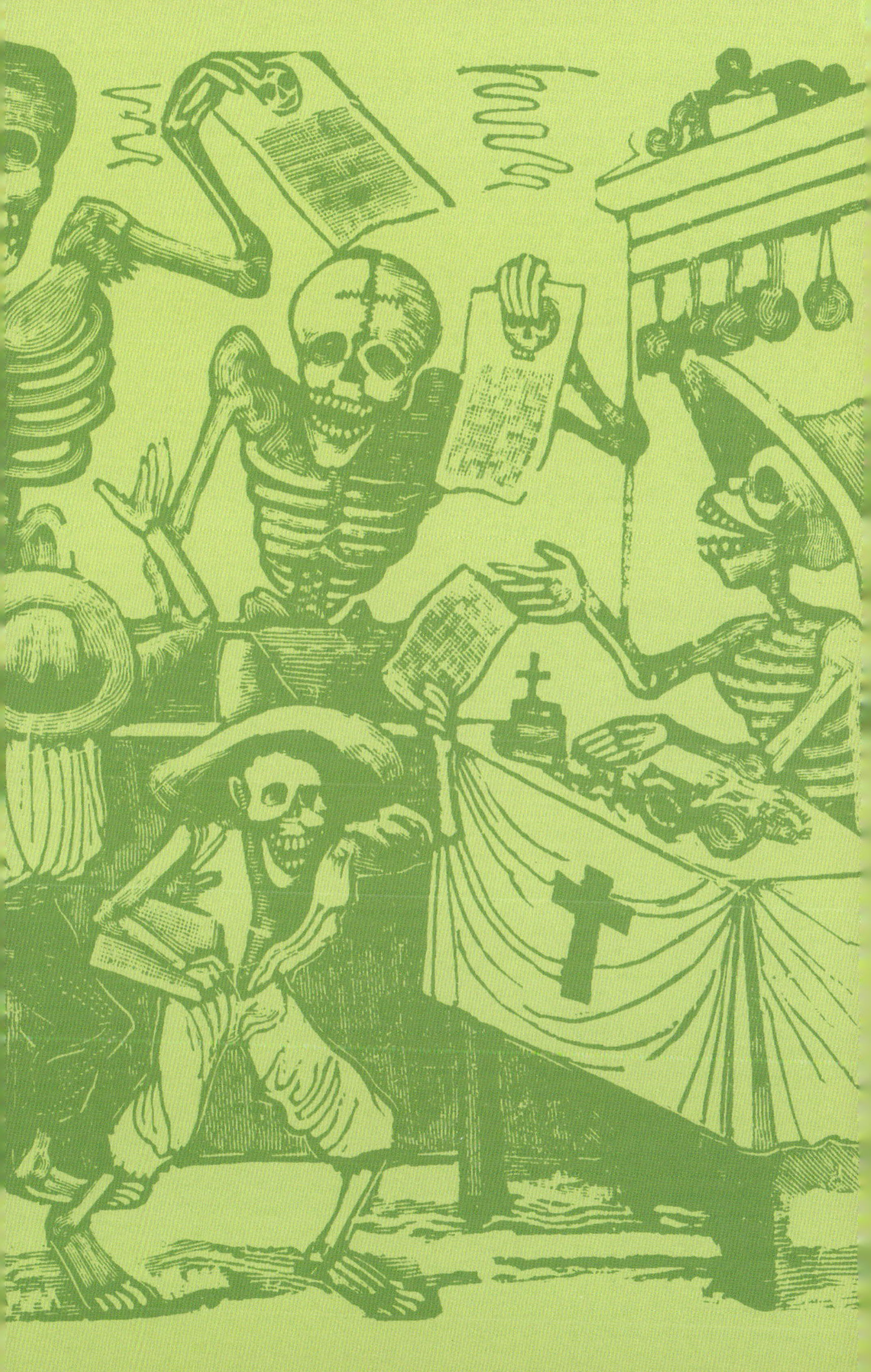

PARTICIPATING ARTISTS (ARTISTAS PARTICIPANTES)

La Mano Press

Wishes to thank the artists who submitted work for this humble book.

Agradece a los artistas por permitirnos usar su obra en este humilde libro.

Including | Incluyendo

MANUEL MANILLA

JOSÉ GUADALUPE POSADA

◆ José Guadalupe Posada *Calavera del siglo xx*
◆◆ Artemio Rodríguez *Fine Art*

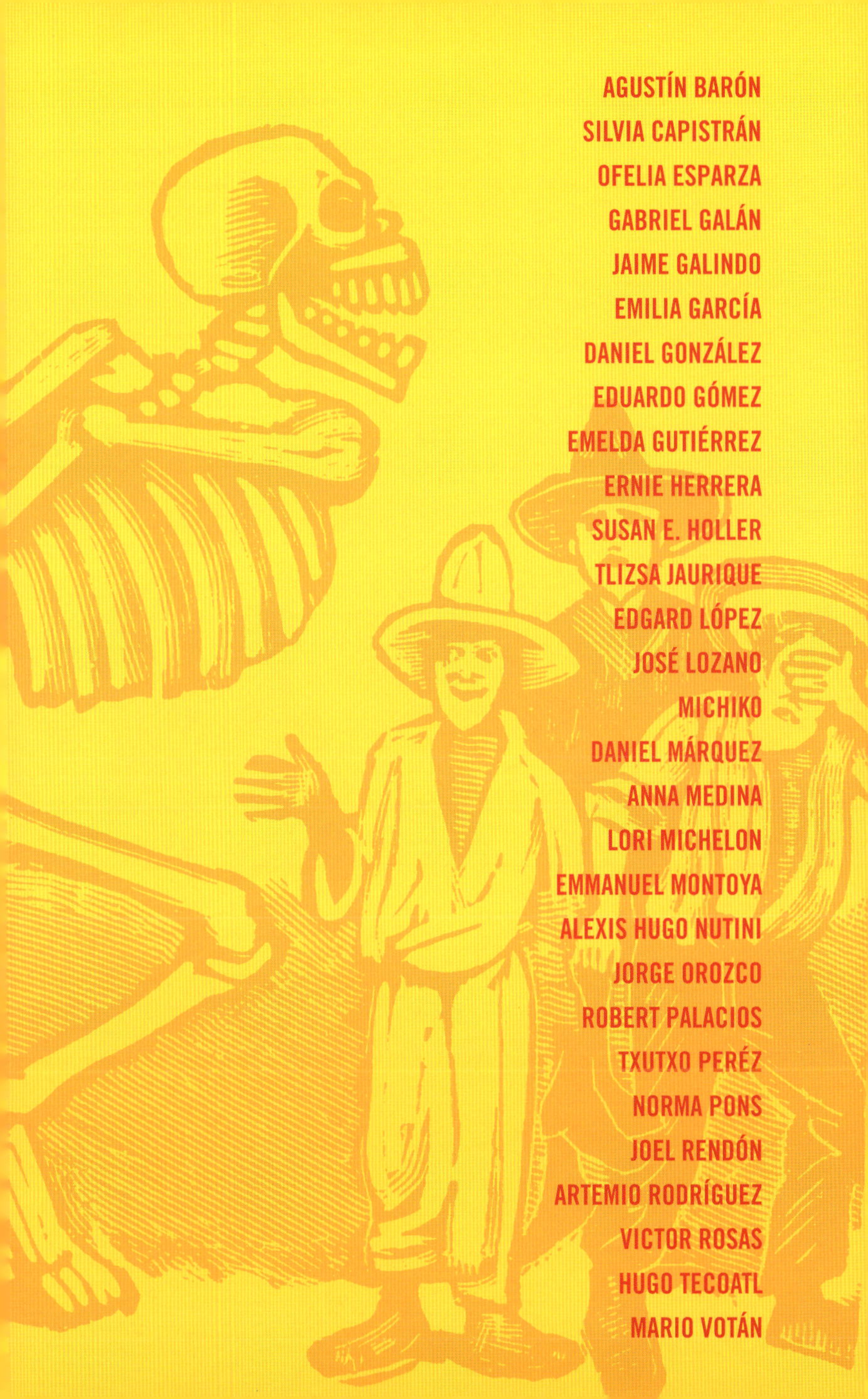

AGUSTÍN BARÓN
SILVIA CAPISTRÁN
OFELIA ESPARZA
GABRIEL GALÁN
JAIME GALINDO
EMILIA GARCÍA
DANIEL GONZÁLEZ
EDUARDO GÓMEZ
EMELDA GUTIÉRREZ
ERNIE HERRERA
SUSAN E. HOLLER
TLIZSA JAURIQUE
EDGARD LÓPEZ
JOSÉ LOZANO
MICHIKO
DANIEL MÁRQUEZ
ANNA MEDINA
LORI MICHELON
EMMANUEL MONTOYA
ALEXIS HUGO NUTINI
JORGE OROZCO
ROBERT PALACIOS
TXUTXO PERÉZ
NORMA PONS
JOEL RENDÓN
ARTEMIO RODRÍGUEZ
VICTOR ROSAS
HUGO TECOATL
MARIO VOTÁN

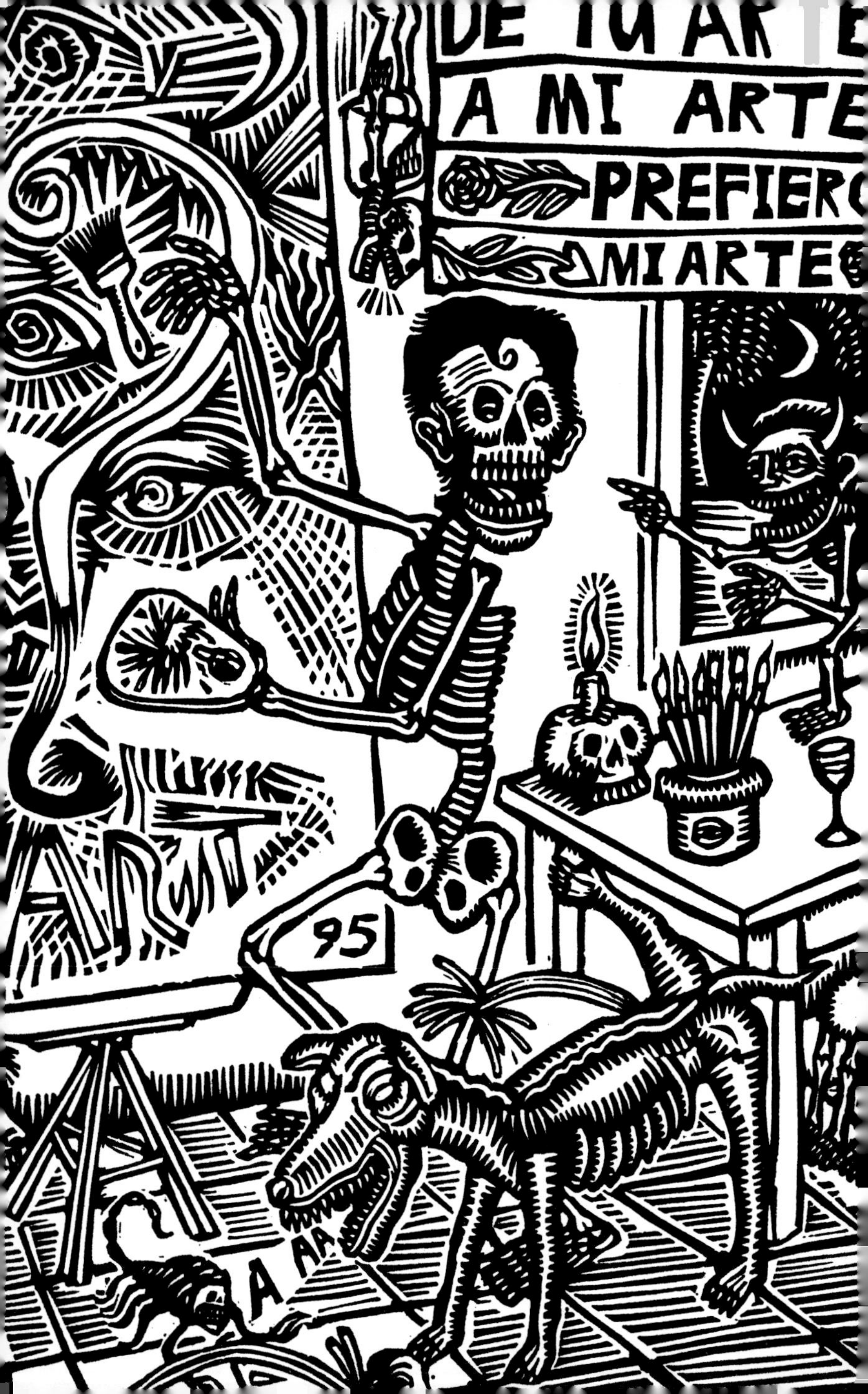

DE
A MI ARTE
PREFIER
MI ARTE
95

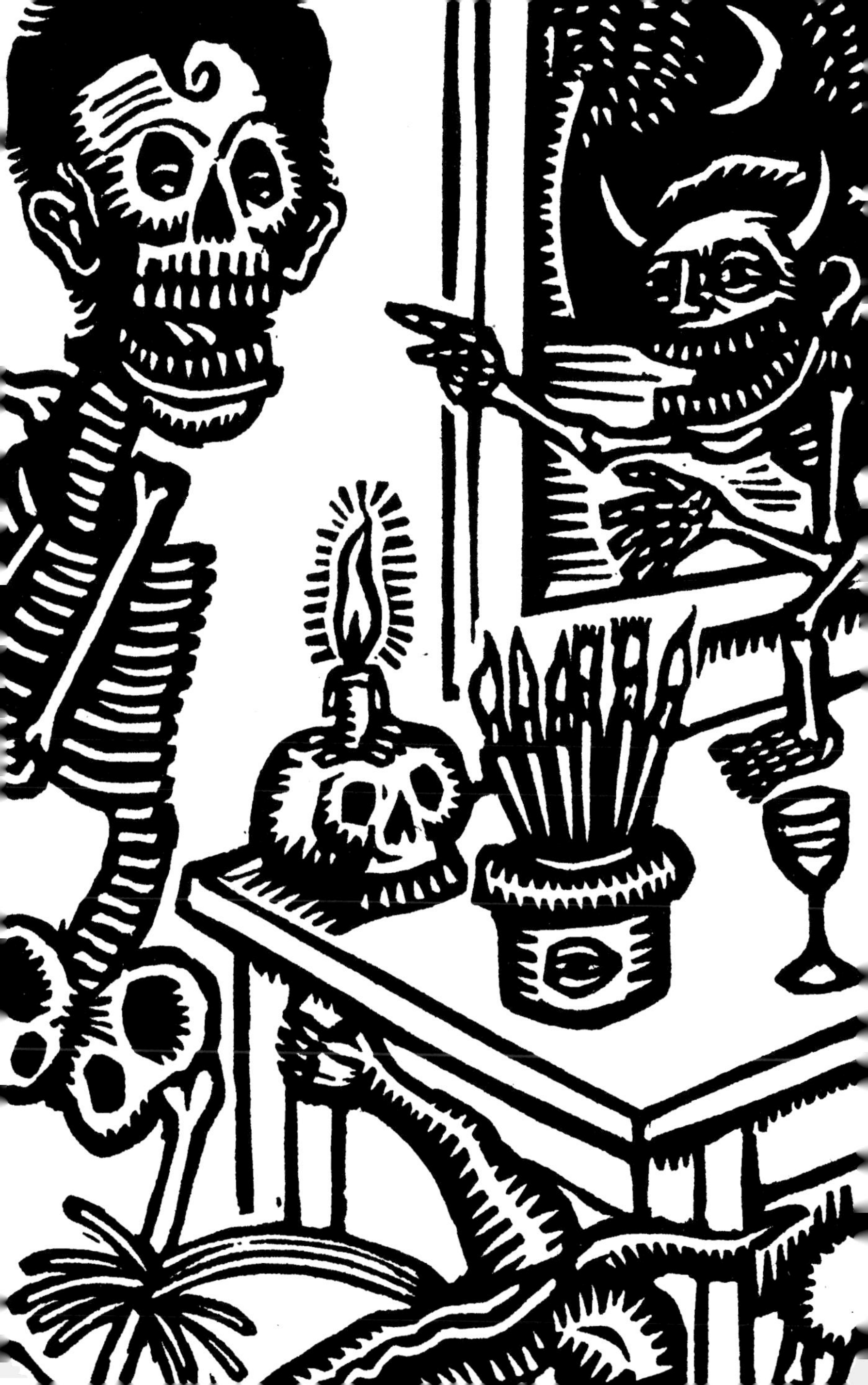

INTRODUCTION

Dear reader, the book you have in your hands, the book whose pages have beckoned you like a siren from beyond, contains some of the best graphic art works inspired by the Day of the Dead celebration (November 1, 2). Most of the artists represented here are from Los Angeles. Along with their work, we have included a selection of images by two of the greatest Mexican illustrators of the 20th century: Manuel Manilla and José Guadalupe Posada.

If you don't already know the answer, the first question you must be asking yourself is: What is the Day of the Dead? Well, the Day of the Dead is an incredibly important traditional Mexican celebration that takes place every year on November 1st and 2nd. November 1st, is dedicated to dead children. Nov. 2nd, is for everyone else. All over Mexico, and in some homes in the United States (and, I guess, in many other places), regular life gets suspended because everybody who has a dead relative, a dead lover or a dead friend (and that includes -as you know- EVERYBODY) participates in rituals that are over 500 years old. Some people visit their dearly departed at the local cemetery, others build altars in their homes, and some simply devote a moment of silence to the memory of the souls who come to visit and hang around with the living. The living, in order to be good hosts, and ensure that the dead feel at home in this, the world they used to inhabit, make offerings of flowers, candles, food, drink, and smokes.

While the origins of the tradition are pre-Hispanic, the celebrations we now see are the result of a complex mixture of indigenous beliefs and practices and those imposed by Spanish Catholics. Catholics celebrate All Souls Day, which like all celebrations commemorating the dead (think Halloween) happen during the dead time in autumn, after the harvests have come in. This coincidence of timing and belief, allowed Day of the Dead to survive the

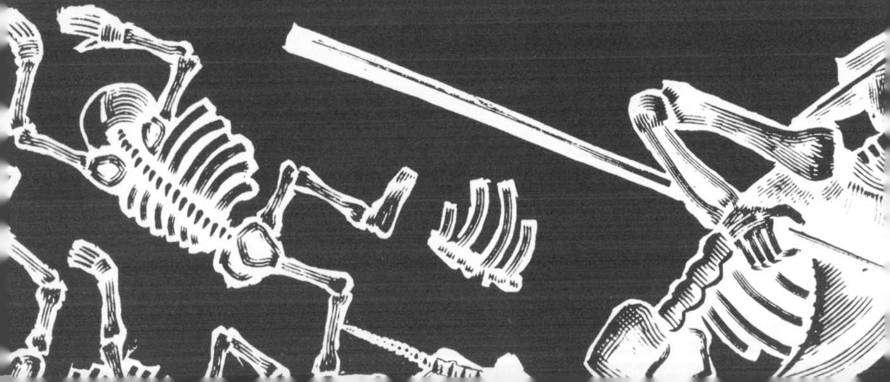

Spanish Conquest of Meso-Americans, and accounts for its continued existence n modern Mexico.

But why do artists create artwork for the Day of the Dead? The answers re as varied as there are artists. Still, one can say that the Day of the Dead inpires artists because artists are inspired by life, and life is nothing without the ertainty of death to give it limits and meaning. As you very well know, every ulture and its artists are concerned with death. In Mexico, the cult of death vas central to most ancient civilizations; the Aztecs being only the last and most amous. In modern Mexico the artistic expression of death reached a zenith with he Mexican broadsides of José Guadalupe Posada (1852-1913). Posada's was a enius who made death as rich and complex as life. It is this way of seeing death hat is reflected in the graphic works included in this book.

Here, dear reader, you will see works that express the range of human motions: love, hate, irony, sadness, fun, ecstasy and dreariness. Why wouldn't rtists be attracted to such a vibrant palette of emotion? Artists who are attracted o the Day of the Dead know that our dead ones are not gone. They know that he dead occupy another level of reality, but that they are around the corner, that hey live in this planet, and that their condition mirrors ours.

The artists included in this book are keenly aware of their mortaly. They know we all must die and they understand that this knowledge reeals a lesson as profound as those found in any of the holy texts: In this life we hould be good, otherwise, well, nobody is going to bring us mole and tequila on November 2nd.

Artemio Rodríguez & José Orozco
Los Angeles, 2005

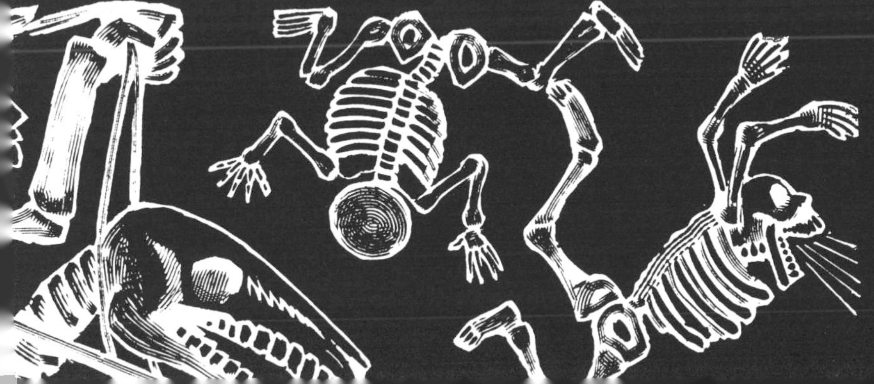

INTRODUCCION

Estimado lector: este libro, que como sirena de lejanos mares ha venido a dar a tus manos, contiene algunas de las mejores obras gráficas inspiradas en Día de Muertos (noviembre 1 y 2). La mayoría de los artistas aquí representados vive en Los Ángeles, aunque hay algunos de San Francisco y de la ciudad de México Tambien hemos incluido trabajos de dos de los más grandes ilustradores mexicanos: Manuel Manilla y José Guadalupe Posada.

Si acaso no supieras la respuesta, la primera pregunta que te estarás haciendo es: ¿Qué es el Día de Muertos? Día de Muertos es una muy importante tradición mexicana que se celebra cada año en noviembre 1 y 2. Noviembre 1 es dedicado a los niños muertos. Noviembre 2 es para todos los muertos En México, y en algunos hogares en Estados Unidos (y me imagino que también en otros sitios), la vida regular se suspende, ya que todos aquellos que tienen un amigo o un familiar muerto (y eso incluye a la mayoría) participan de un modo u otro en rituales que han sobrevivido por mas de 500 años. Mucha gente visita a sus muertos en los cementerios locales, otros les dedican altares en sus casas y otros simplemente dedican un momento de silencio en memoria de las almas que vienen a visitar y andar por un momento en el mundo de los vivos. Los vivos para ser buenos anfitriones, y asegurarse de que los muertos se sientan en casa en este mundo que fue suyo, les dedican ofrendas de flores, velas, comida, bebida cigarros y demás.

Aunque los orígenes de esta tradición son prehispanicos, las celebraciones actuales son resultado de una compleja mezcla de las creencias y prácticas indígenas con las impuestas por el catolicismo español. Los católicos celebran e Día de Todos los Santos en el otoño, por las mismas fechas, cuando han finalizado las cosechas. Esta coincidencia en buena parte explica el por qué sobrevivió e

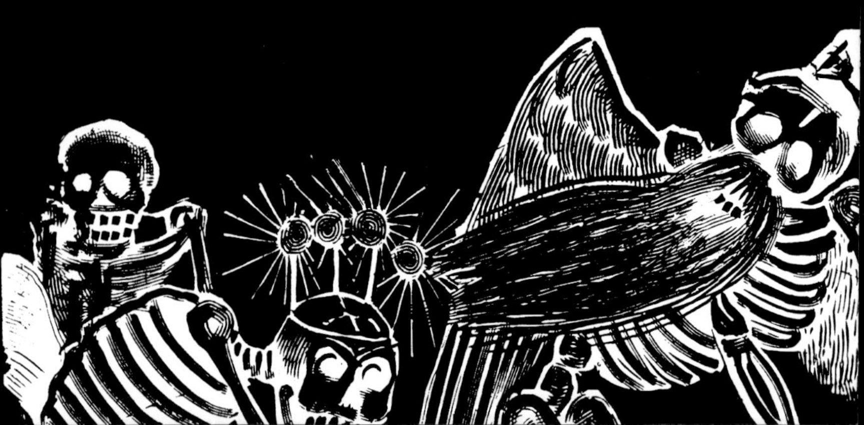

Día de Muertos a la conquista española en Mesoamérica, y por qué aún se celebra asta nuestros días.

¿Pero por qué los artistas crean arte para Día de Muertos? La respusta es tan variada como los artistas mismos. Aun así, podemos decir que Día de Muertos inspira a los artistas porque éstos se inspiran en la vida y la vida es nada in la certeza de la muerte, que da límites y significados a la vida misma. Como ú bien sabras, cada civilizacion y sus artistas tienen una obsesión con la muerte. En México, el culto a la muerte fue algo central para las antiguas civilizaciones; la zteca fue la última y la más famosa. En el México moderno la expresión artística on el tema de la muerte alcanzo su cenit con las hojas sueltas de José Guadaupe Posada (1852-1913). Posada creó imágenes donde la muerte es tan rica y tan ompleja como la vida misma. Este es el modo de ver la muerte que predomina en as obras incluidas en este libro.

Aquí, estimado lector, verás trabajos que expresan todo el arcoiris de las mociones humanas: amor, odio, ironía, tristeza, alegría, éxtasis, cansancio. ¿Como o iban a sentirse los artistas atraídos por tan vibrante paleta de emociones? Ellos aben que los muertos no se han ido para siempre, saben que sólo están en otro ivel de nuestra realidad, que están a la vuelta de la esquina, compartiendo este laneta, en condiciones que se asemejan a las nuestras.

Los artistas incluidos en este libro tienen la certeza de su propia moralidad, saben que no hay de otra. Todos nos vamos a morir; y entienden que este onocimiento revela una lección tan profunda como la de cualquiera de los libros agrados: en esta vida hay que ser bueno; de otro modo, cuando estiremos la pata, adie nos va a llevar mole, ni tequila, el 2 de noviembre.

Artemio Rodríguez y José Orozco,
Los Ángeles, 2005

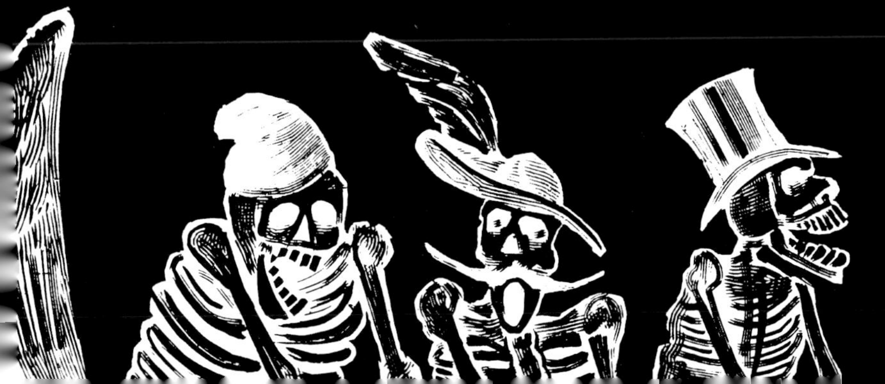

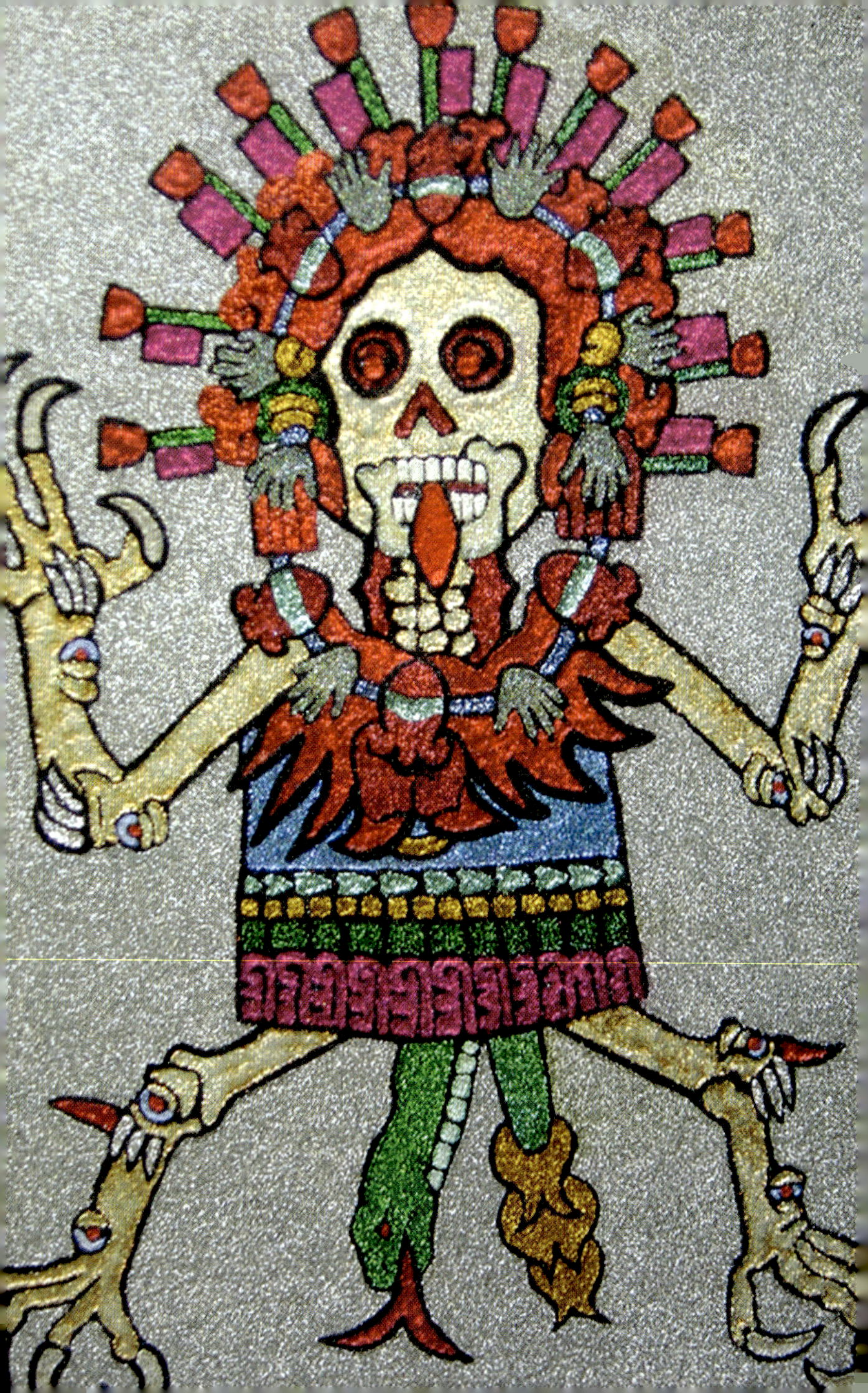

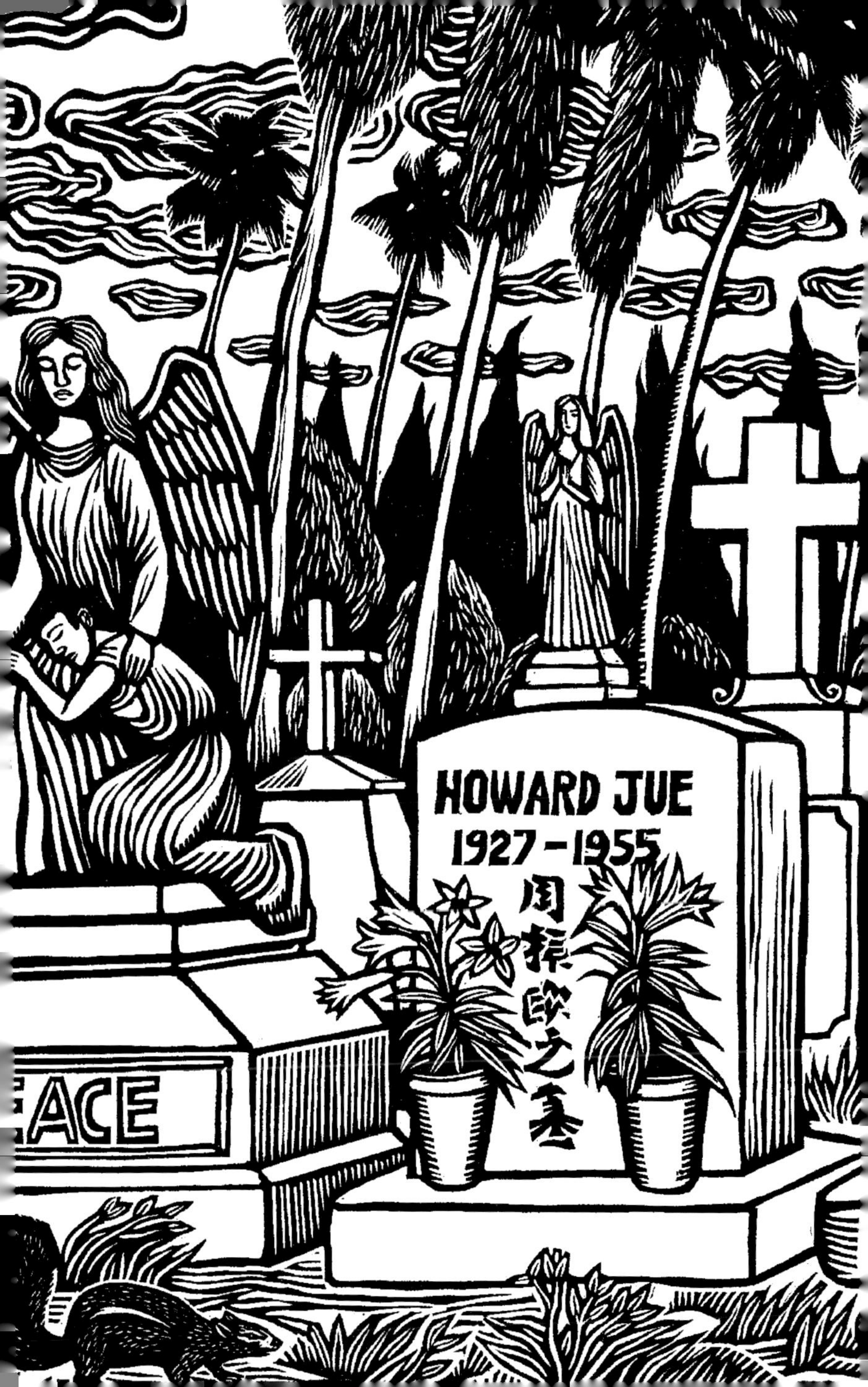
HOWARD JUE
1927 - 1955
EACE

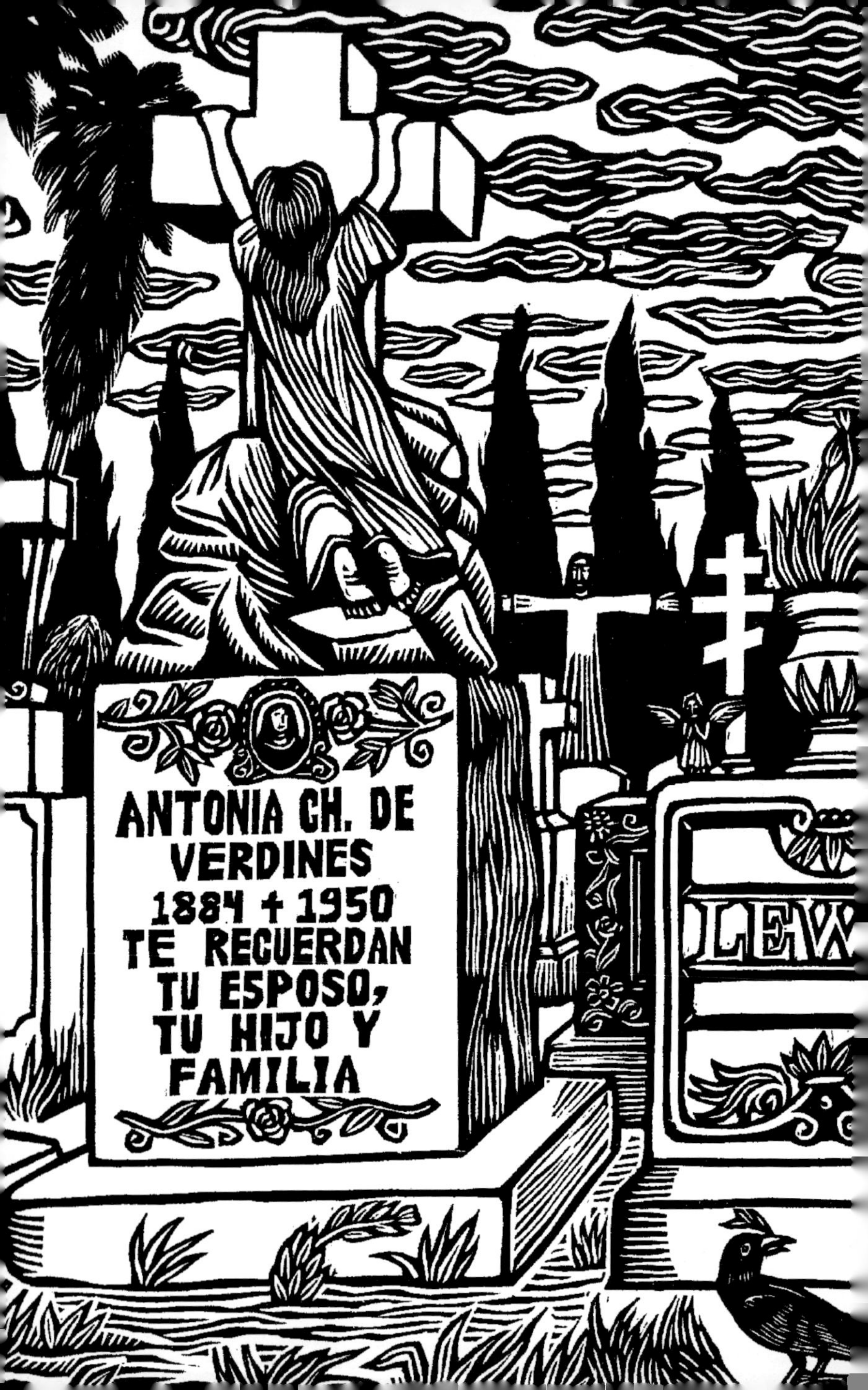
ANTONIA CH. DE
VERDINES
1884 † 1950
TE RECUERDAN
TU ESPOSO,
TU HIJO Y
FAMILIA
LEW

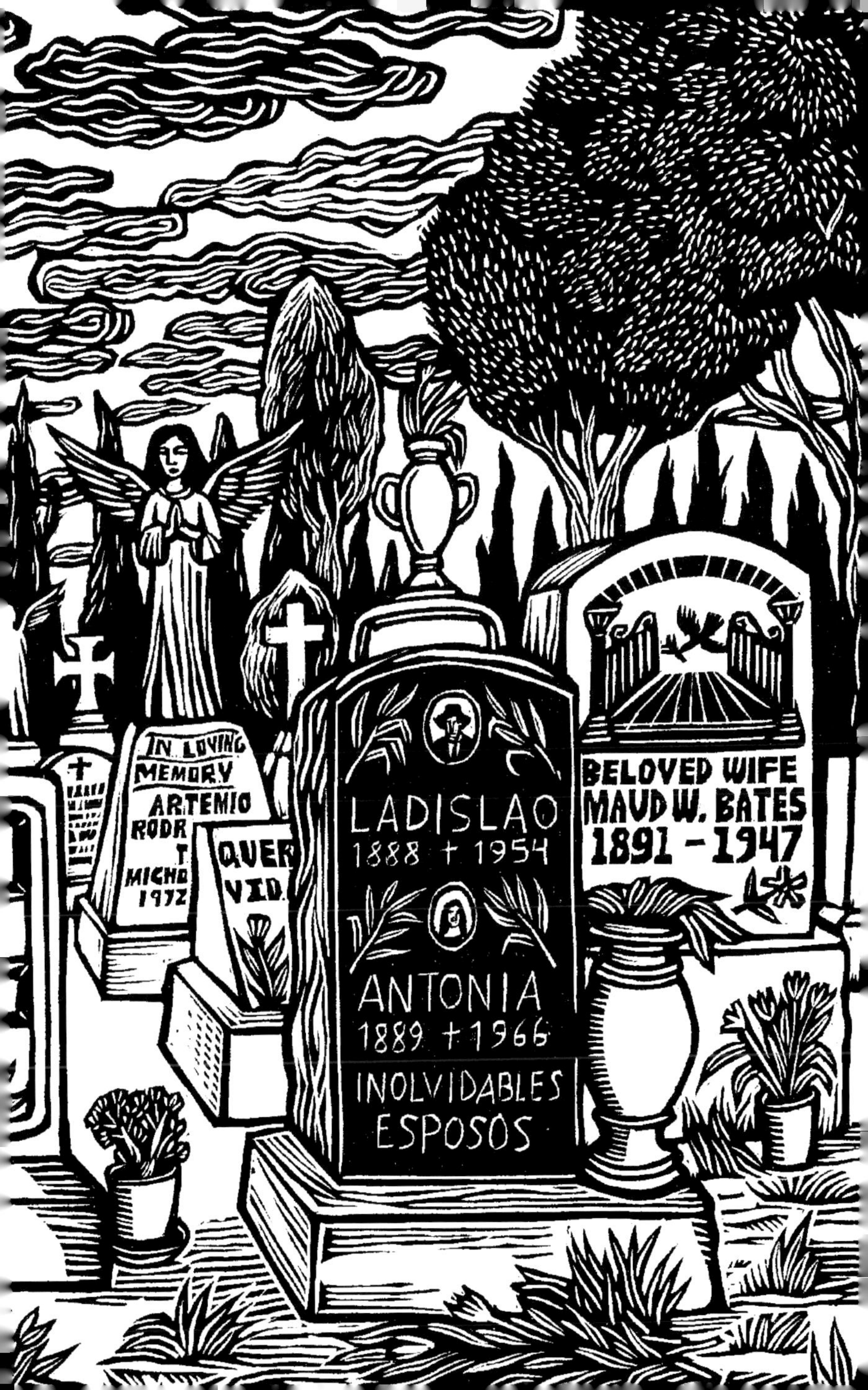
IN LOVING
MEMORY
ARTEMIO
RODR
T
MICHO
1972
QUER
VID.
LADISLAO
1888 + 1954
ANTONIA
1889 + 1966
INOLVIDABLES
ESPOSOS
BELOVED WIFE
MAUD W. BATES
1891 - 1947

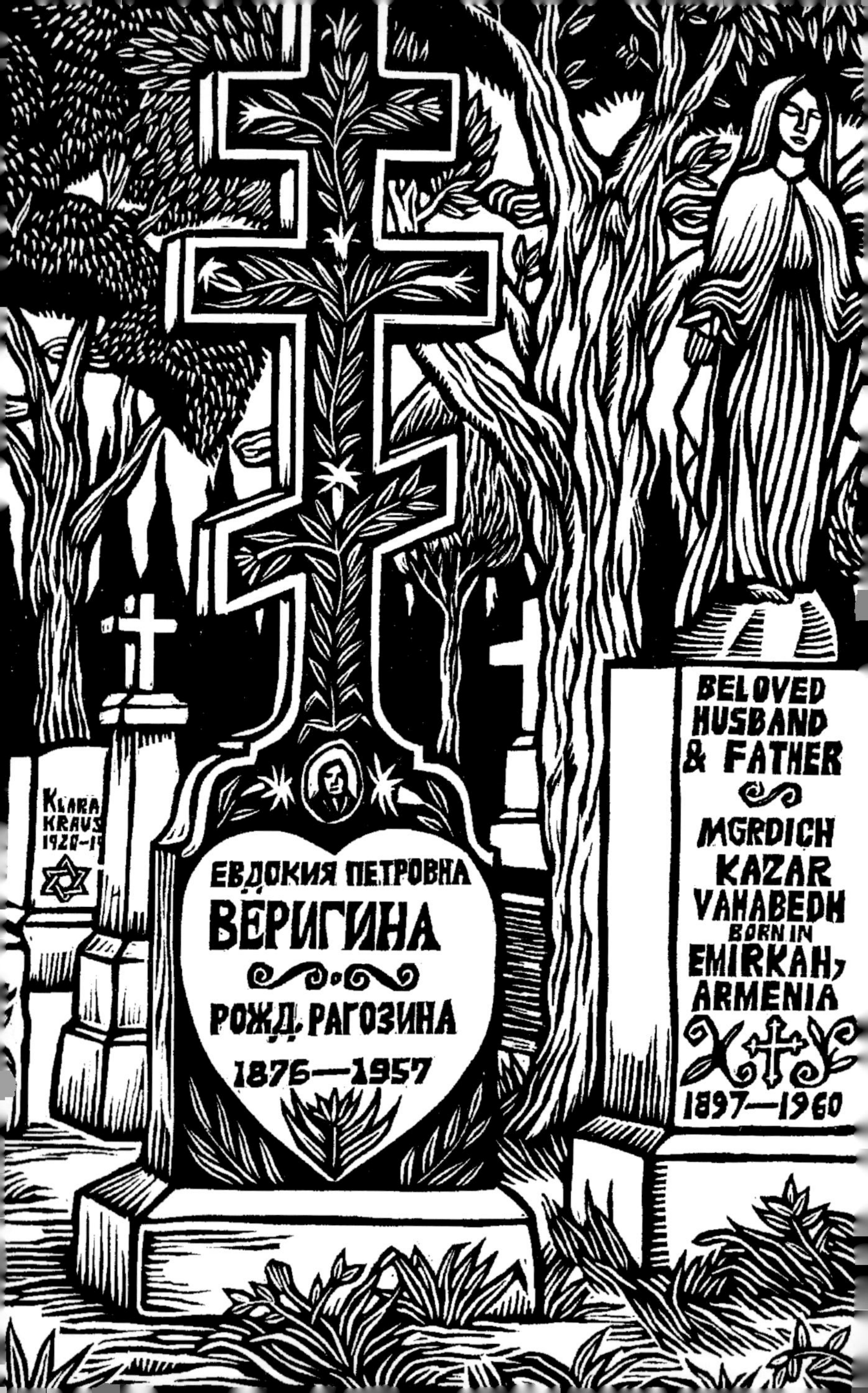

KLARA
KRAUS
1920–19
ЕВДОКИЯ ПЕТРОВНА
ВЕРИГИНА
РОЖД. РАГОЗИНА
1876—1957
BELOVED
HUSBAND
& FATHER
MGRDICH
KAZAR
VAHABEDH
BORN IN
EMIRKAH,
ARMENIA
1897—1960

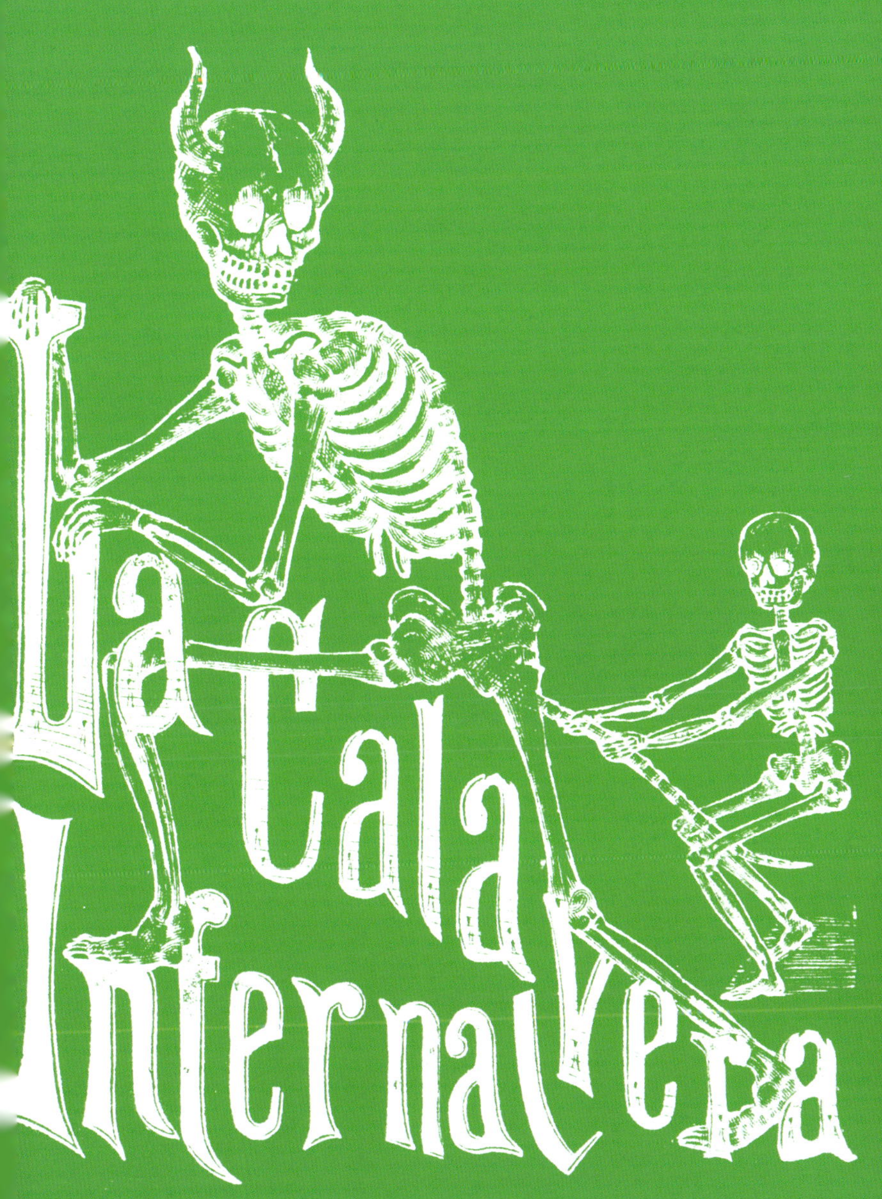

◆◆ Tlizsa Jaurique *Mictecacihuatl*
◆ Artemio Rodríguez *Evergreen*
◆ Manuel Manilla *La calavera*

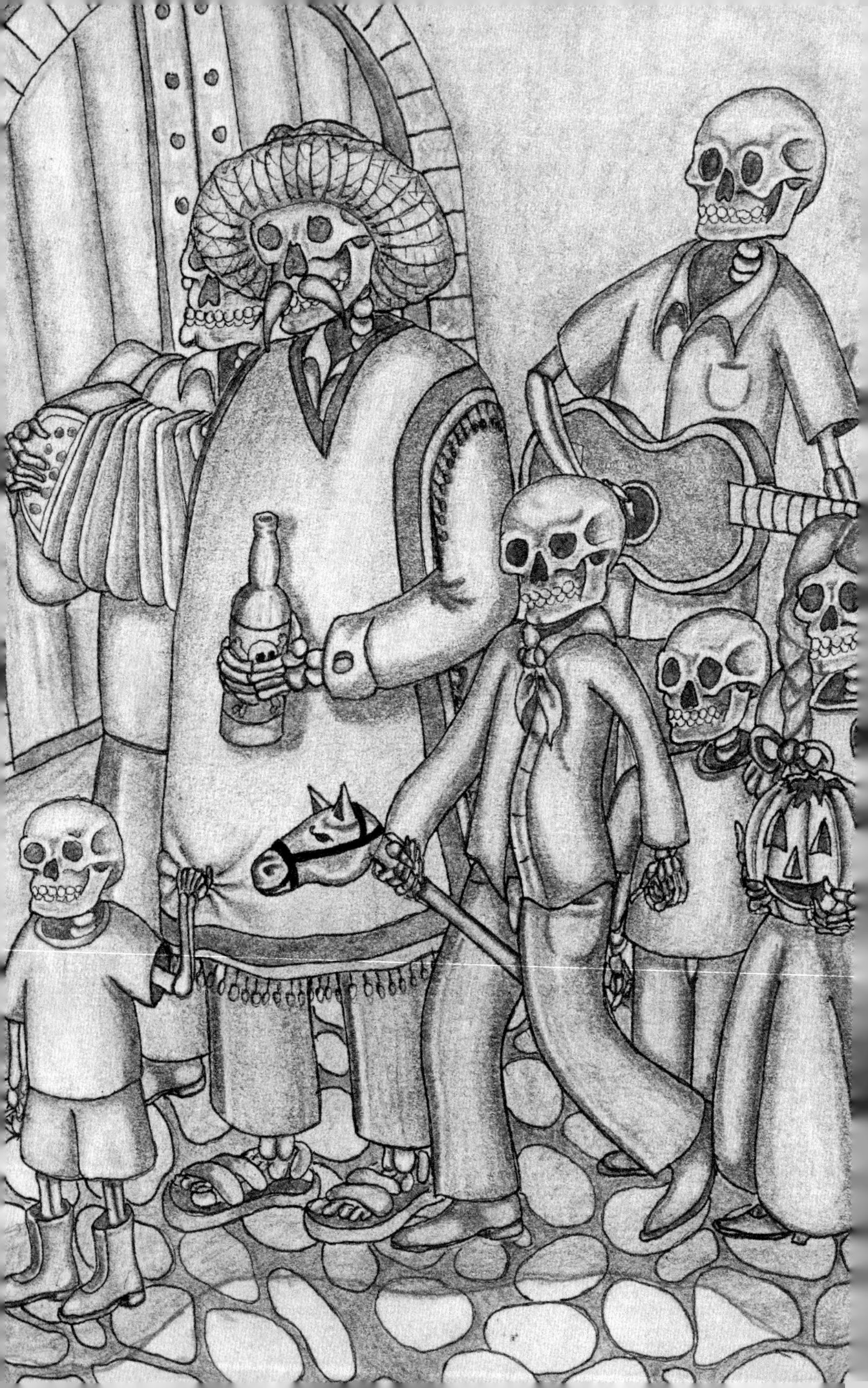

6, 98

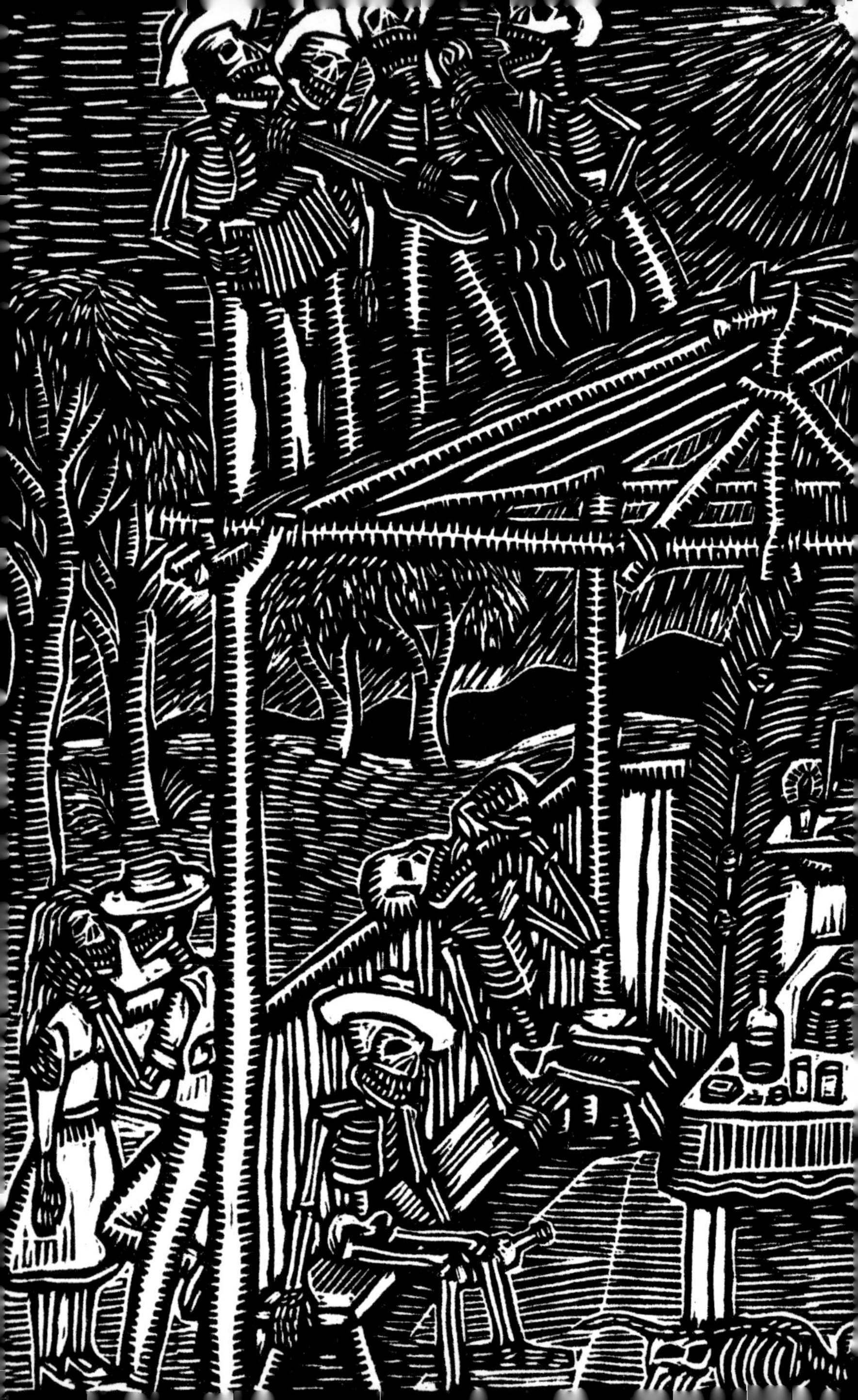

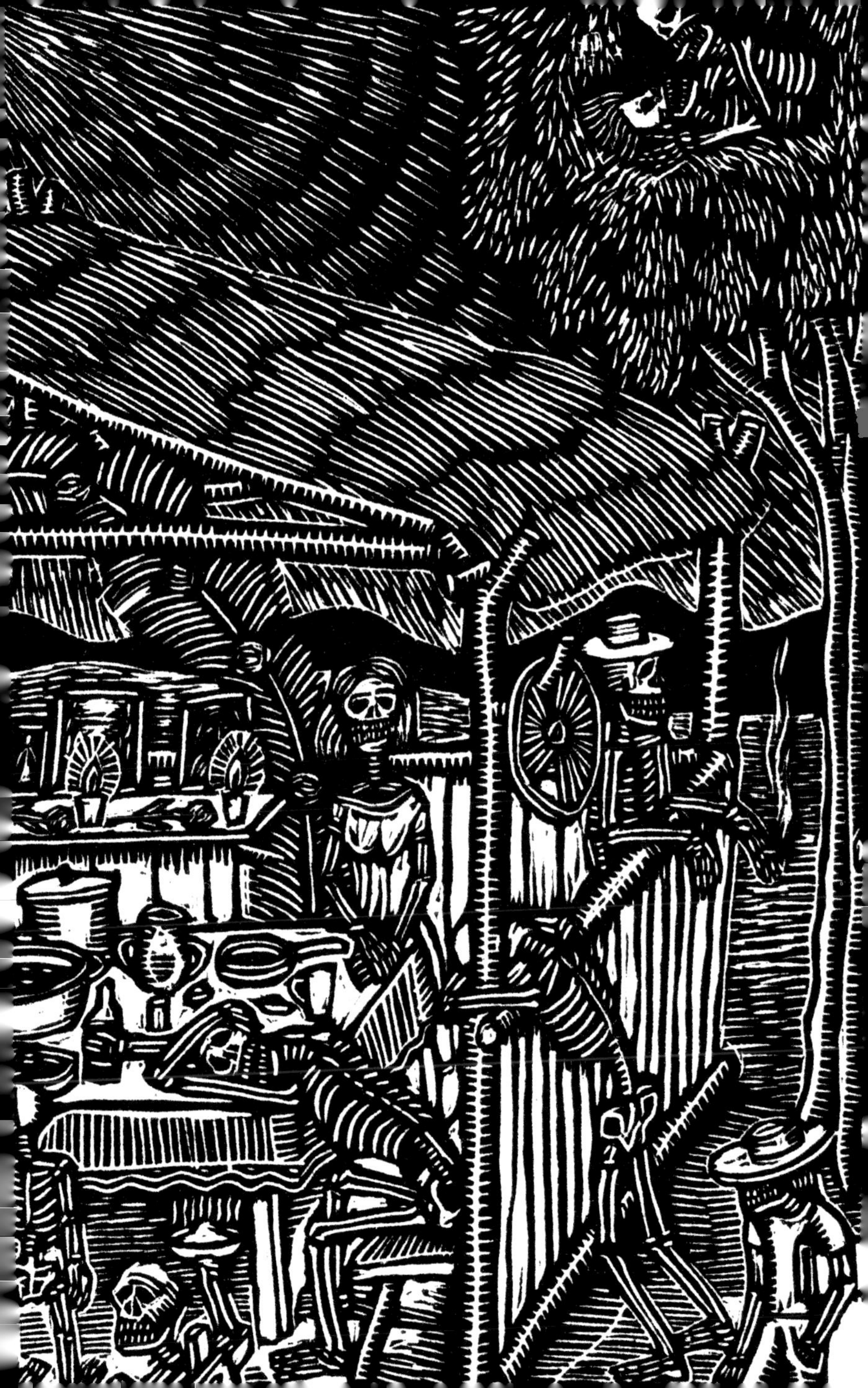

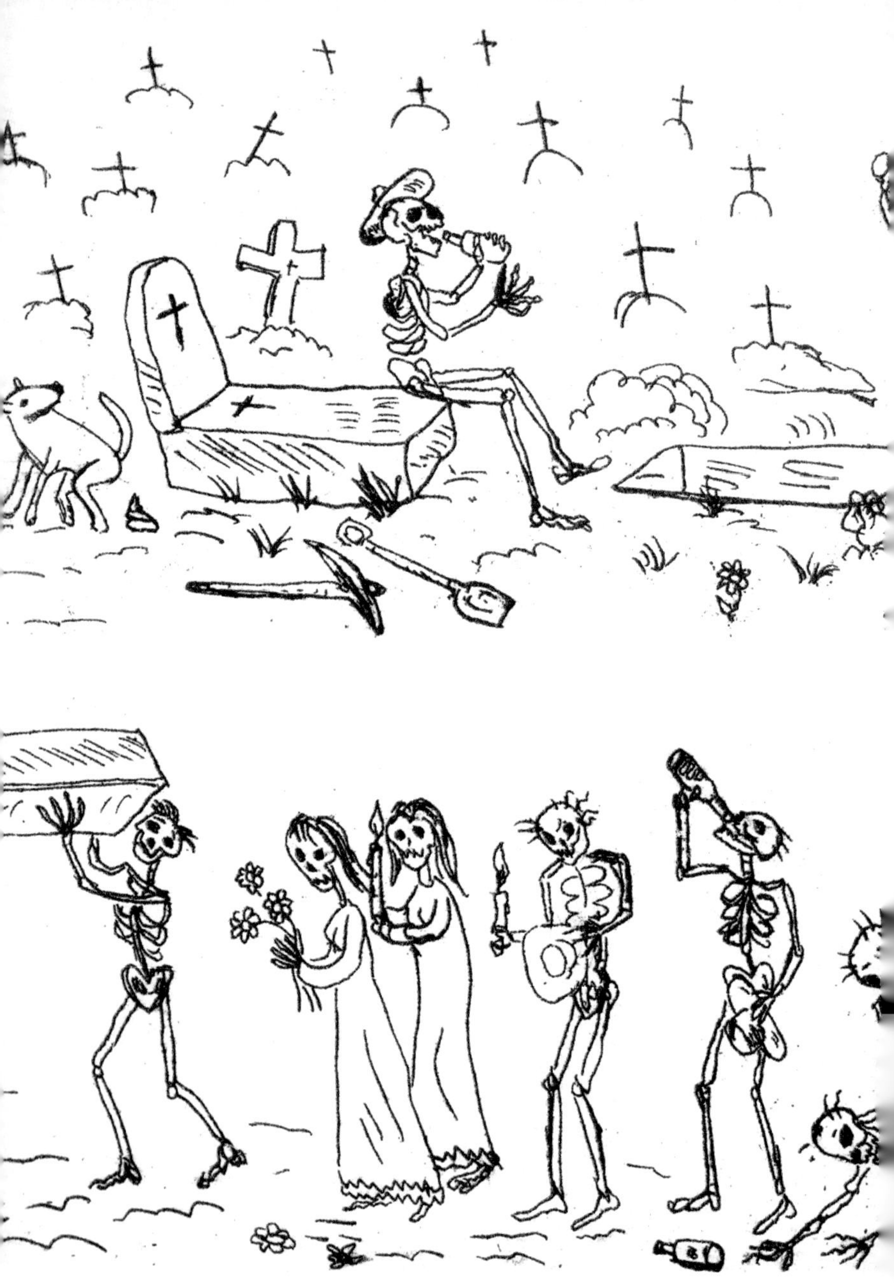

◆◆◆ Gabriel Galán, *Procesión*
◆◆ Artemio Rodríguez *El tiempo llega*

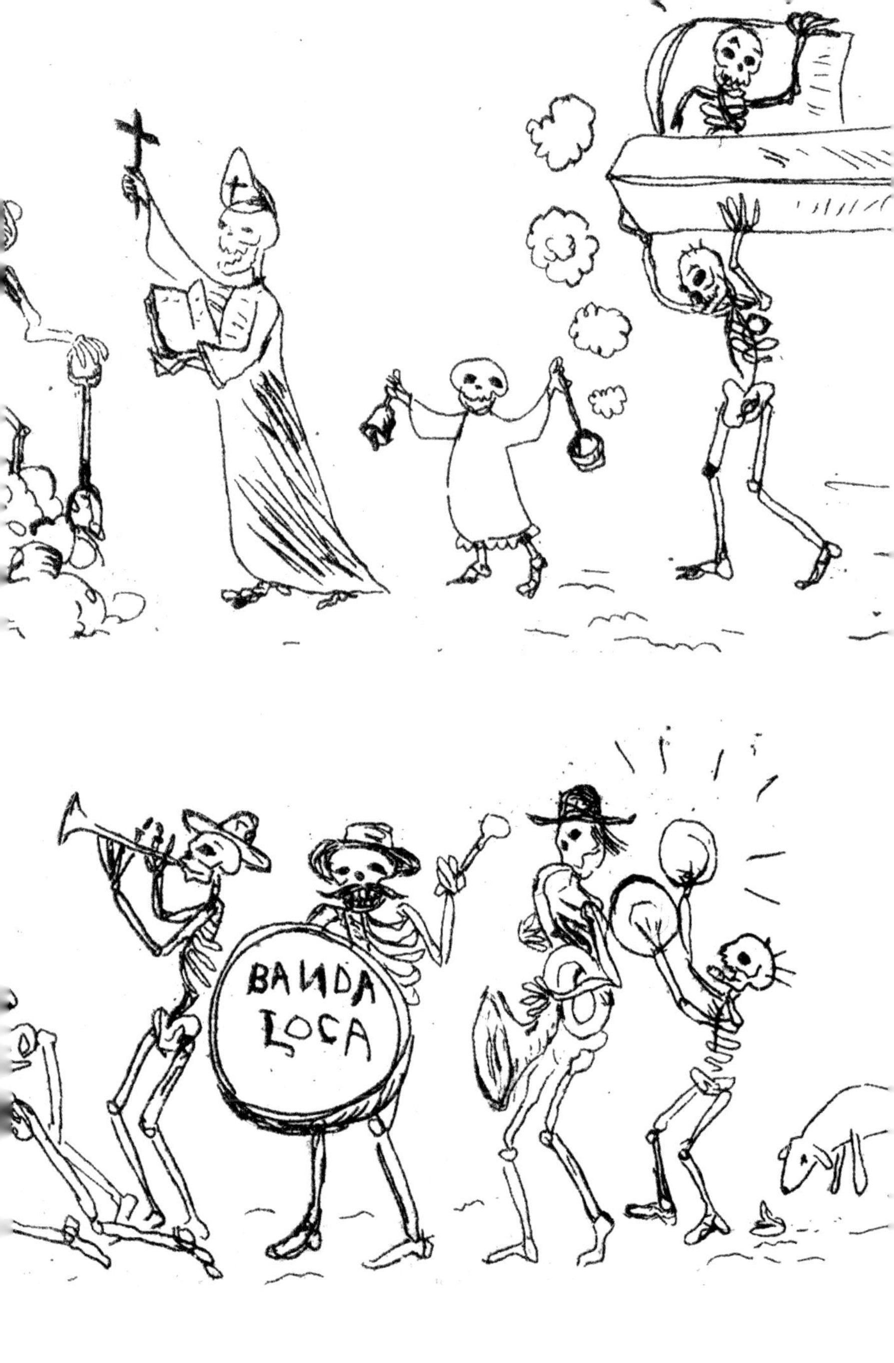

◆◆Agustín Barón *Scenes from the life of the dead*

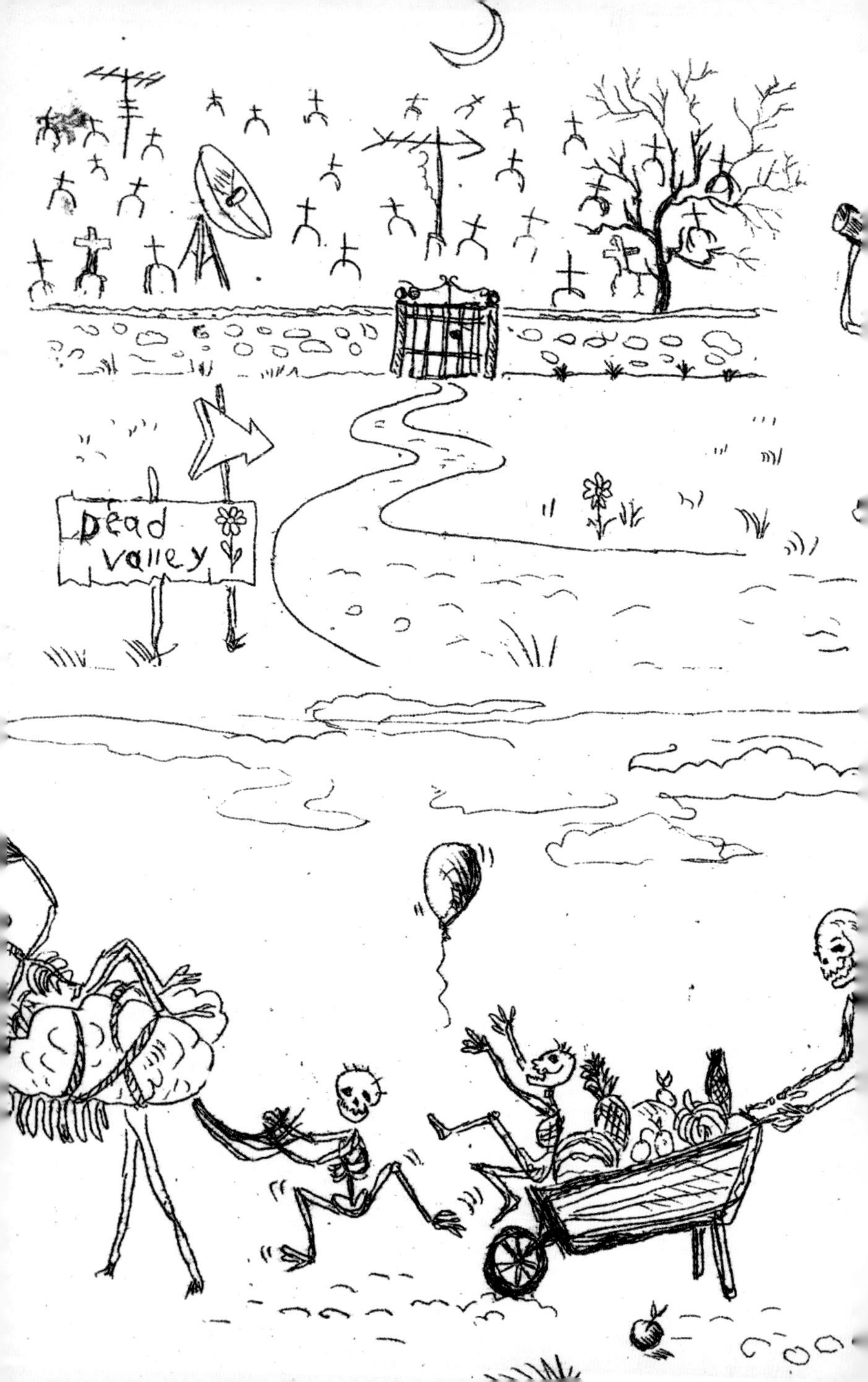
Dead
valley

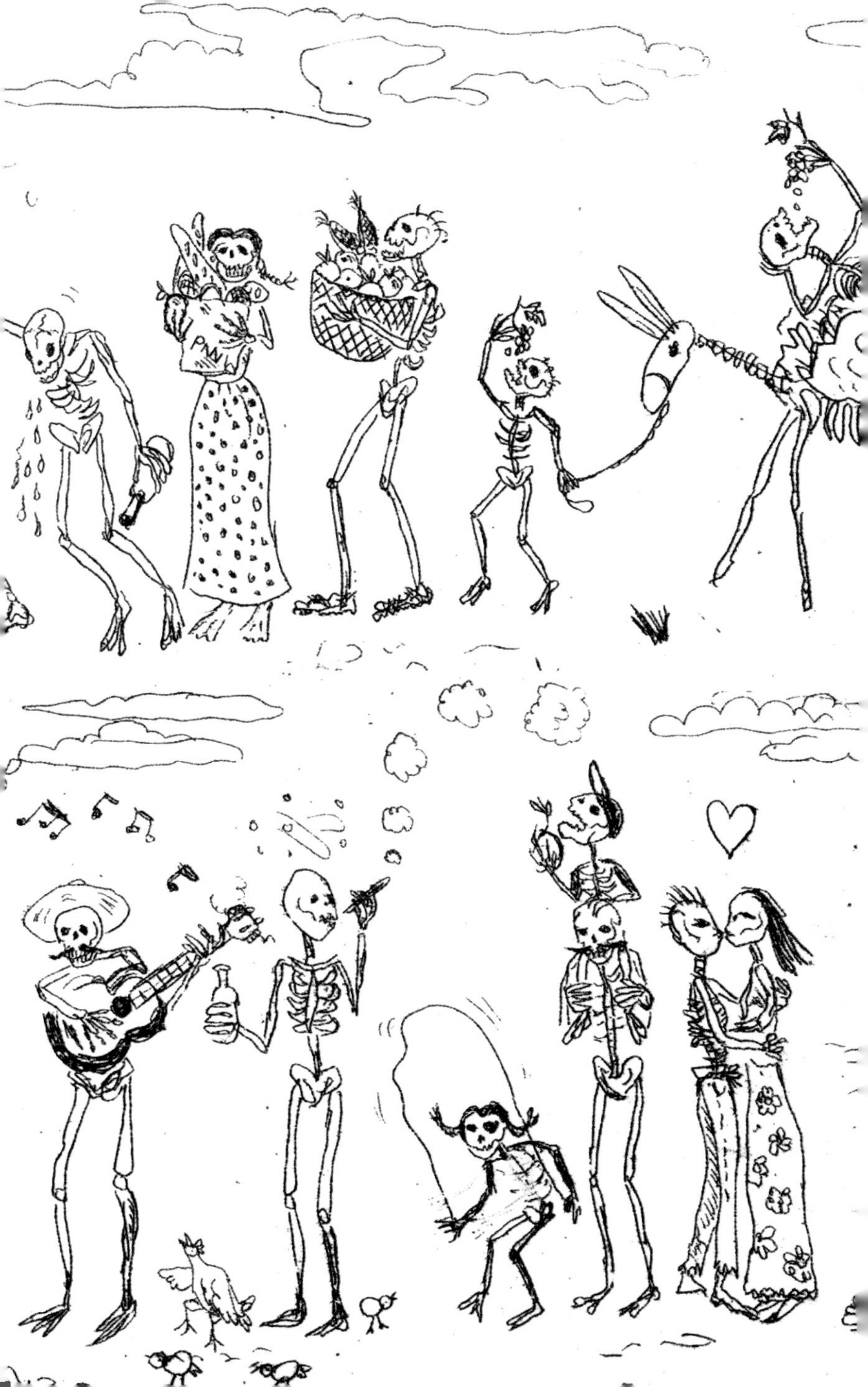

- Manuel Manilla
- José Guadalupe Posada
- Robert Palacios *Trick or Treat*

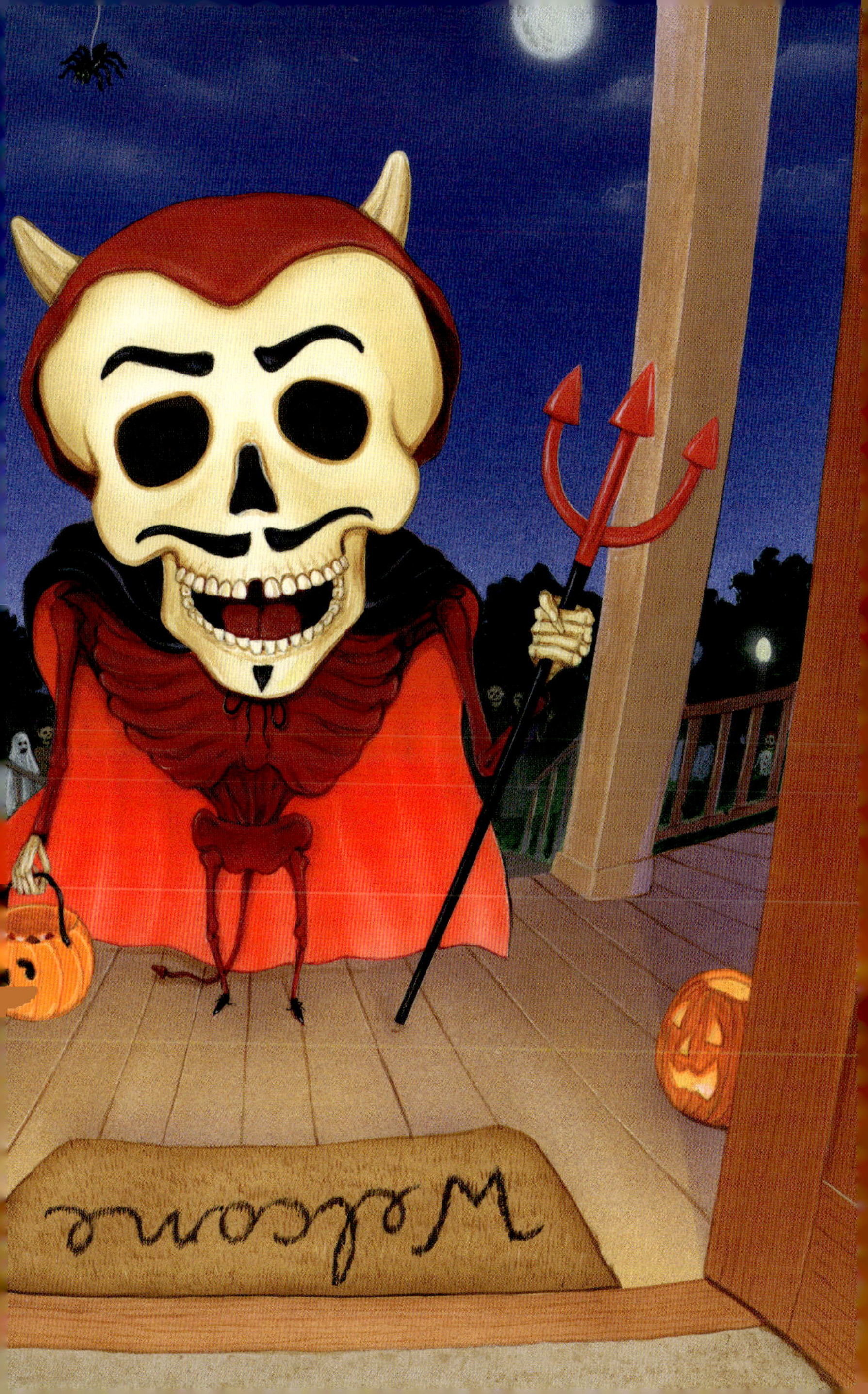
Welcome

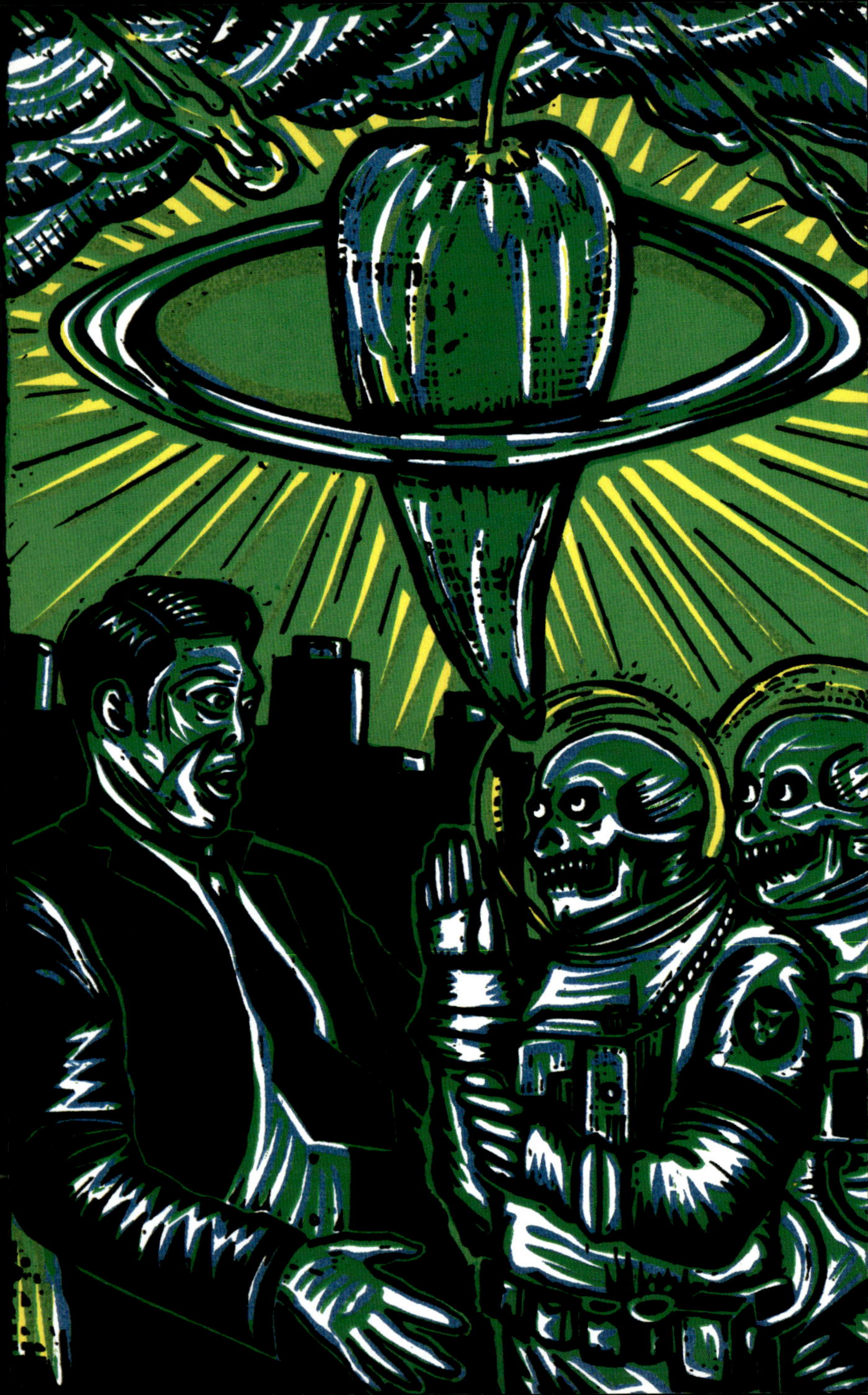

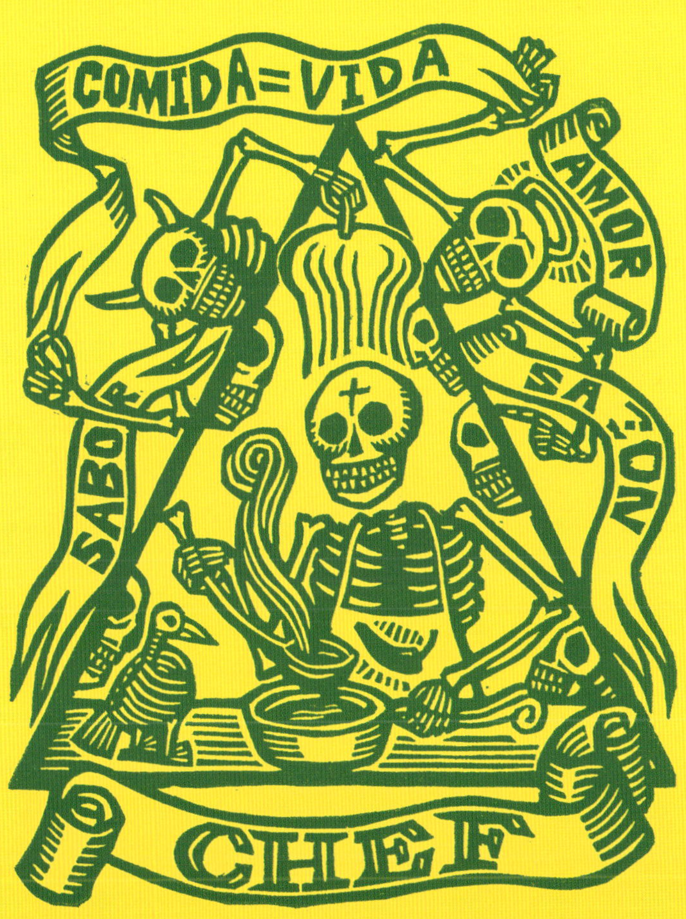

◆ Txutxo Peréz *Calacas from Planet Chile*
◆ Artemio Rodríguez *Chef*

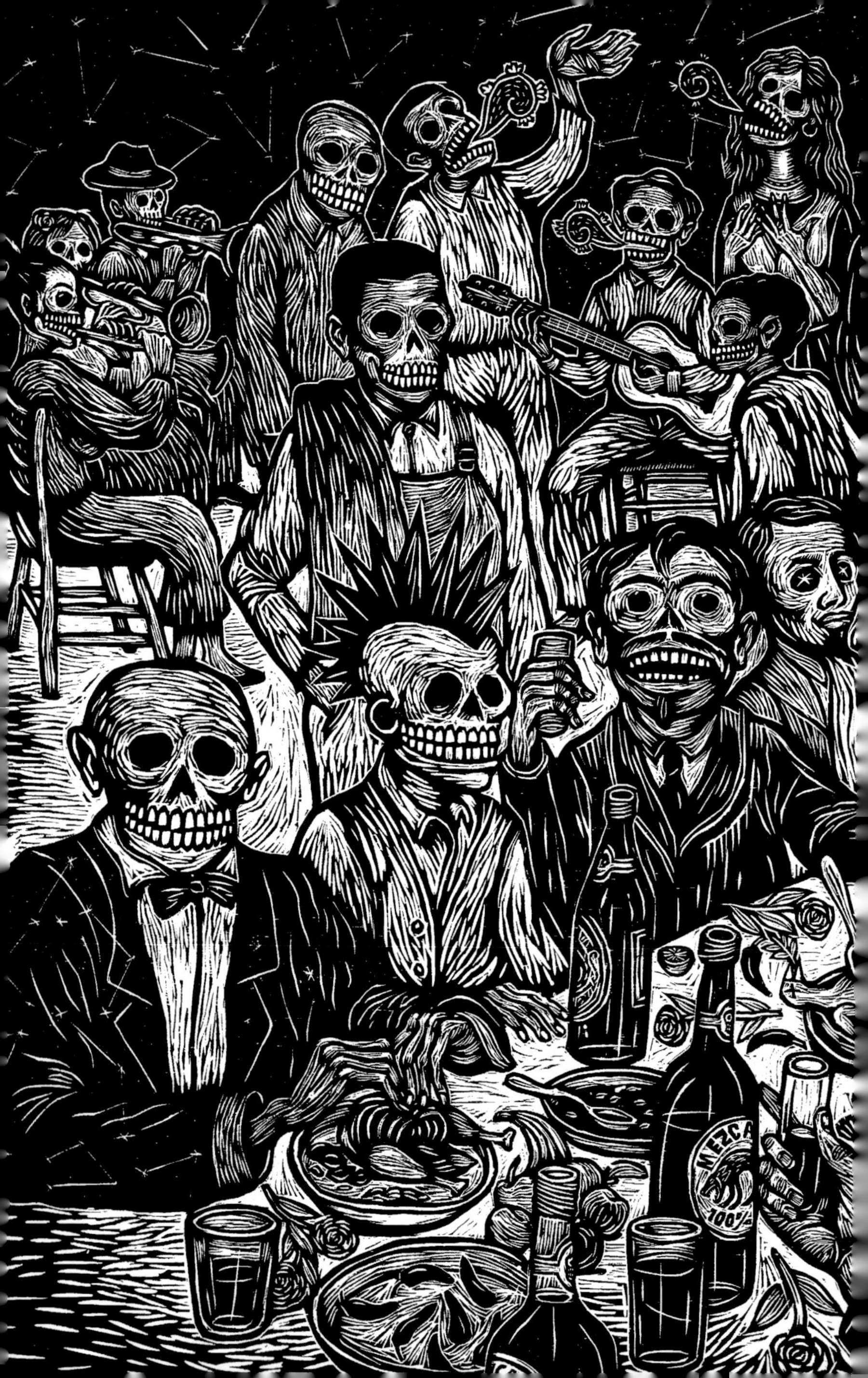
MEZCA
100%

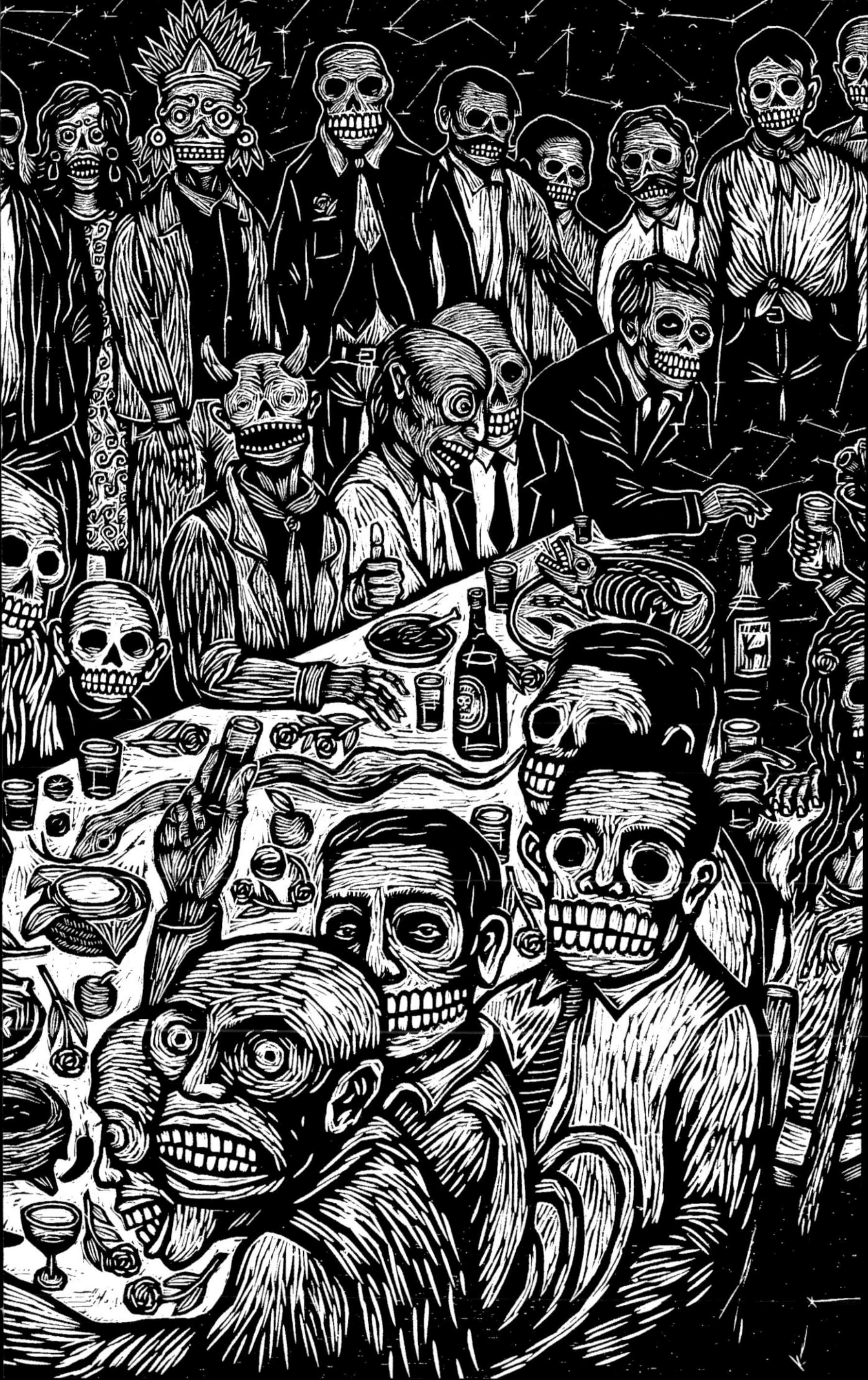

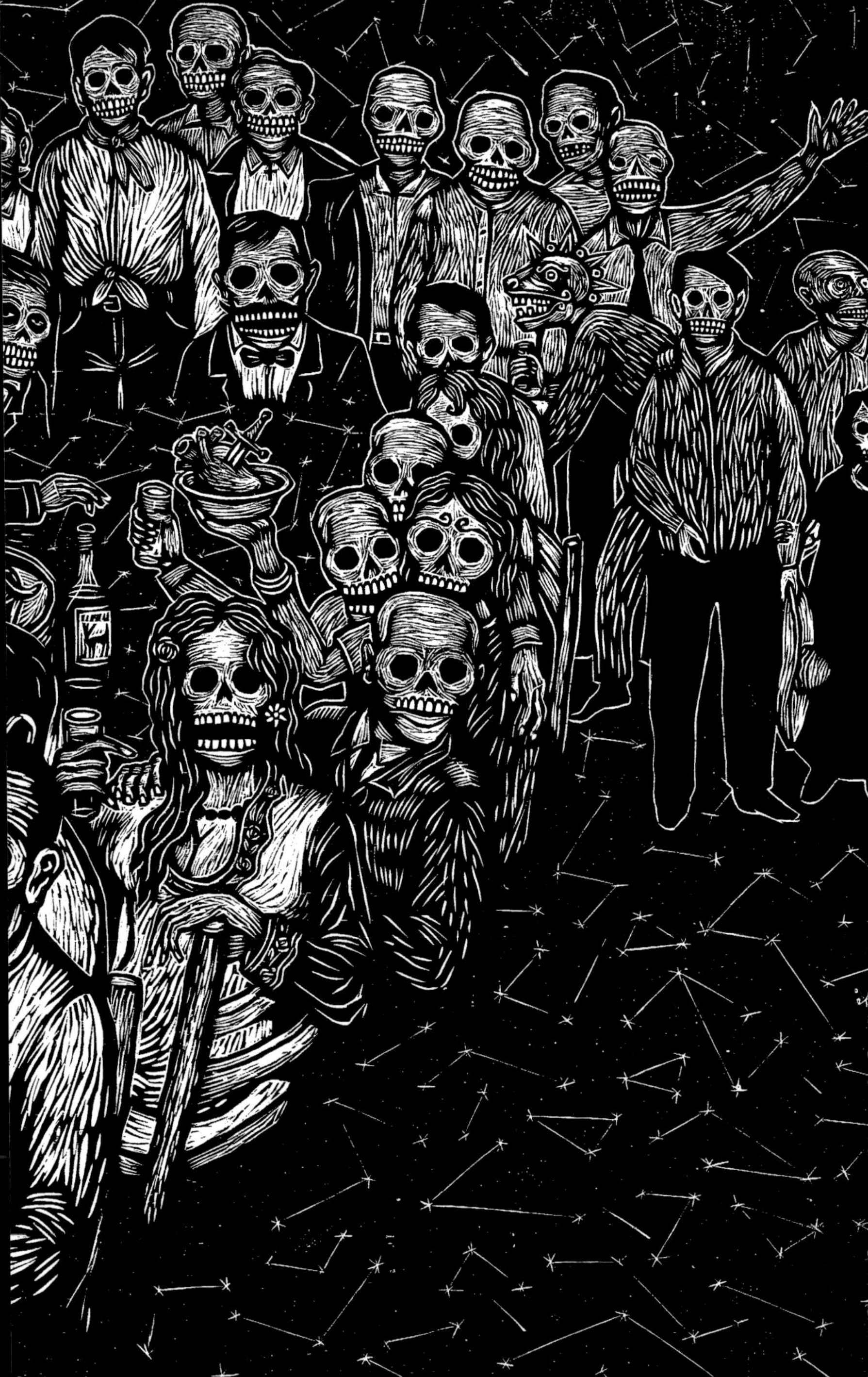

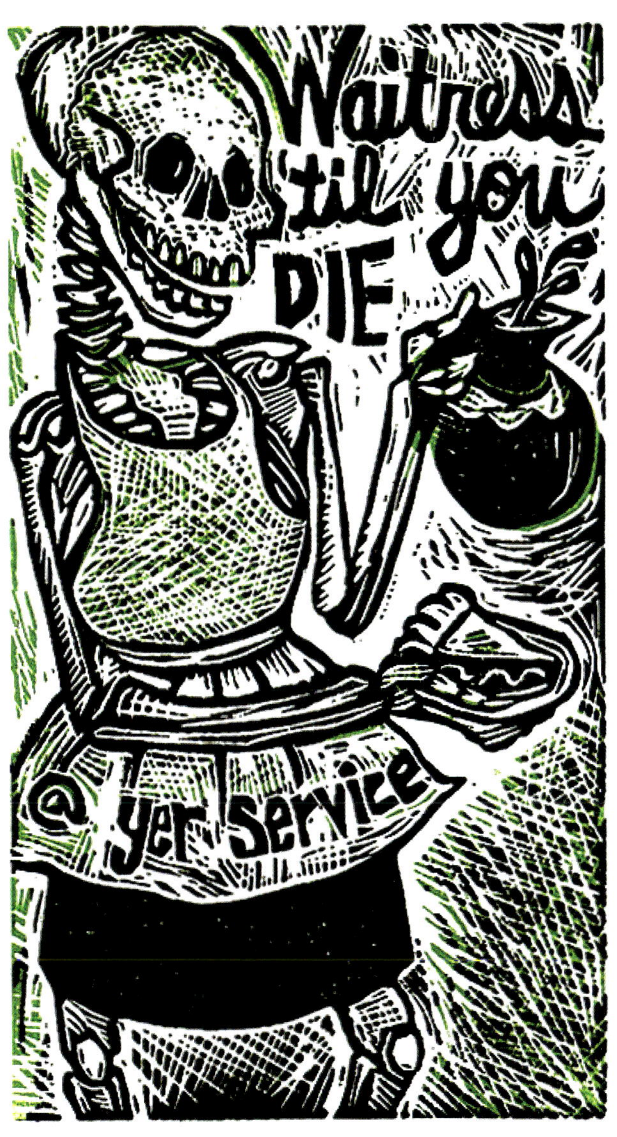

◆◆ Artemio Rodríguez *Infinite Night*
◆ Lori Michelon *Waitress Til You Die*

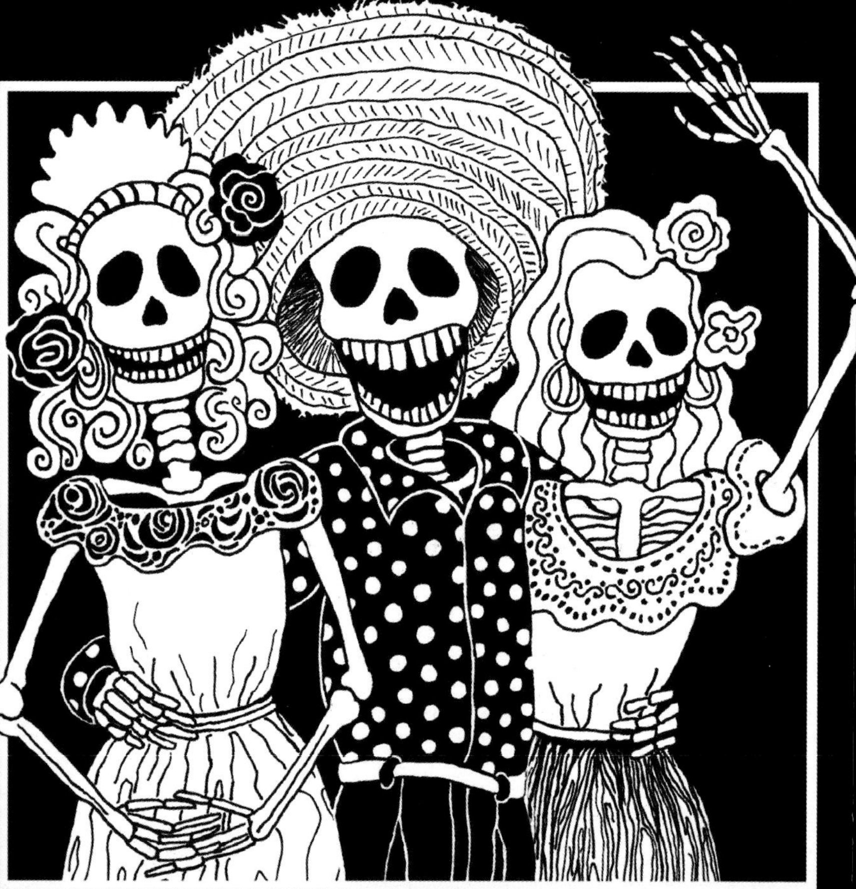

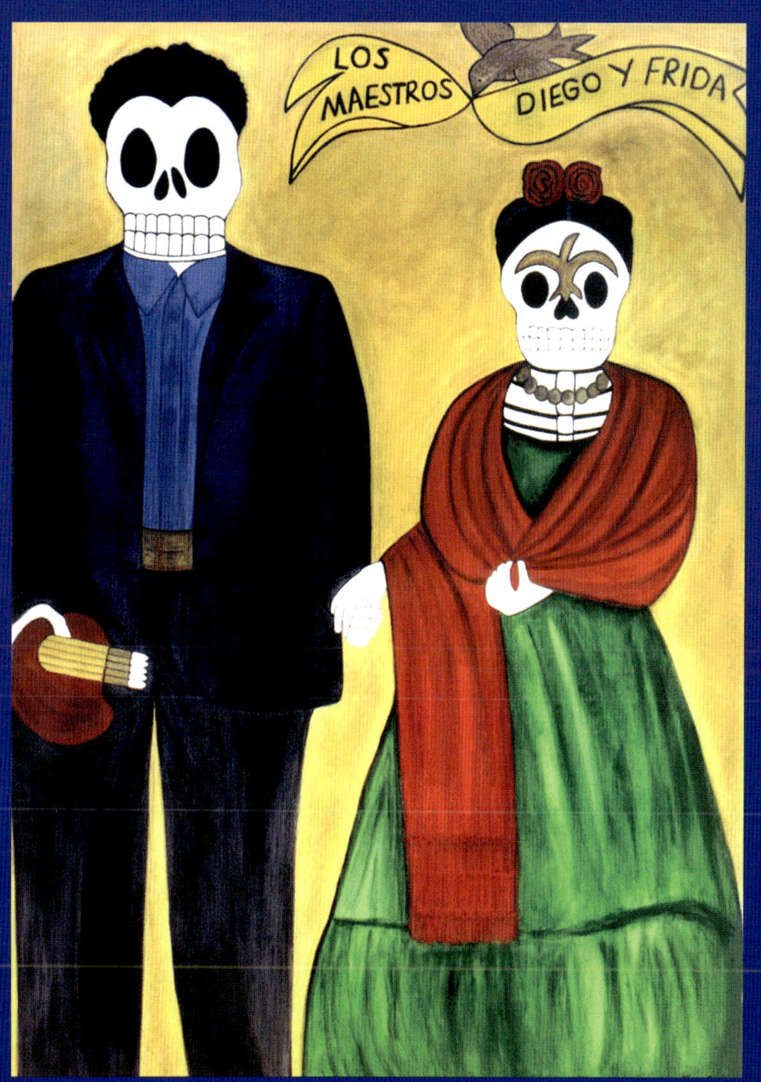

Emilia García *Los Maestros*

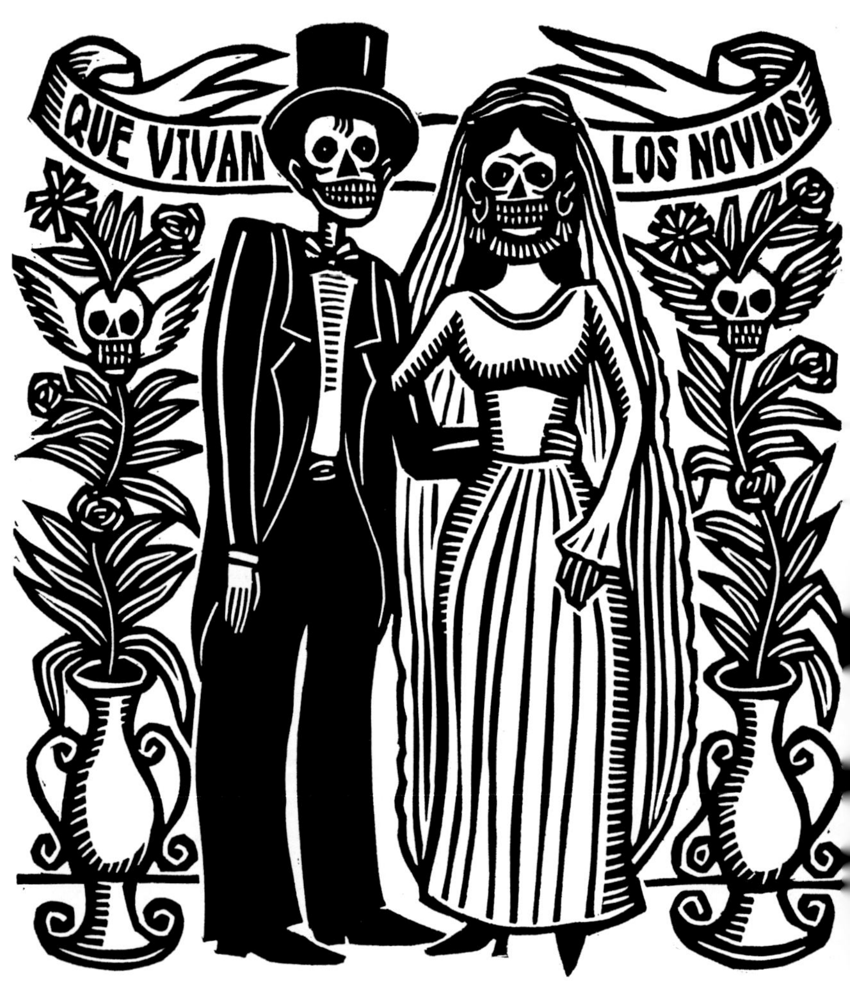

Artemio Rodríguez *Just Married*

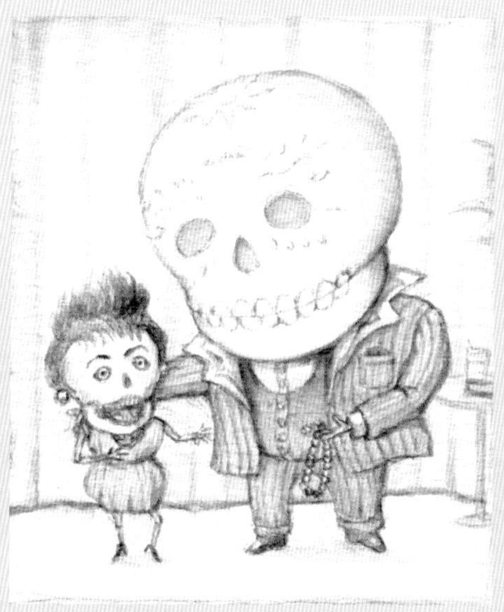

Robert Palacios *Sugar Daddy*

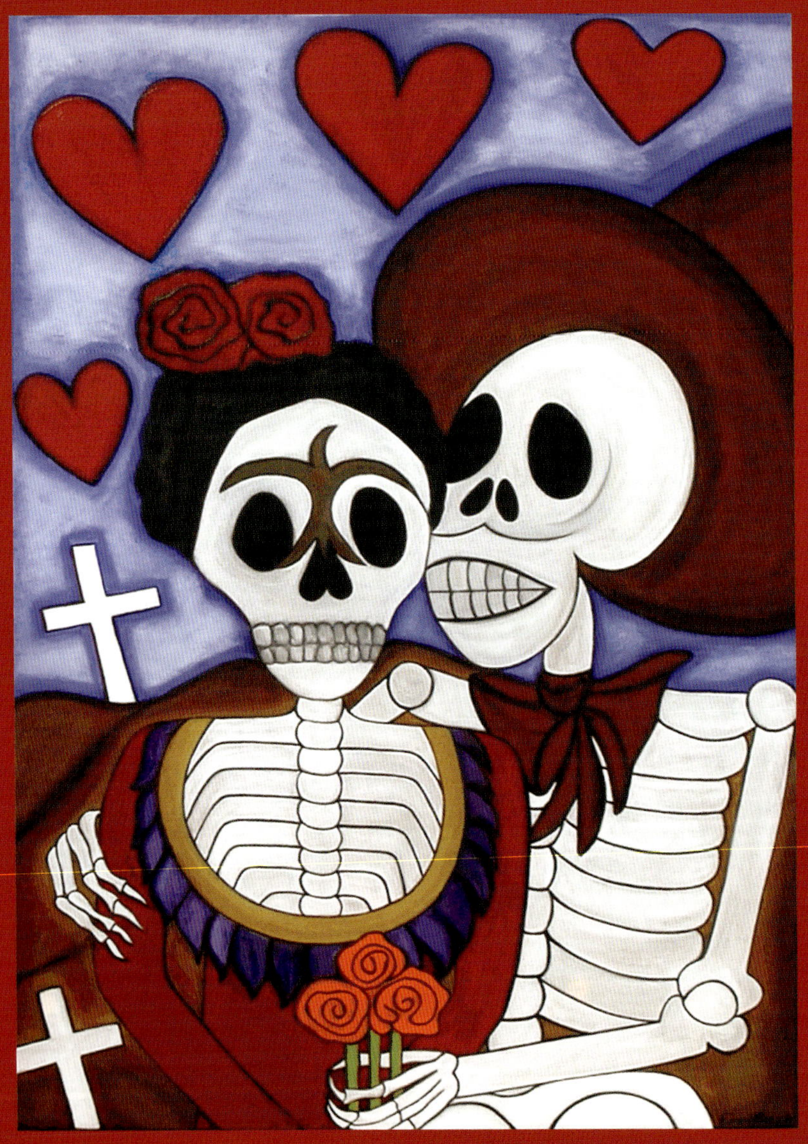

- Emilia García *El Gran Amor*
- Gabriel Galán *Benigno y Celia*

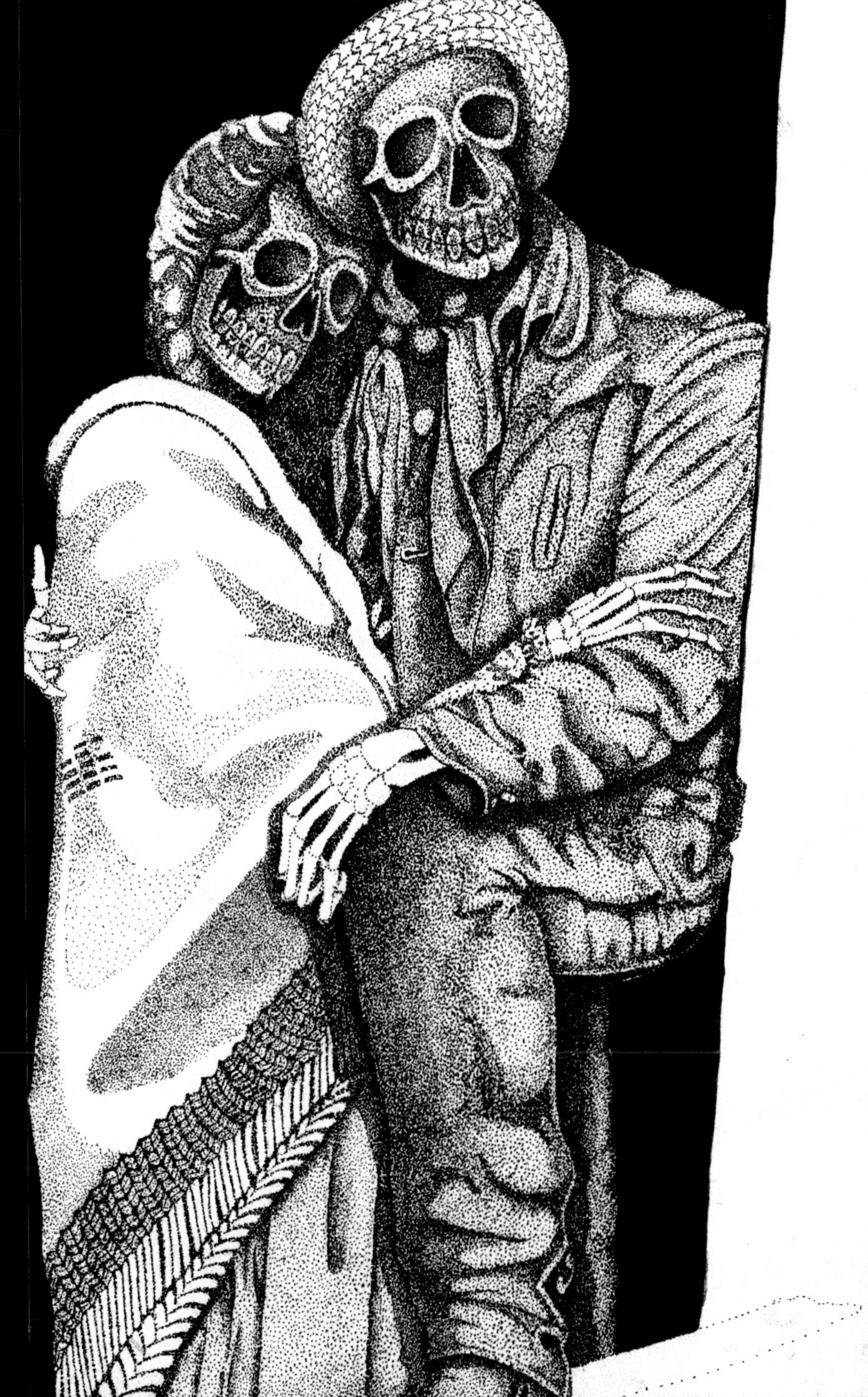

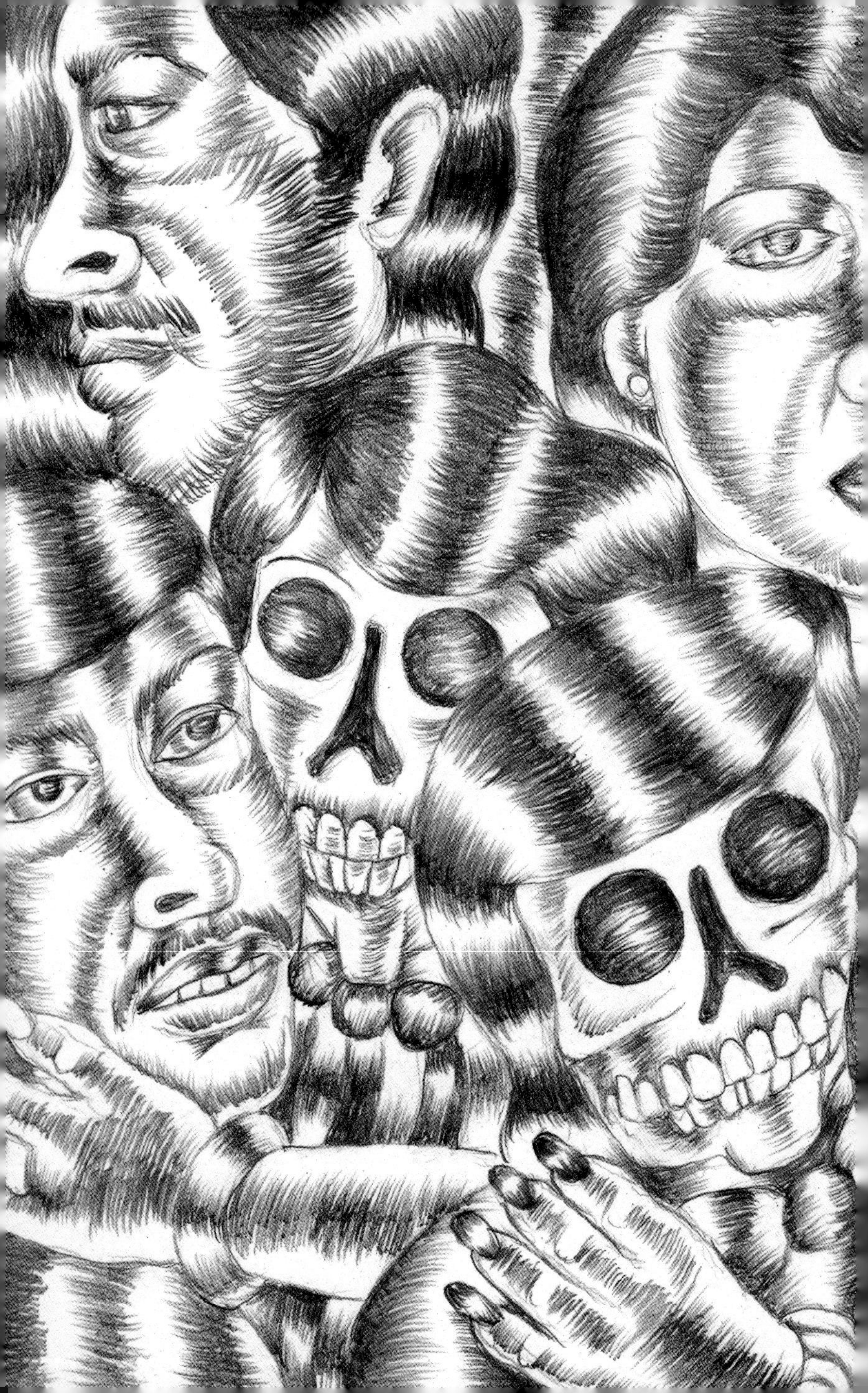

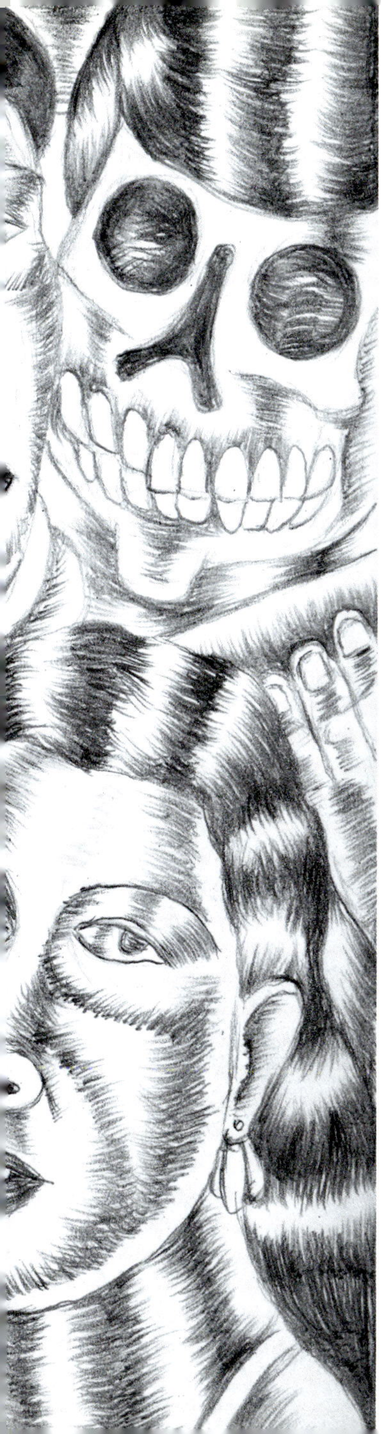

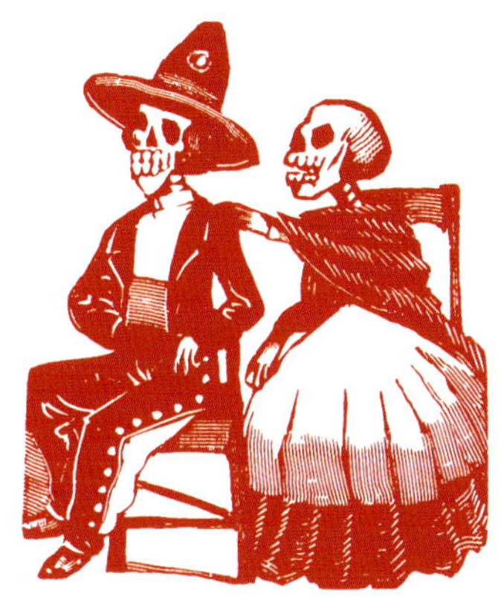

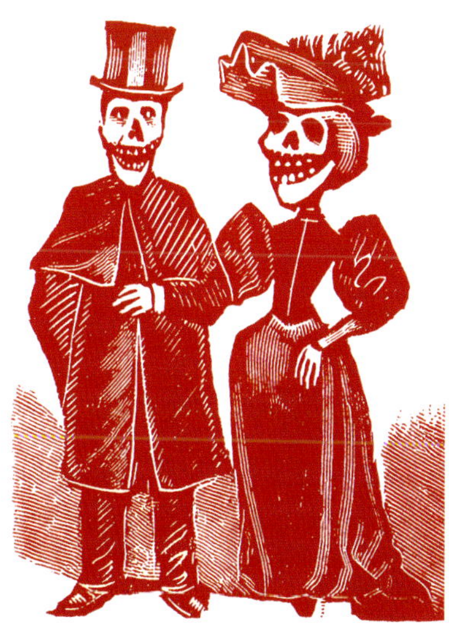

◆ José Guadalupe Posada
◆ José Lozano *Calaca Lounge*

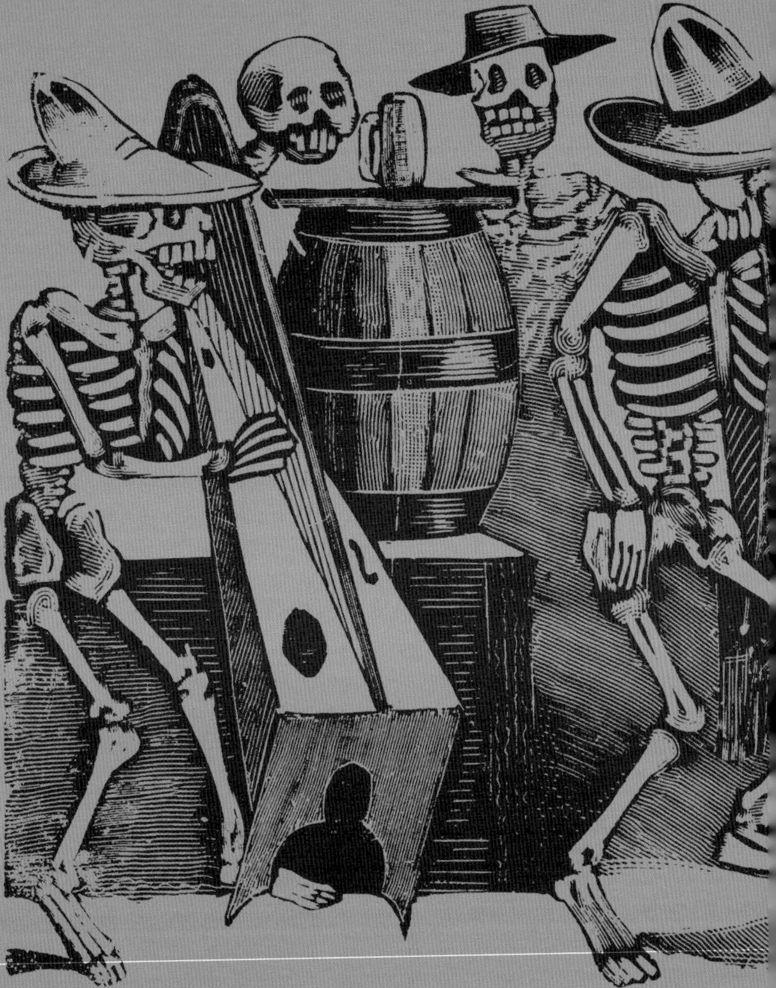

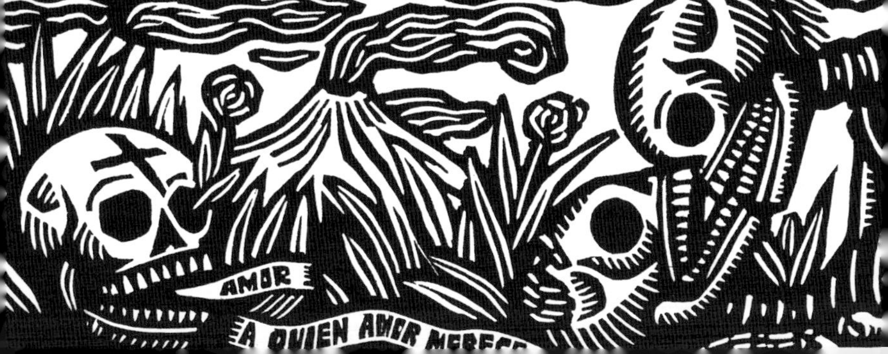
AMOR
A QUIEN AMOR

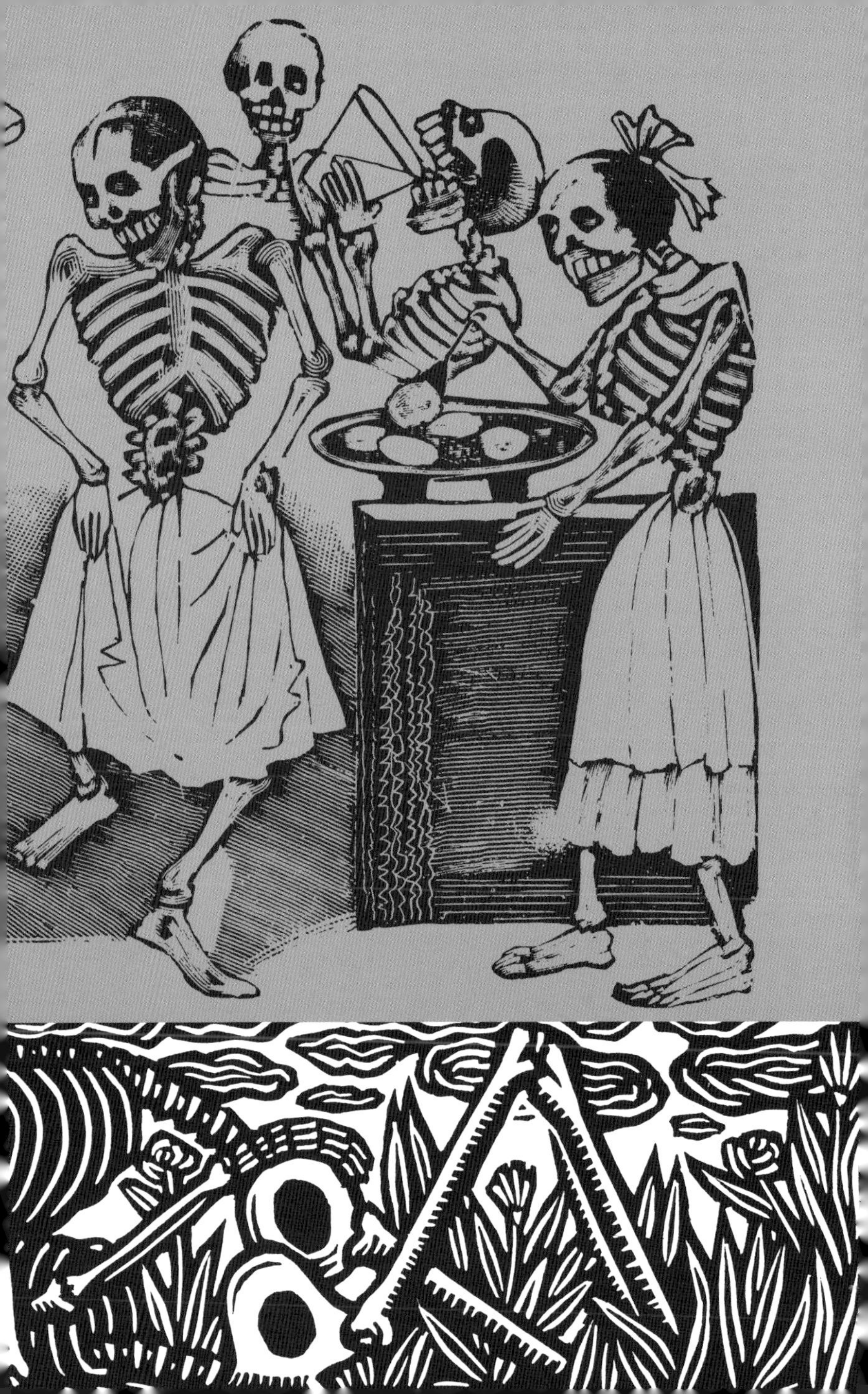

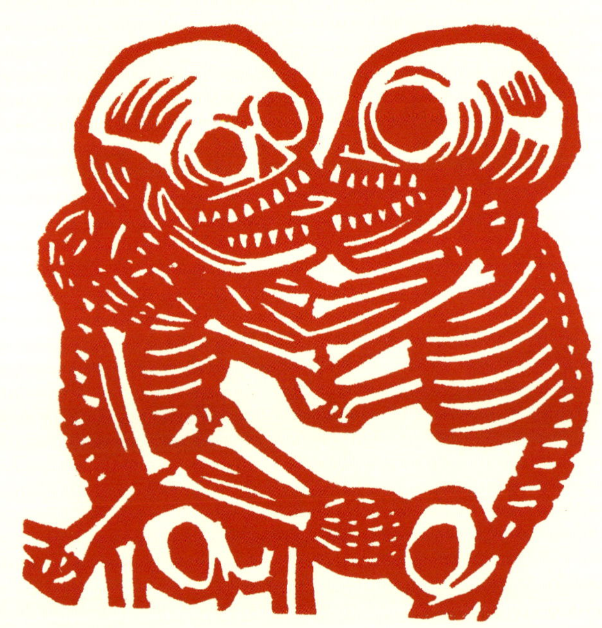

◆◆ José Guadalupe Posada *El fandango*
◆◆ Artemio Rodríguez *Amor a quien amor merece*
◆ Artemio Rodríguez *Loving*

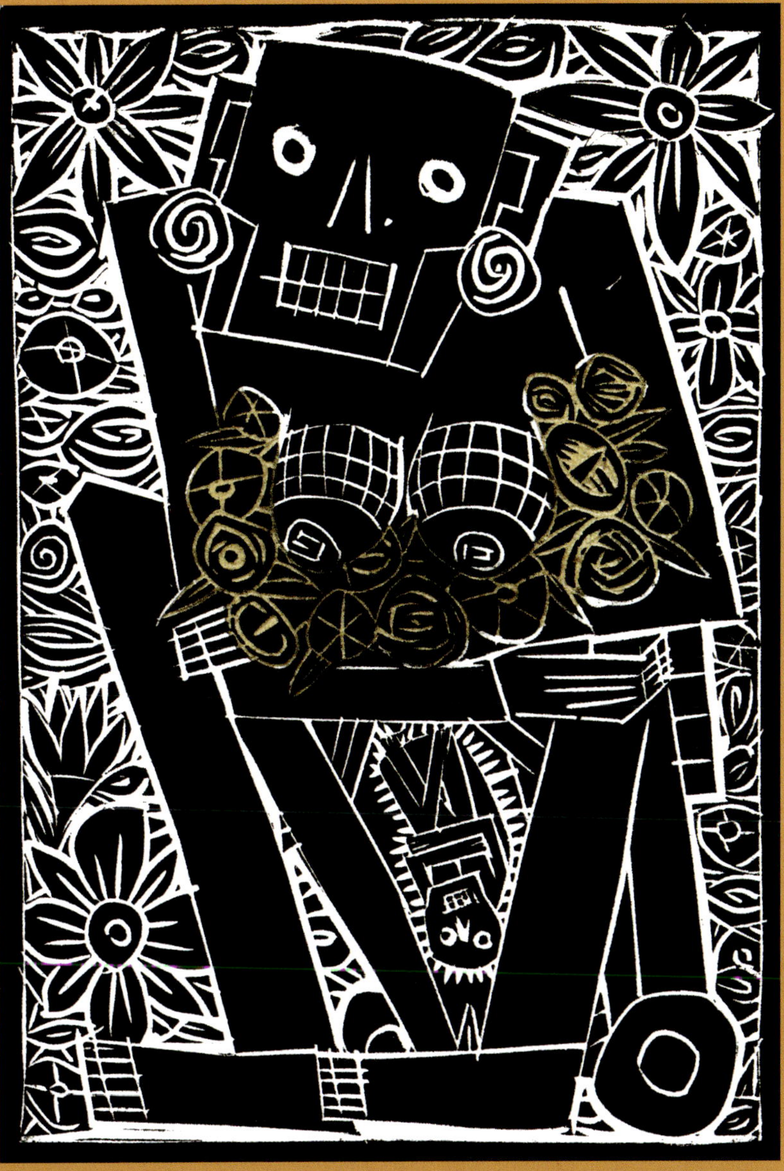

Joel Rendón *Muerta entre flores*

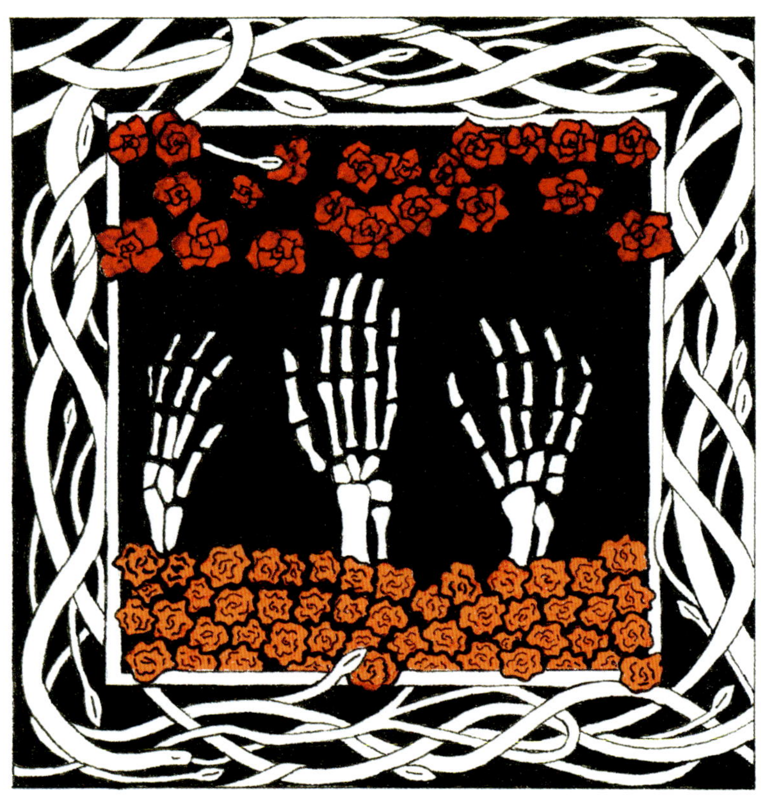

Susan Elizalde Holler *Vivir*

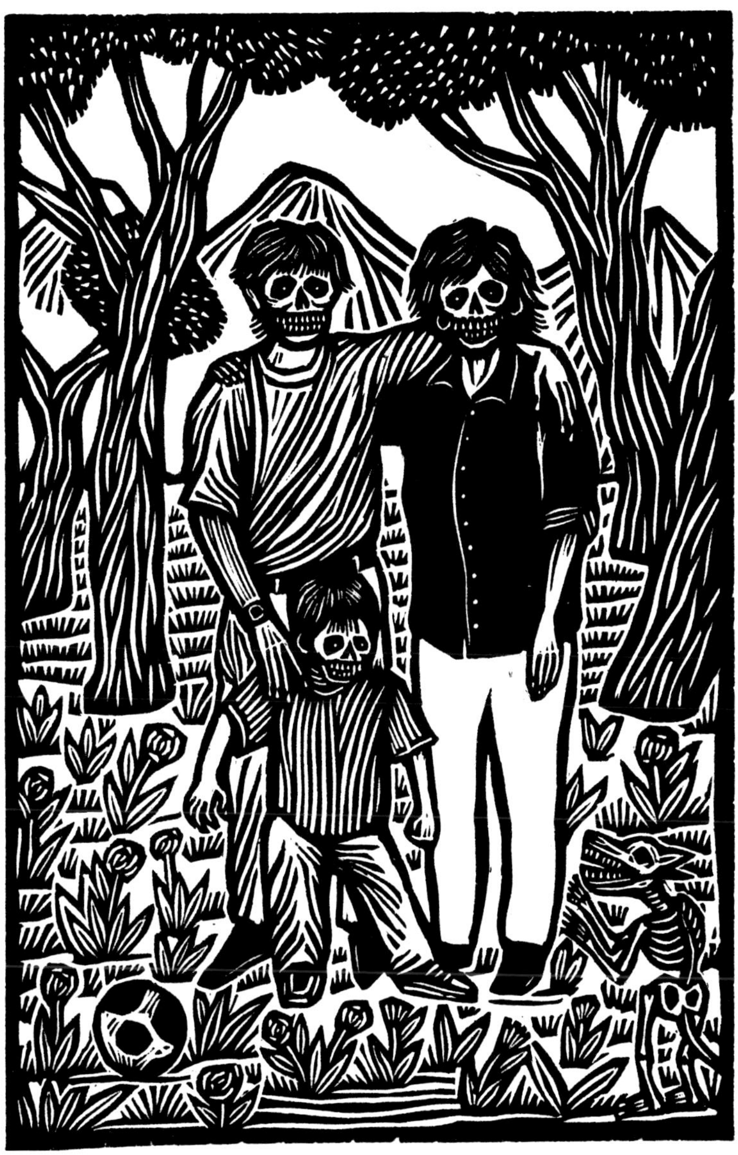

Artemio Rodríguez *Dead Family*

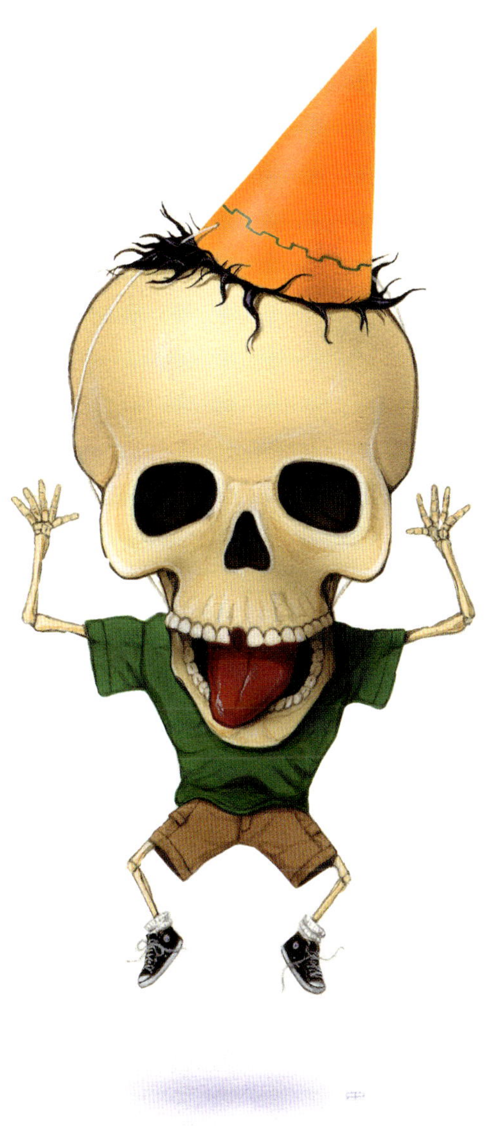

◆ Jaime Galindo *Mictlantecuhtli*
Robert Palacios *Bone Head Party Boy*

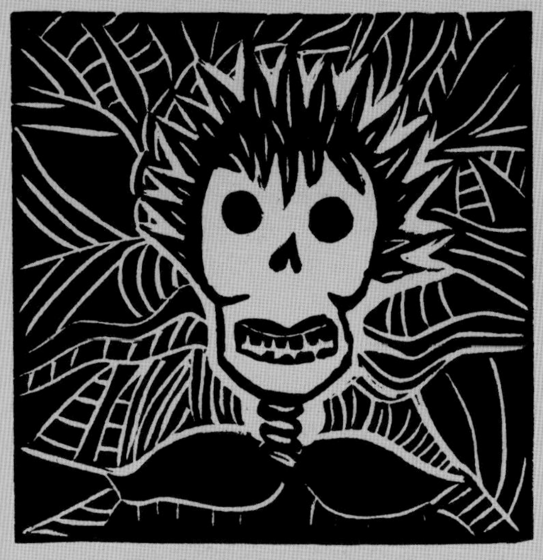

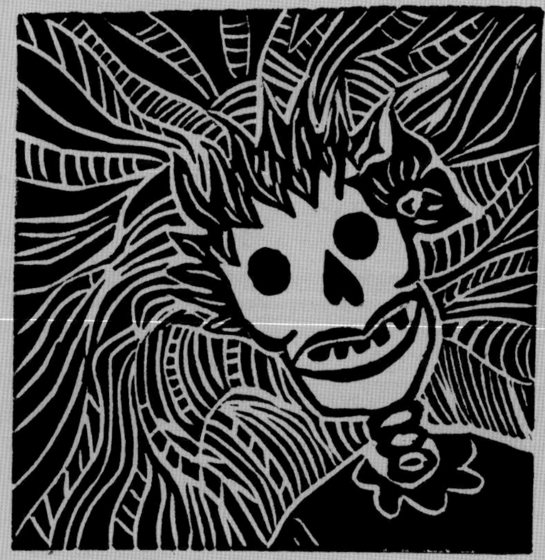

Emelda Gutierrez

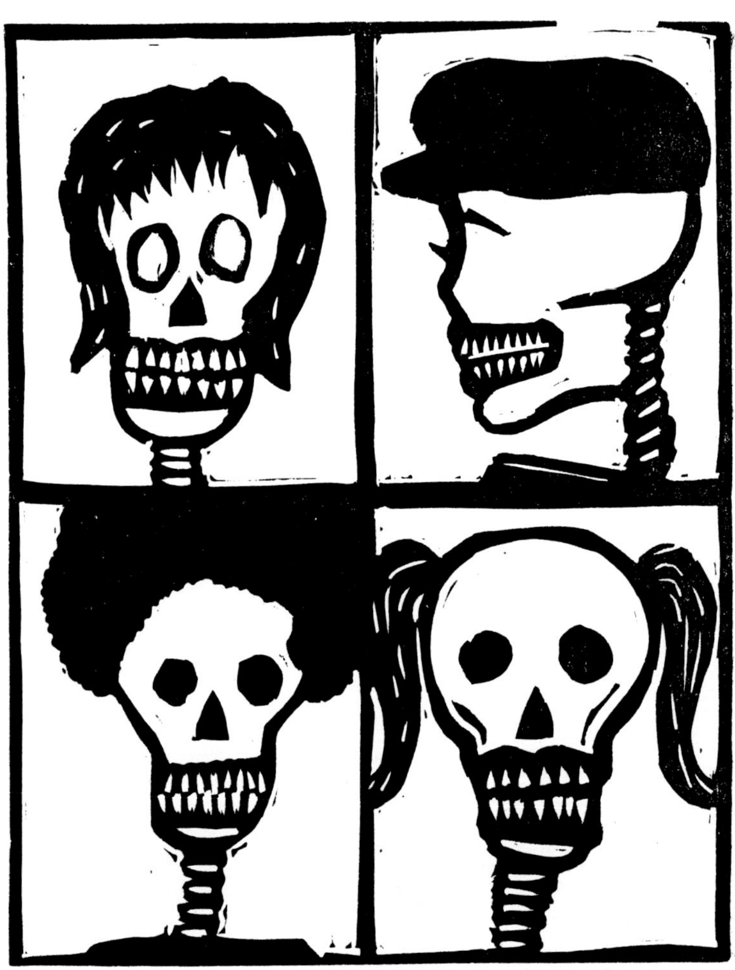

Silvia Capistrán *Cala Cool*

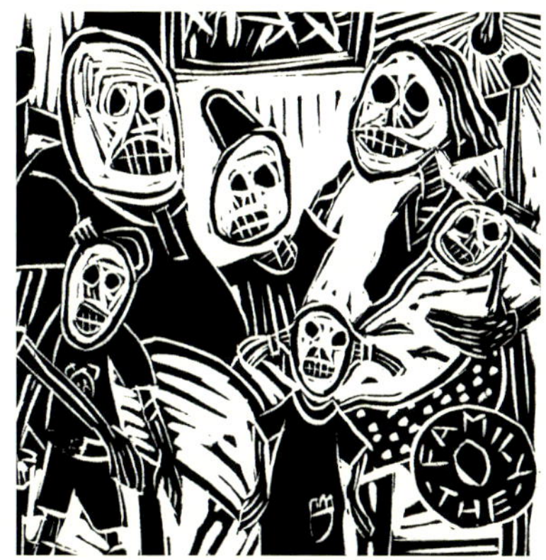

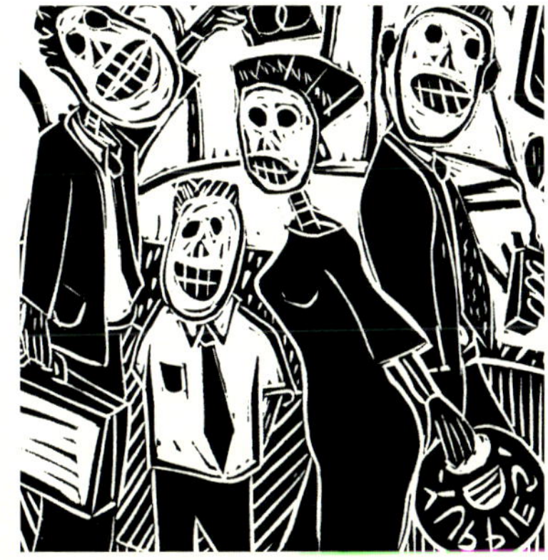

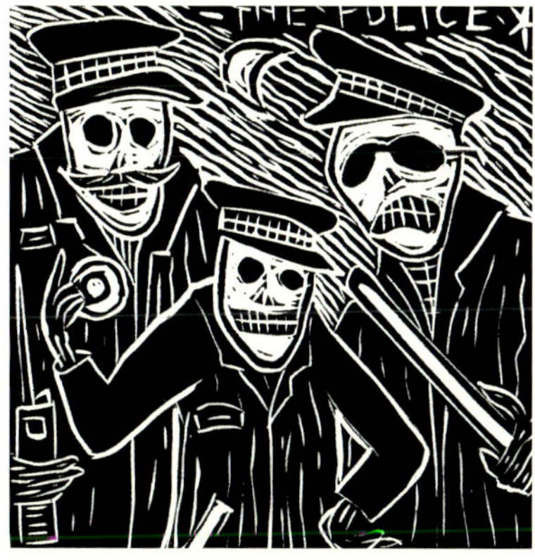

Joel Rendón *Chicago's Life*

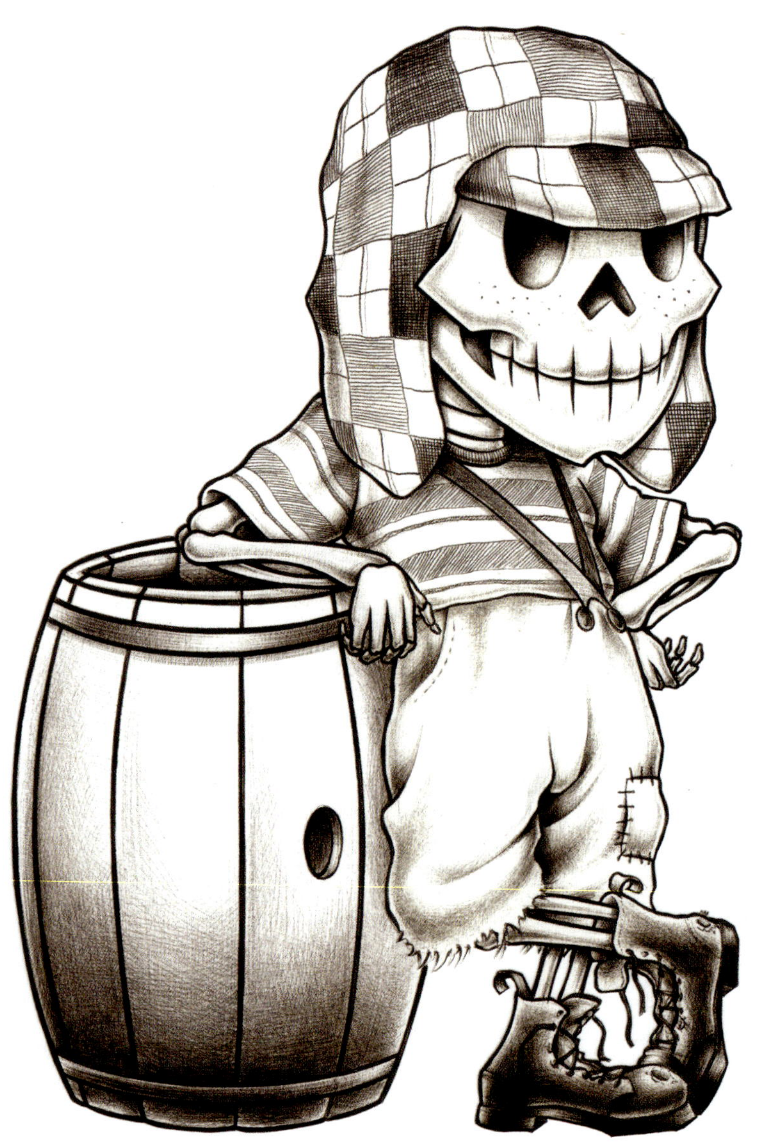

Mario Votán *La kalaka del 8*

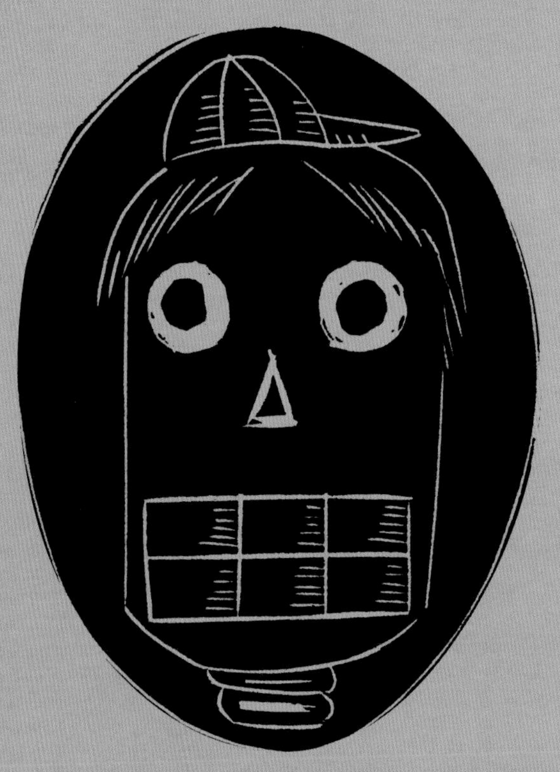

◆ Victor Rosas *Untilted*
◆◆ Daniel González *Yo soy la desintegracion*
◆◆◆ José Guadalupe Posada *La Catrina*

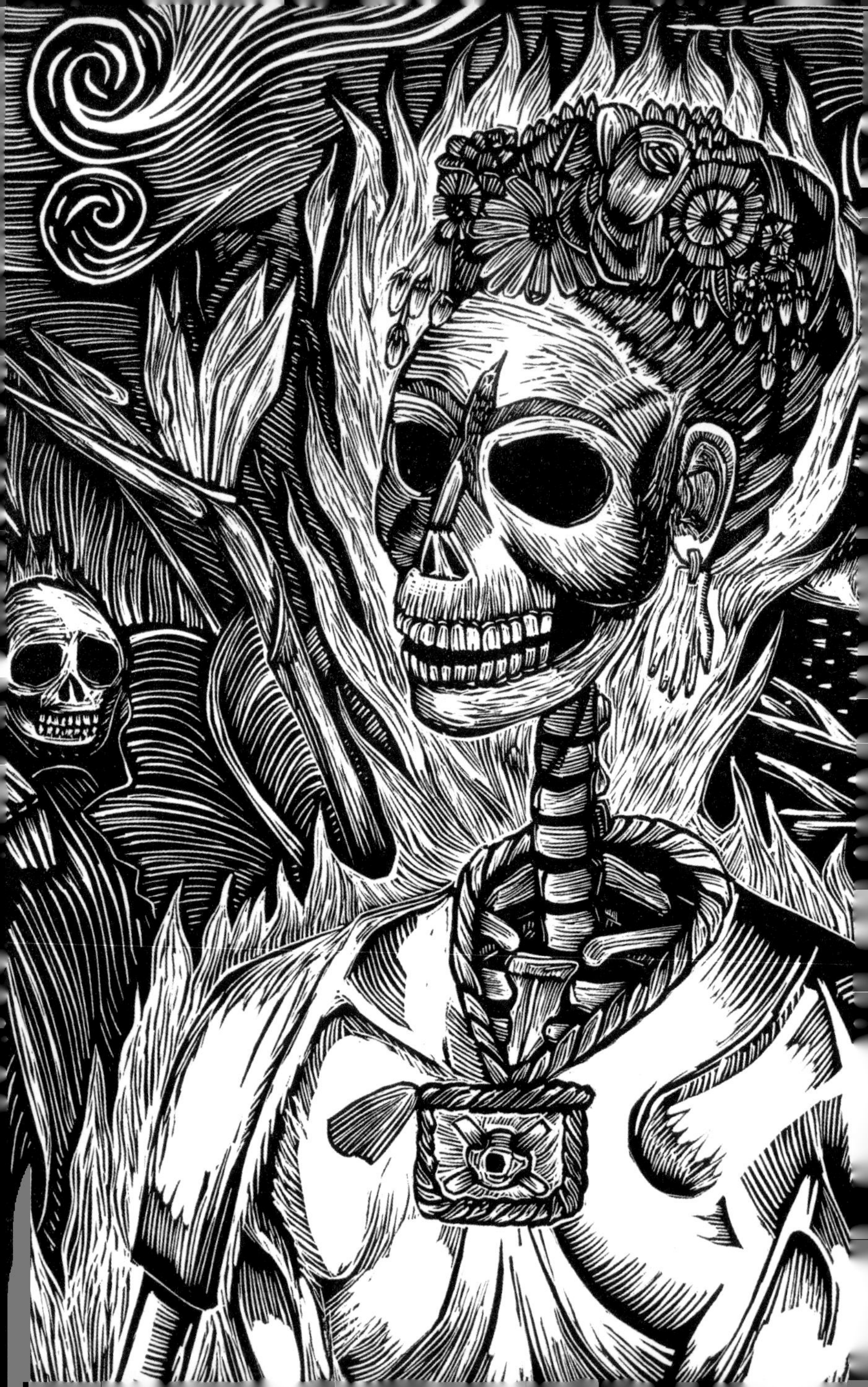

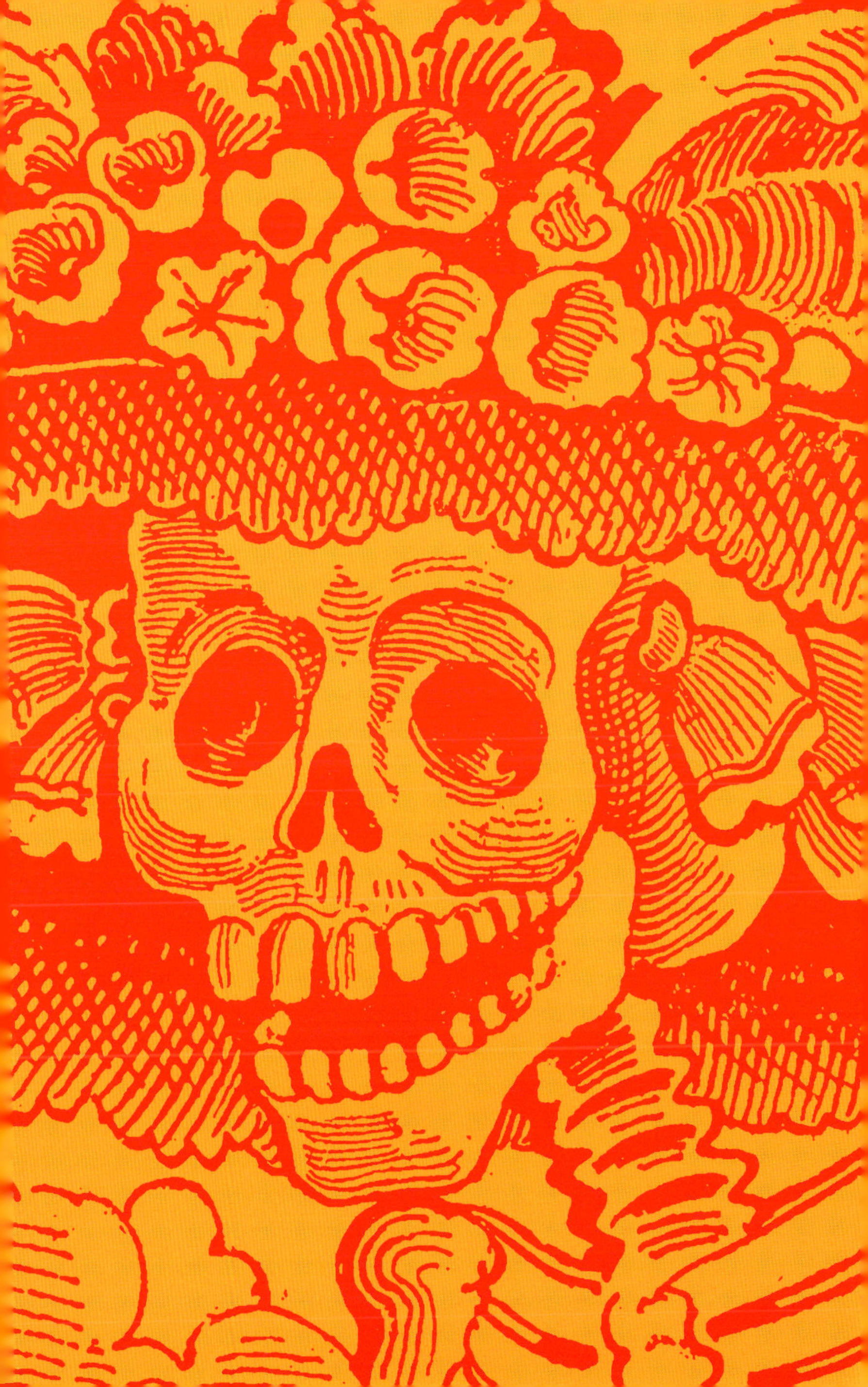

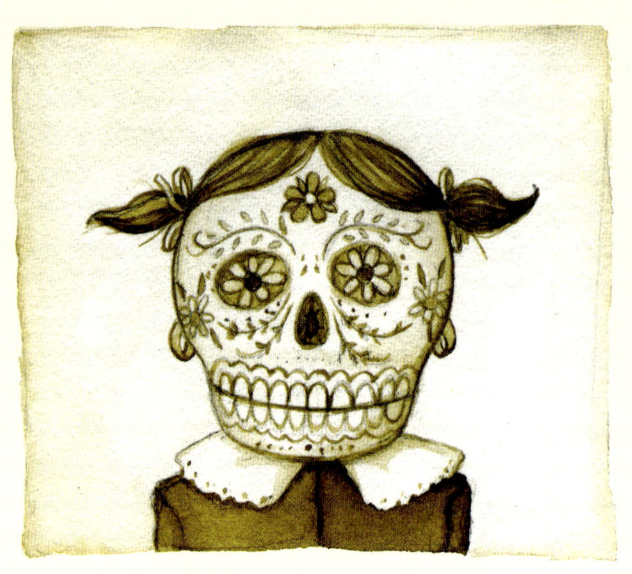

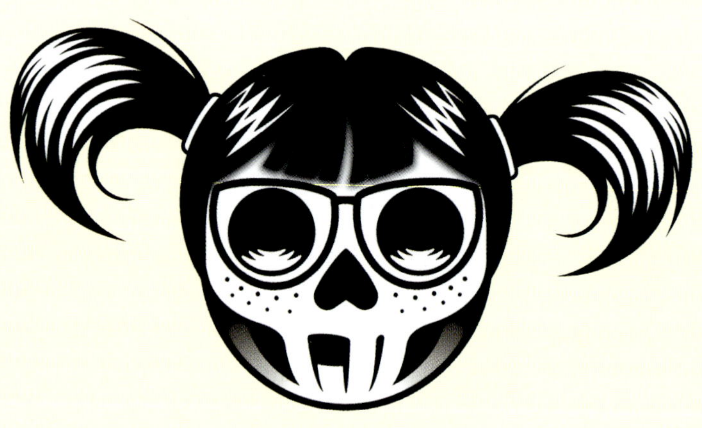

Robert Palacios *Smile*
Mario Votán *La chili vera*

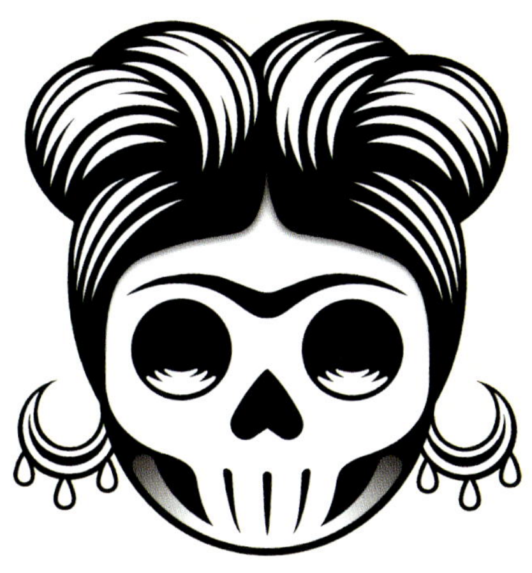

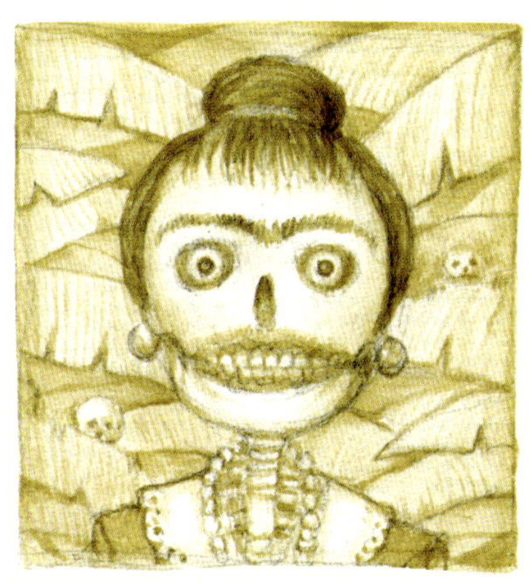

Mario Votán *Frida Kahlakalo*
Robert Palacios *Frida with monkeys*

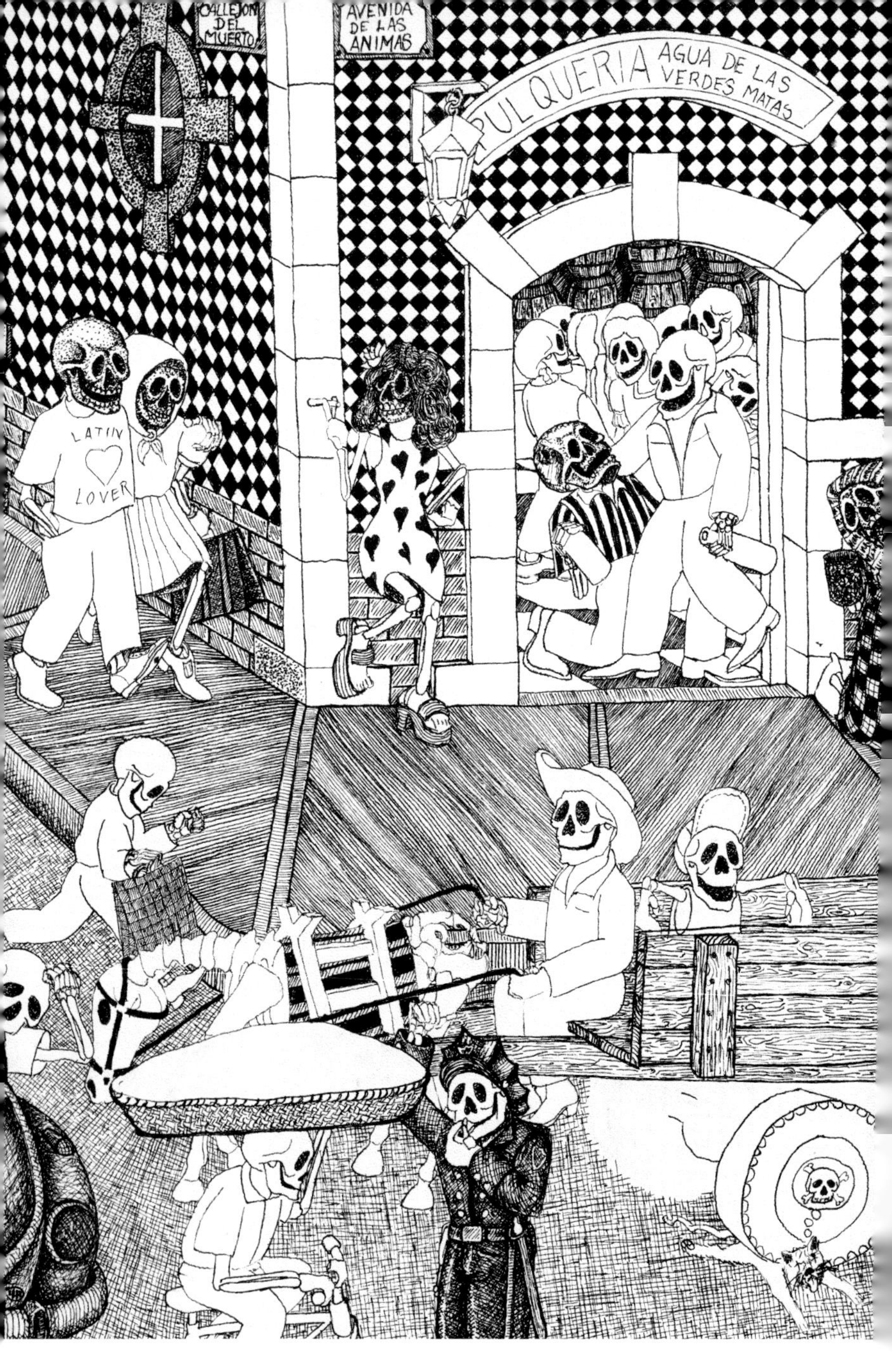

Gabriel Galán *La esquina del muerto*

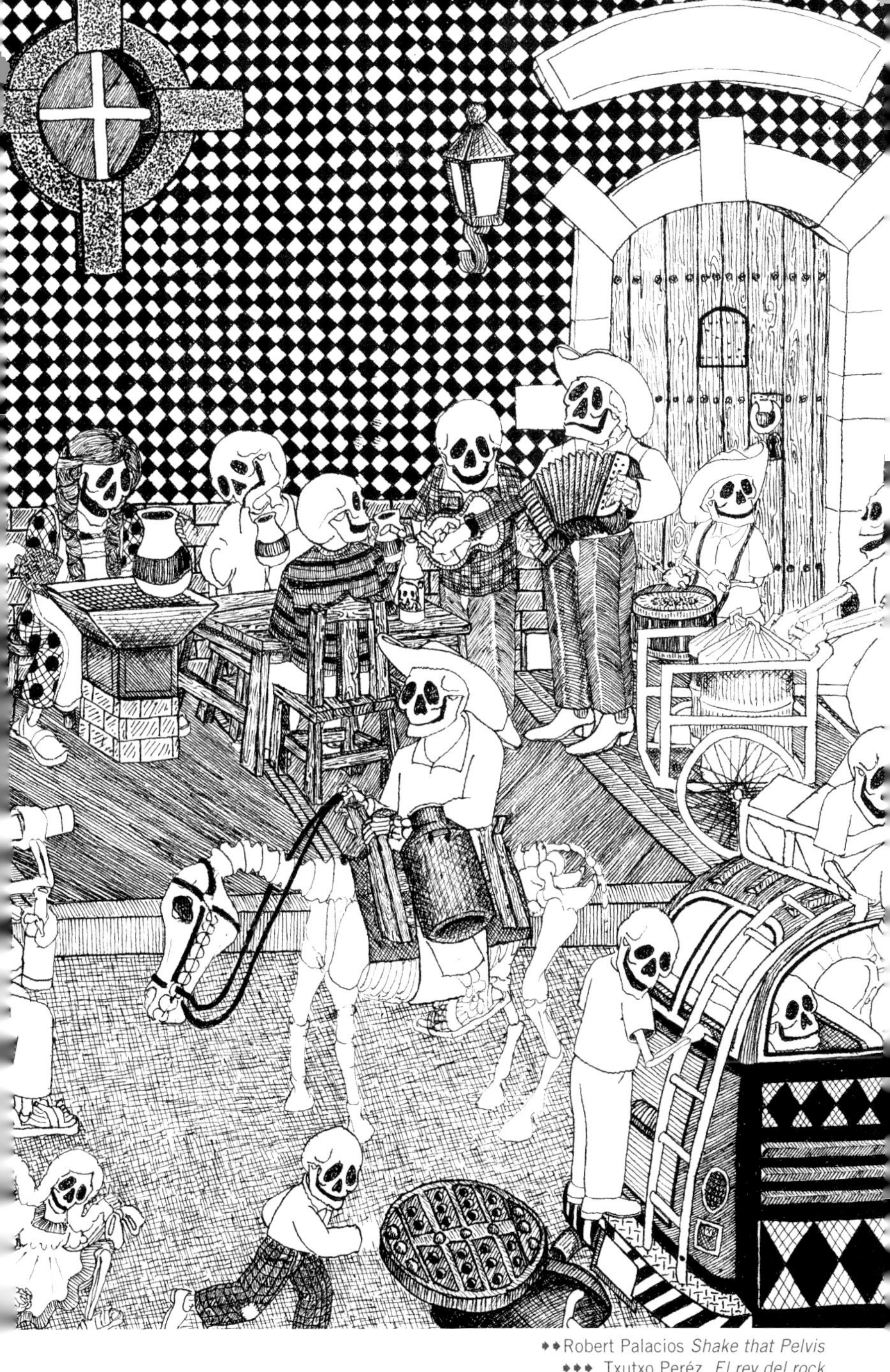

⯌⯌Robert Palacios *Shake that Pelvis*
⯌⯌⯌ Txutxo Peréz *El rey del rock*

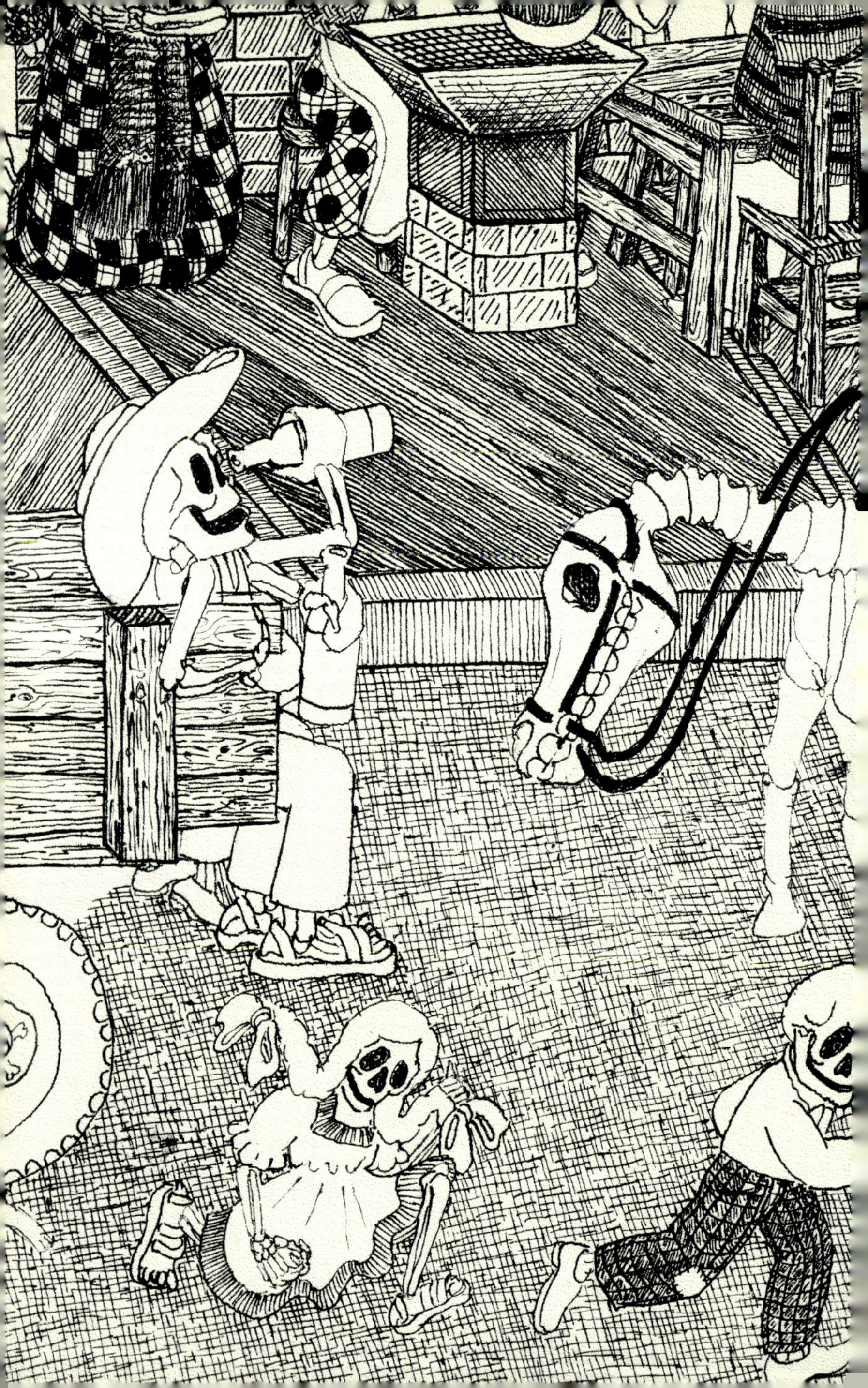

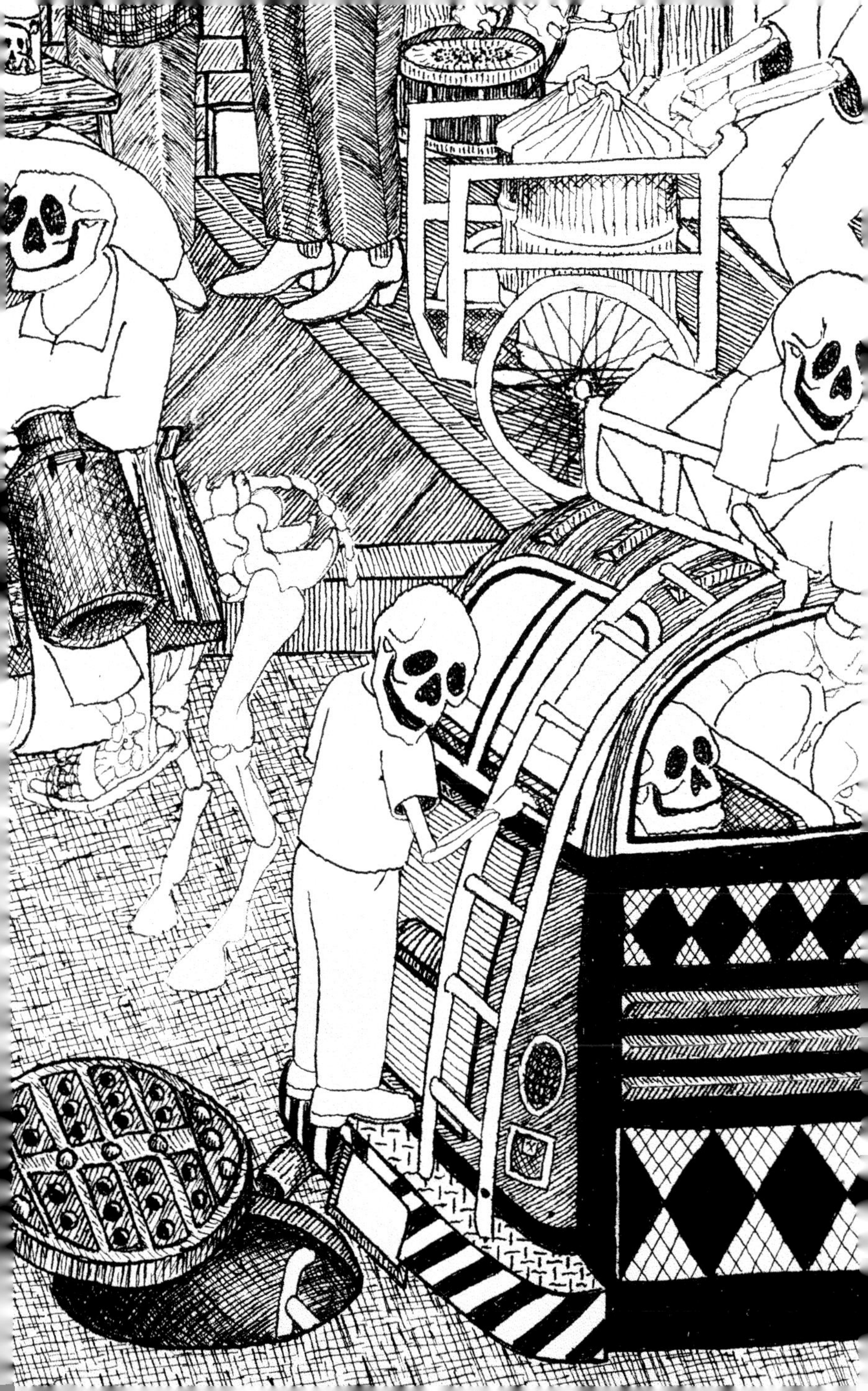

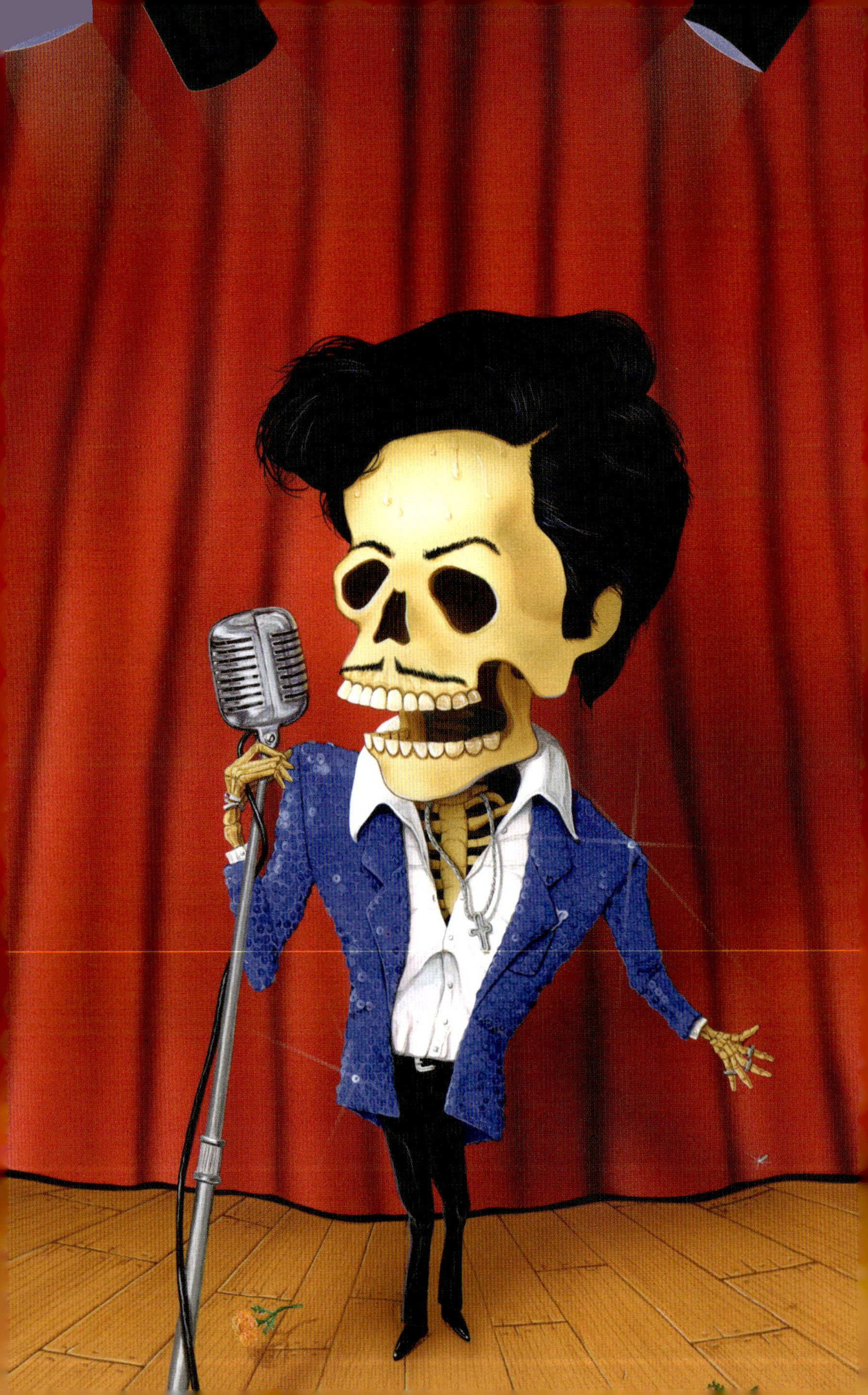

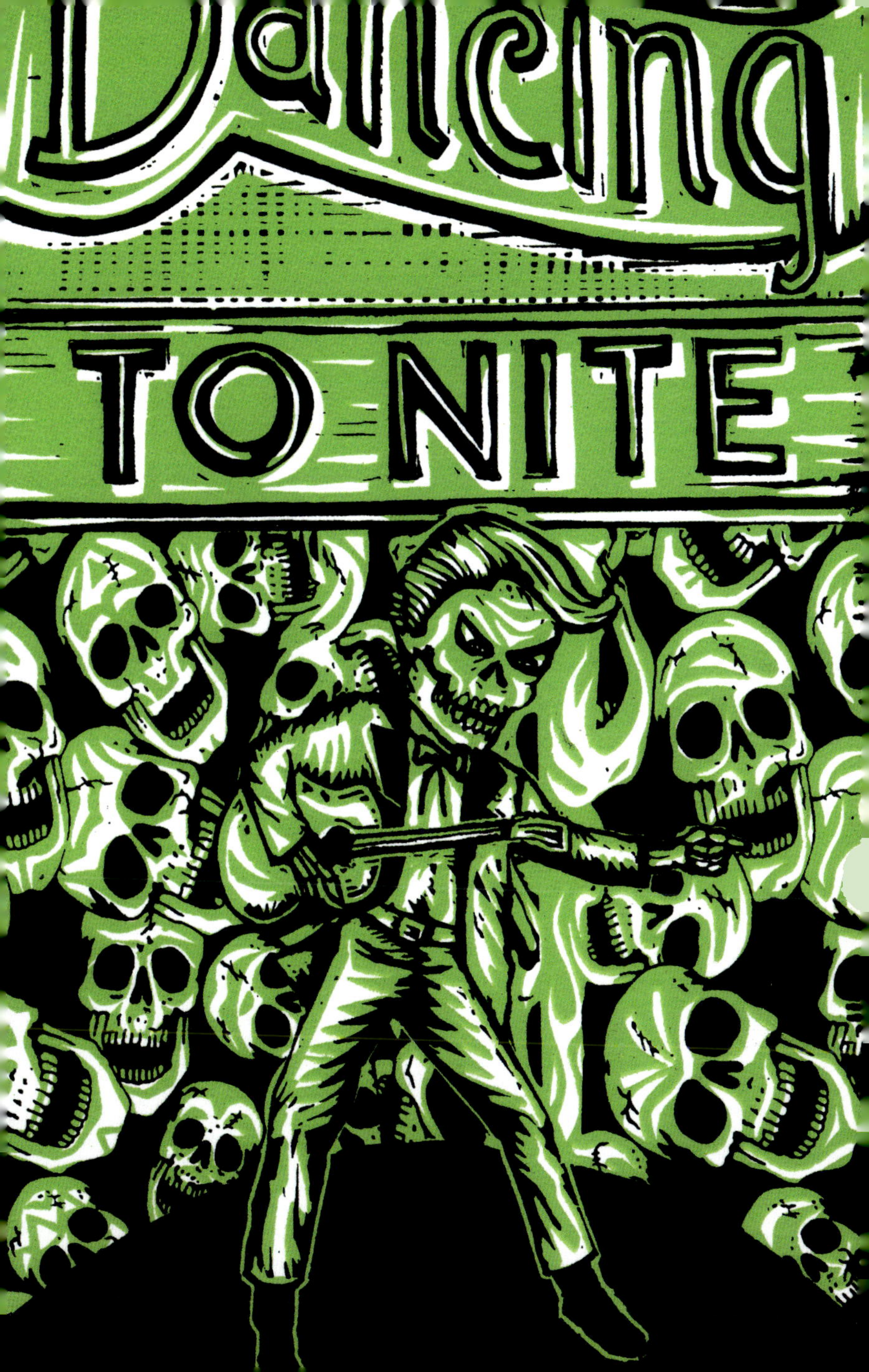
Dancing
TO NITE

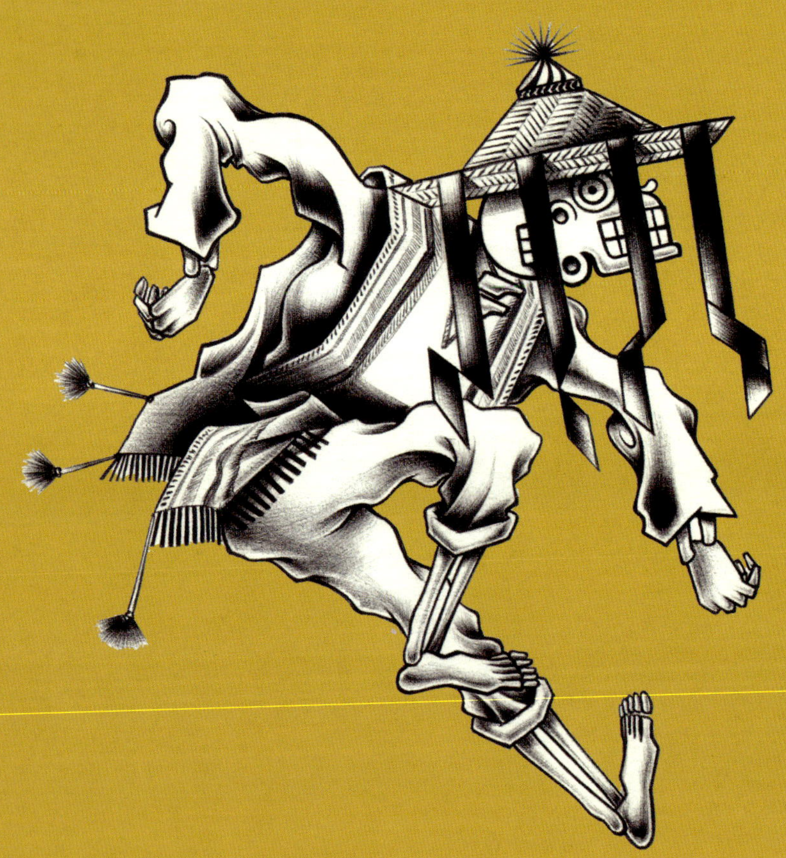

Mario Votán *Danzante Tzotzil*

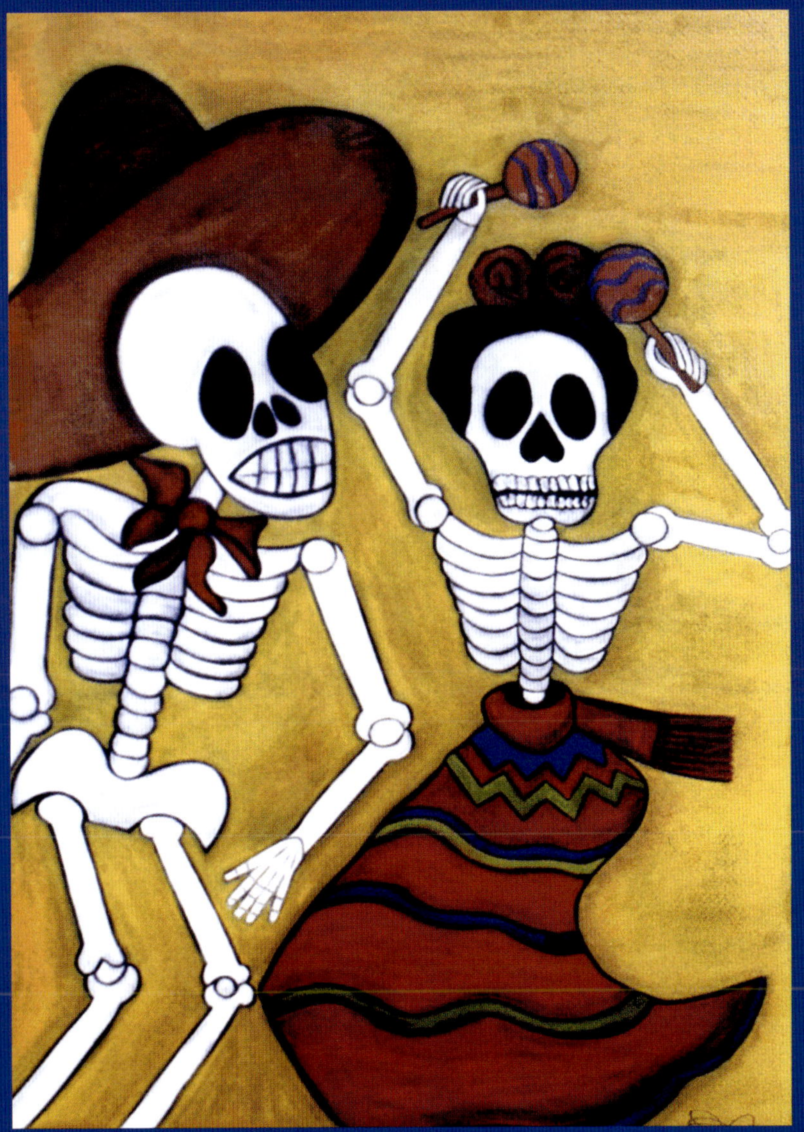

Emilia García *Fiesta Eterna*

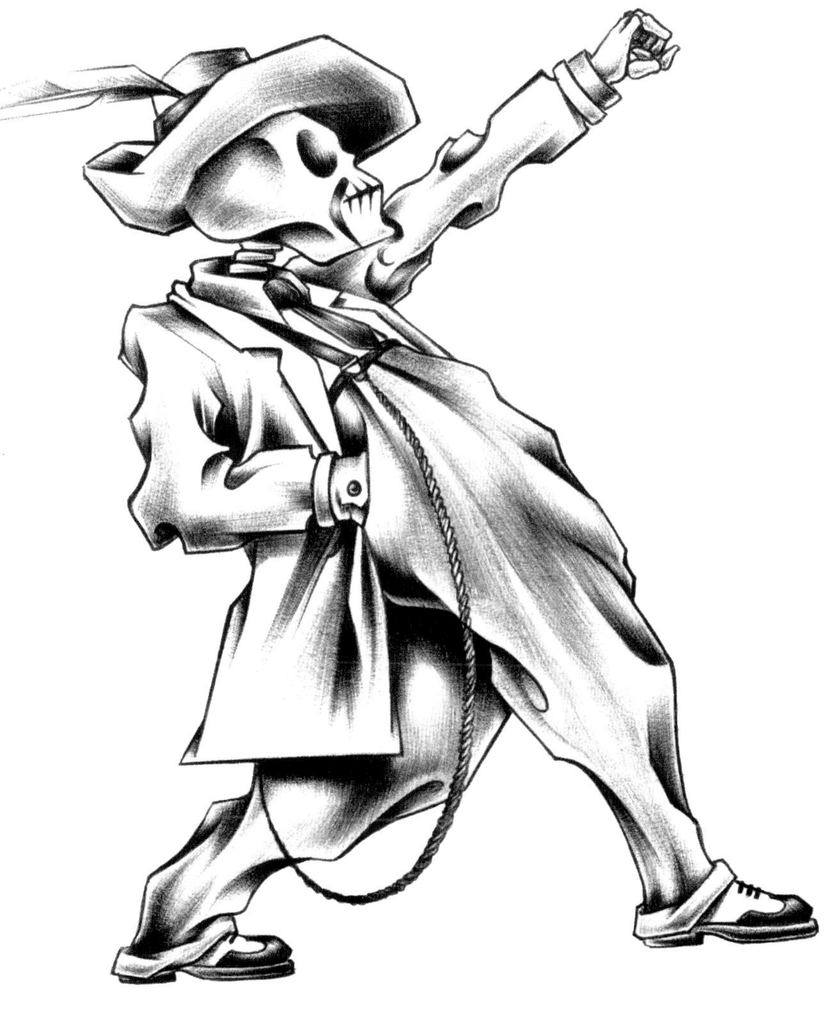

◆ Joel Rendón *Chicago's Life* detail
◆ Mario Votán *Resiste*

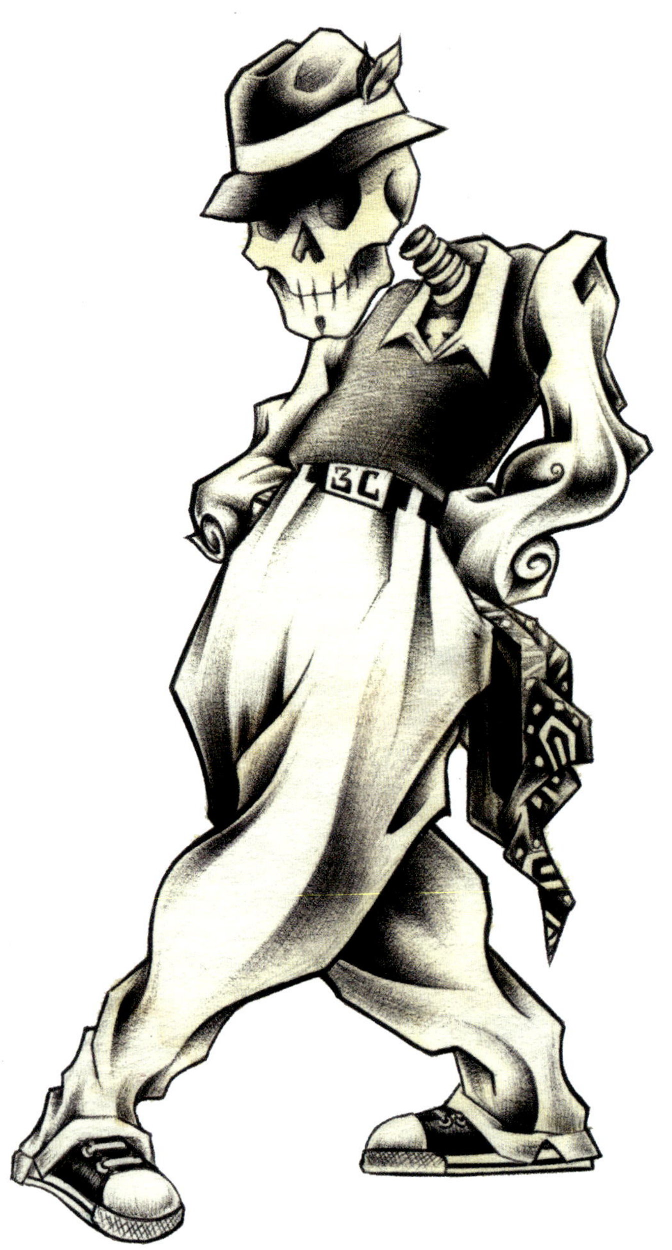

- Mario Votán *Paxukoh*
- Mario Votán *El Klandestino*

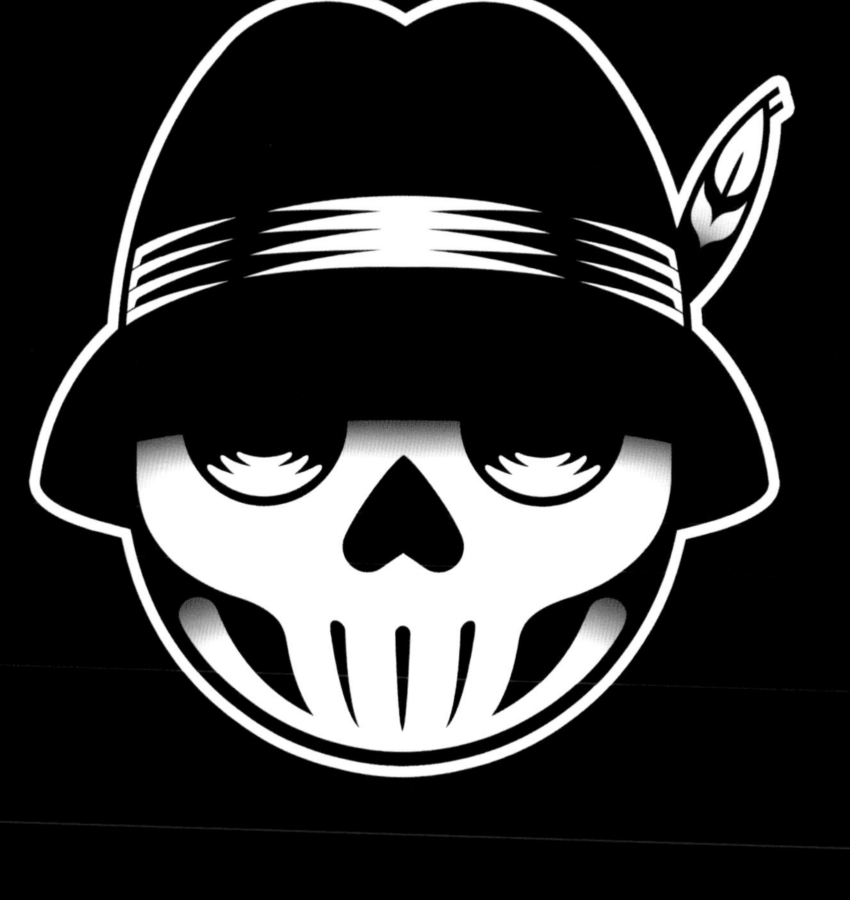

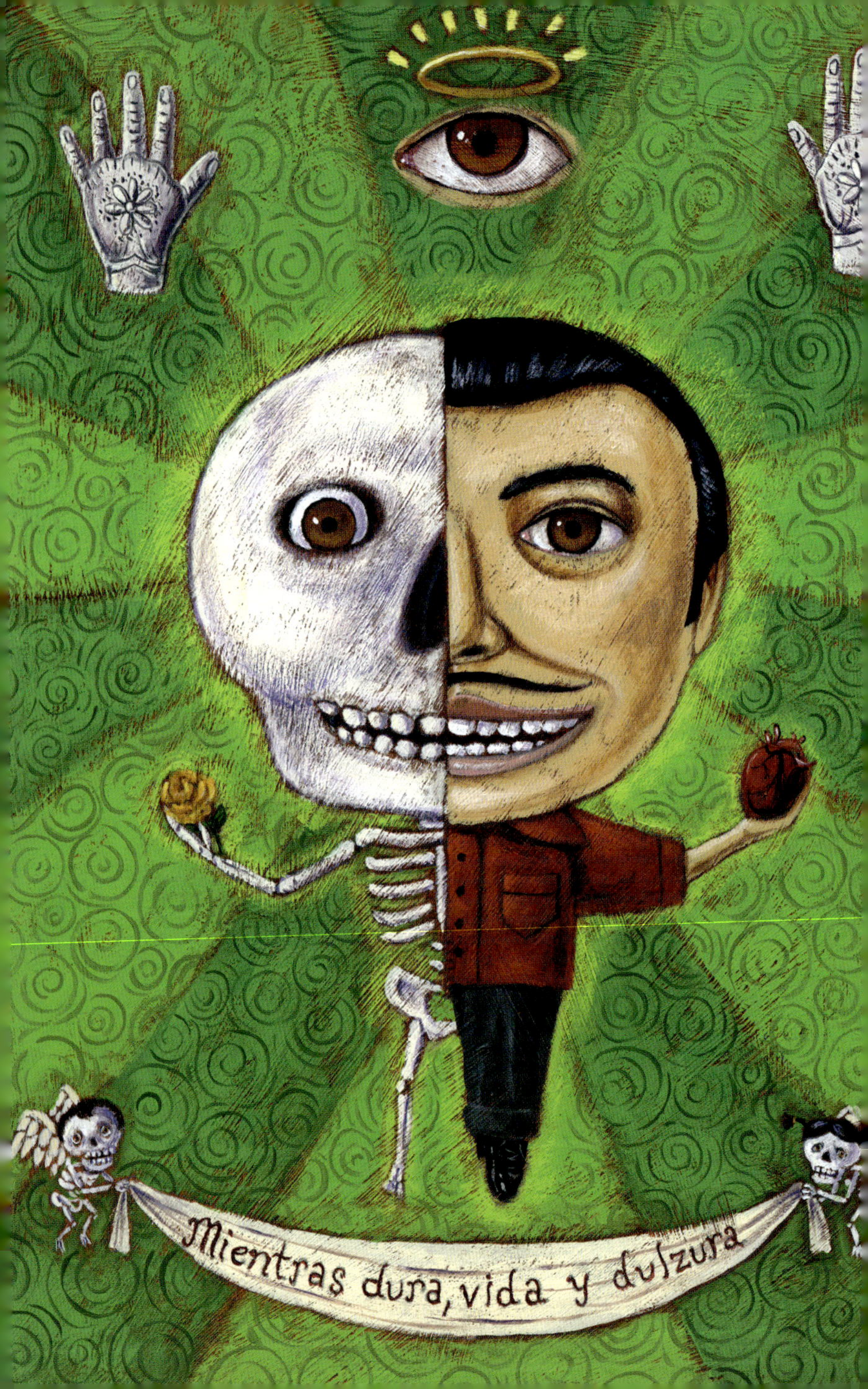
Mientras dura, vida y dulzura

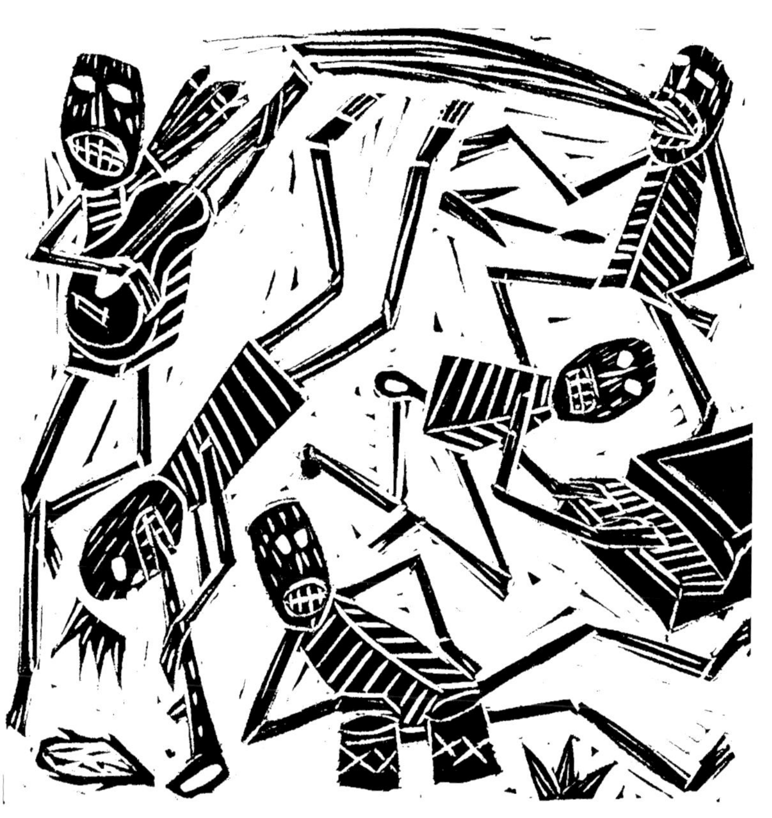

- Robert Palacios *Untitled*
- Joel Rendón *Los Músicos*

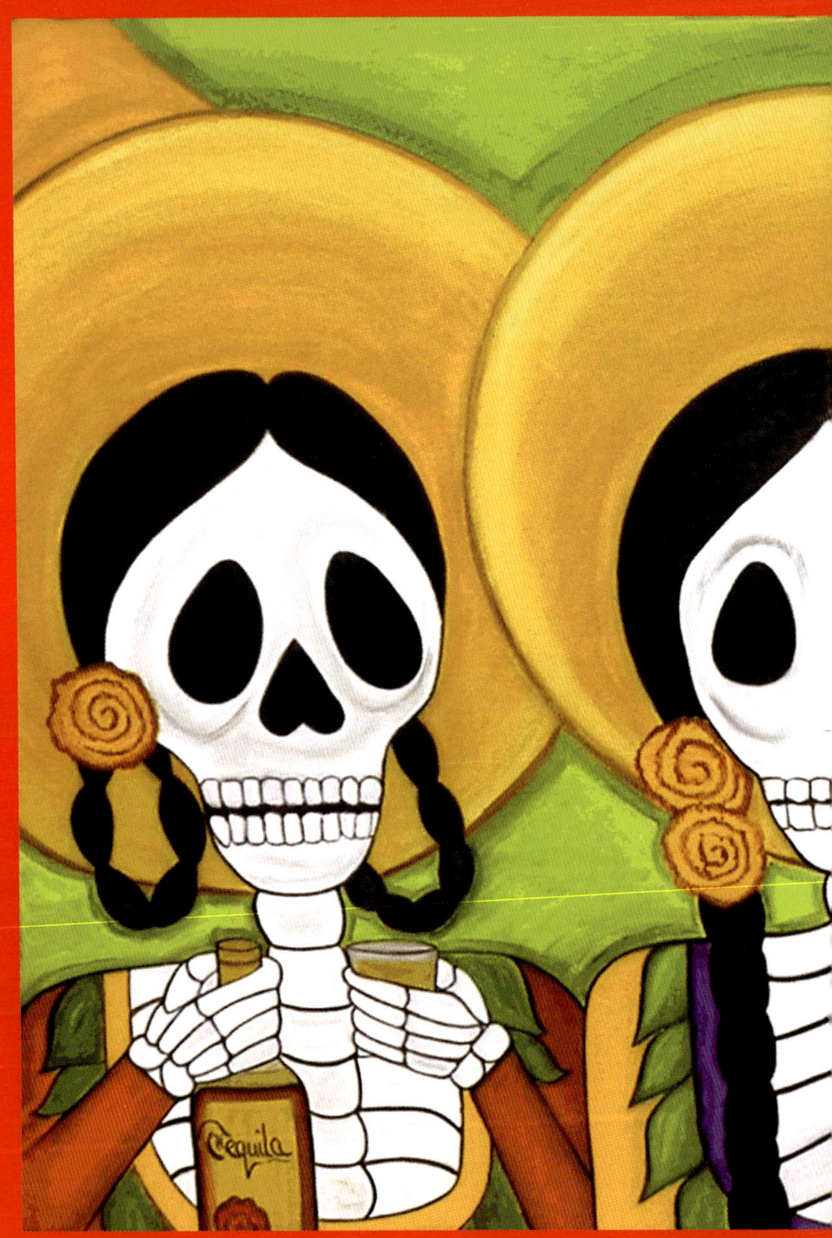

Emilia García *Trio Las Panchas*

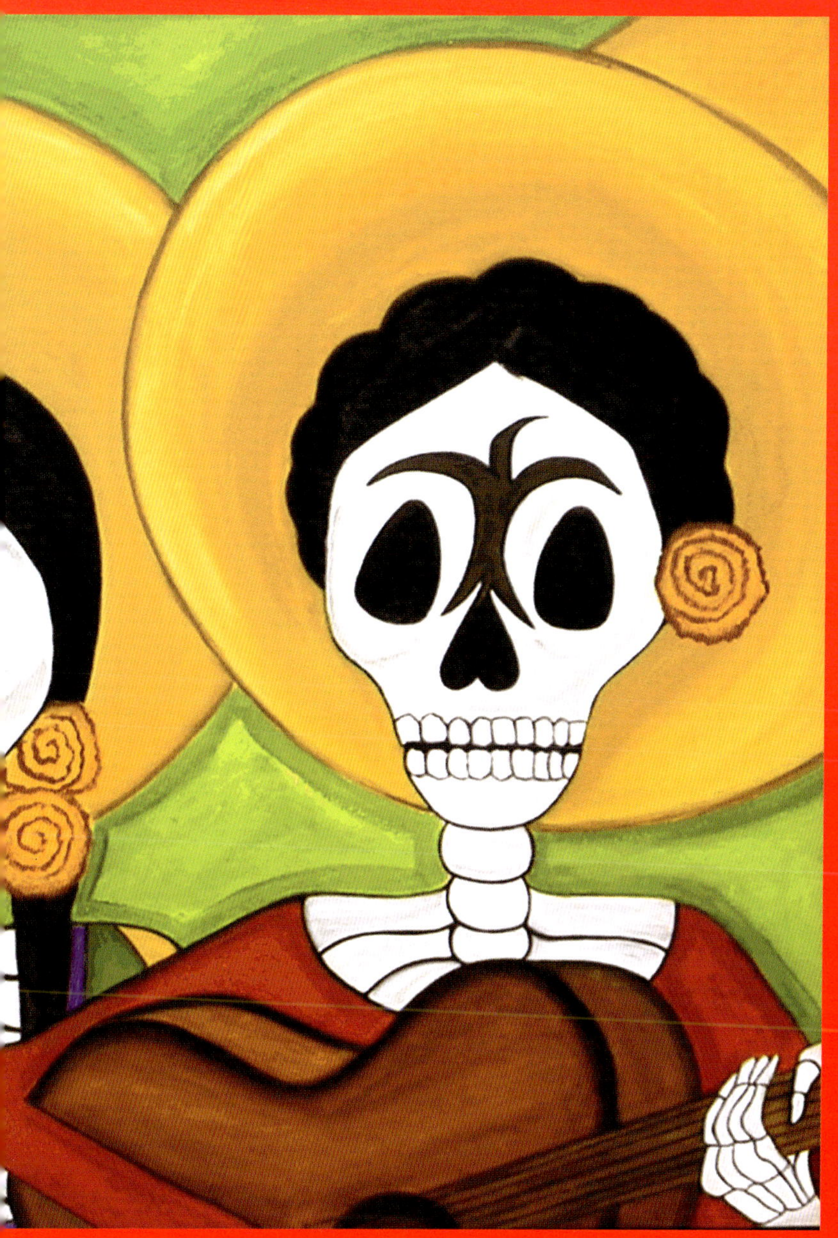

◆◆Emmanuel Montoya *Homenaje a Eugenio Abrego calavera norteña*

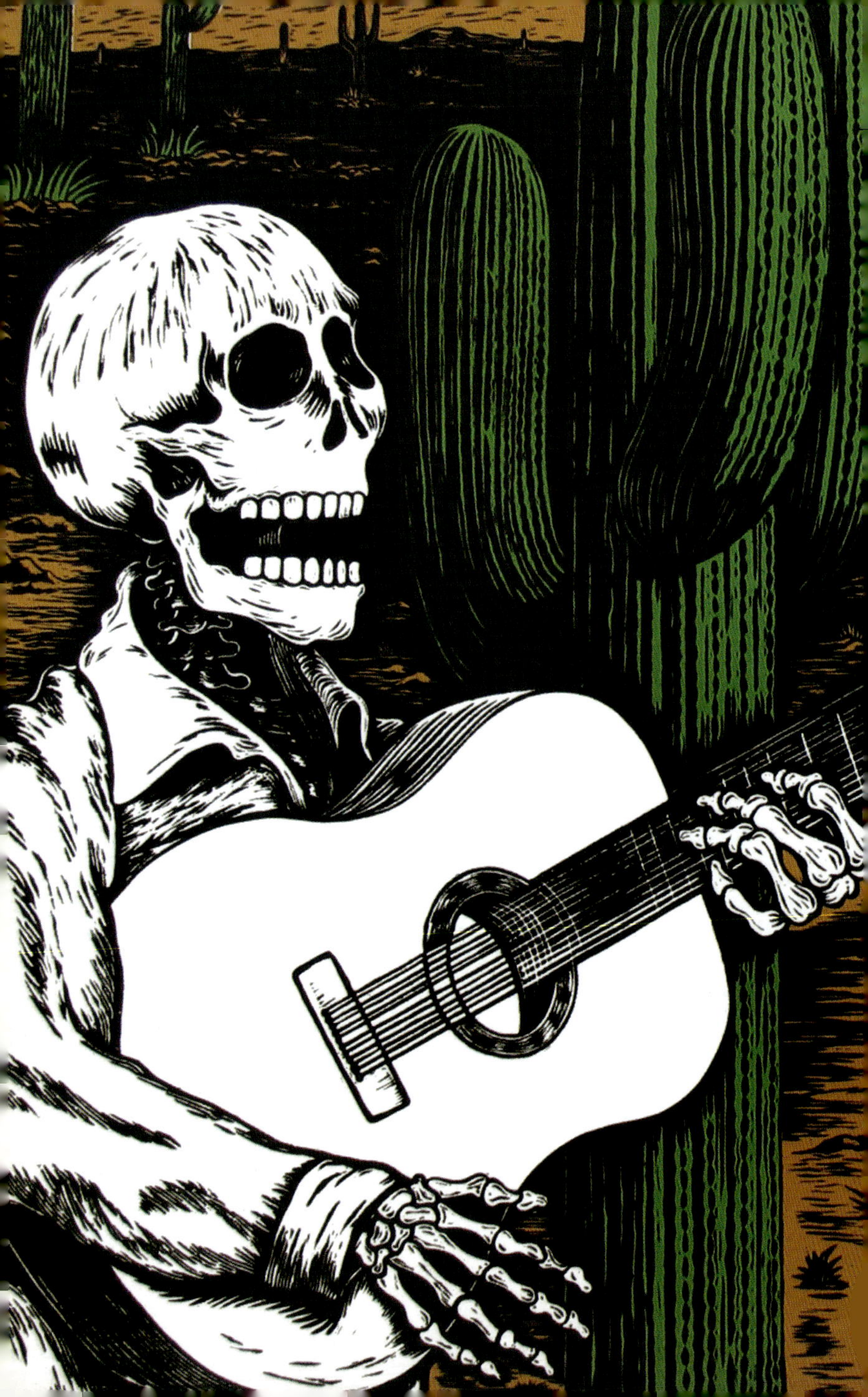

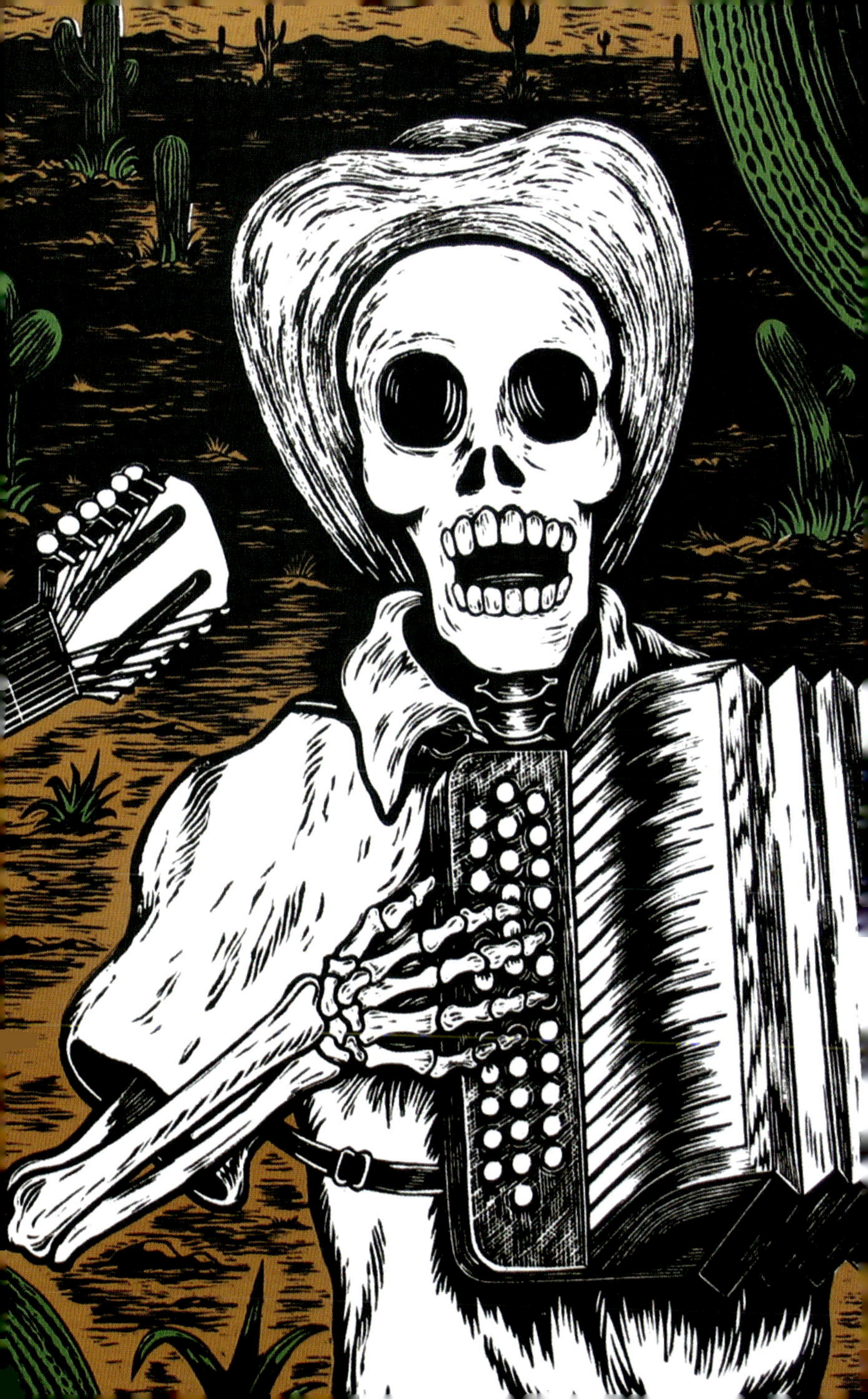

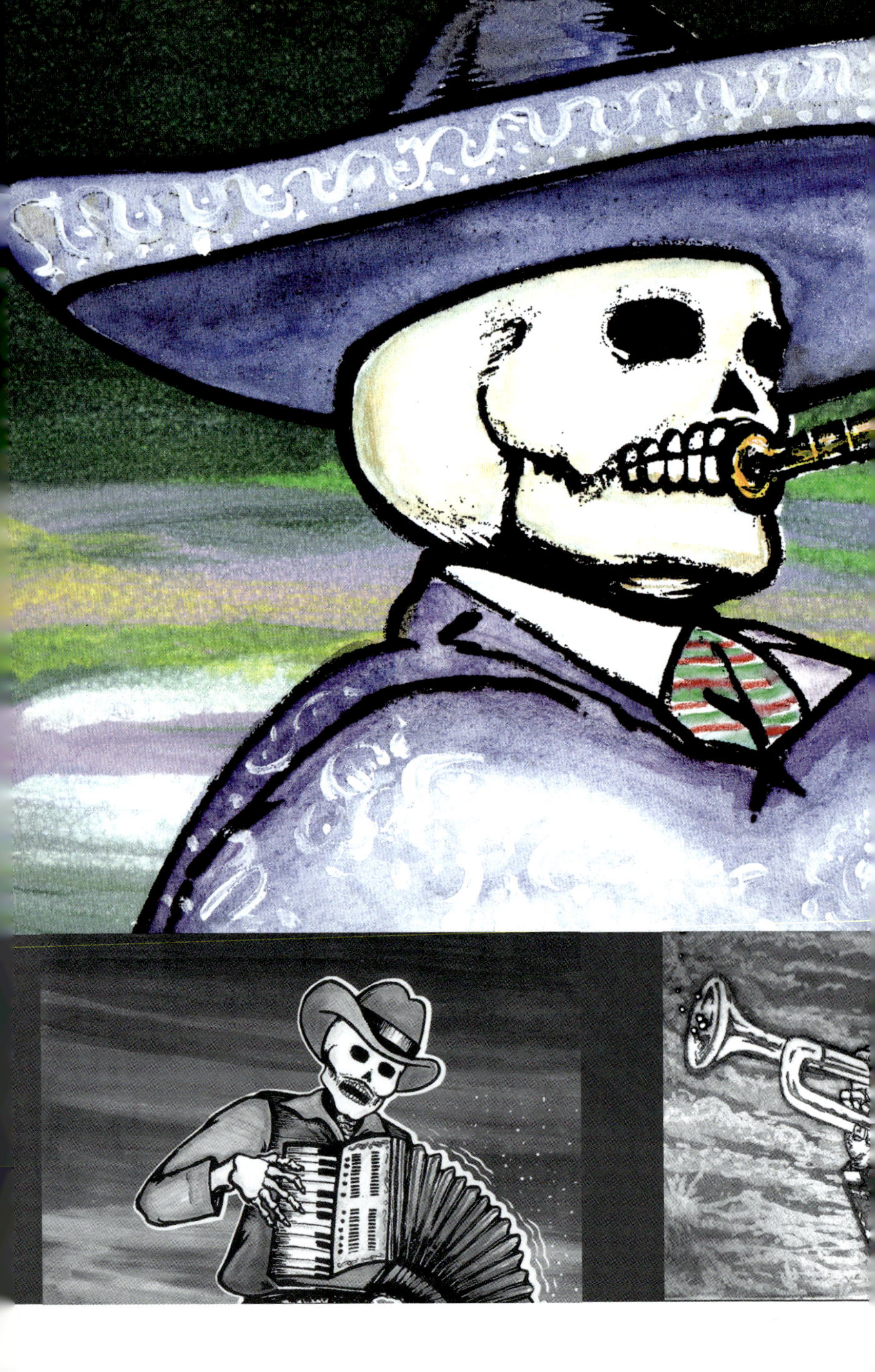

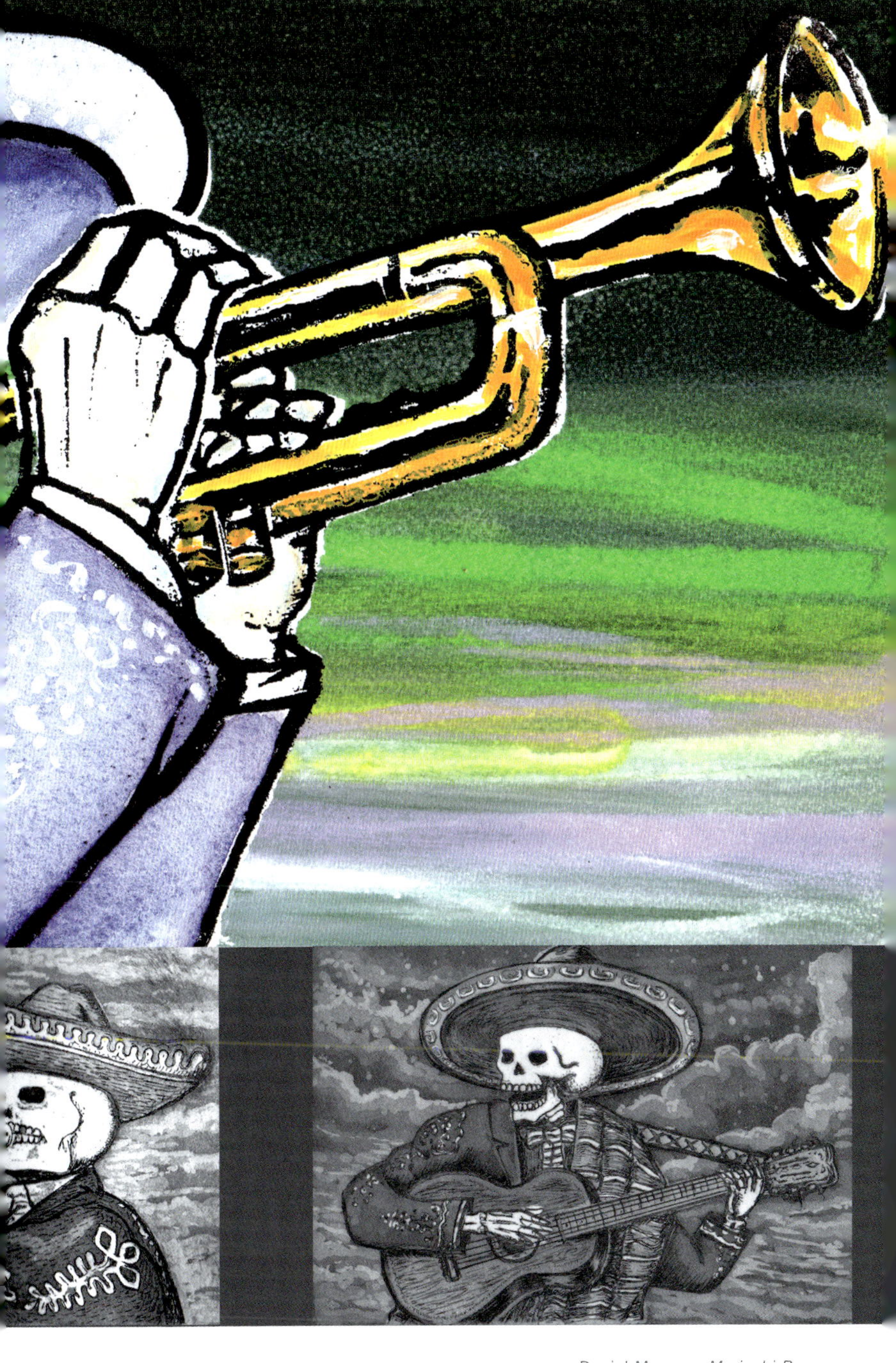

Daniel Marquez *Mariachi Brass*

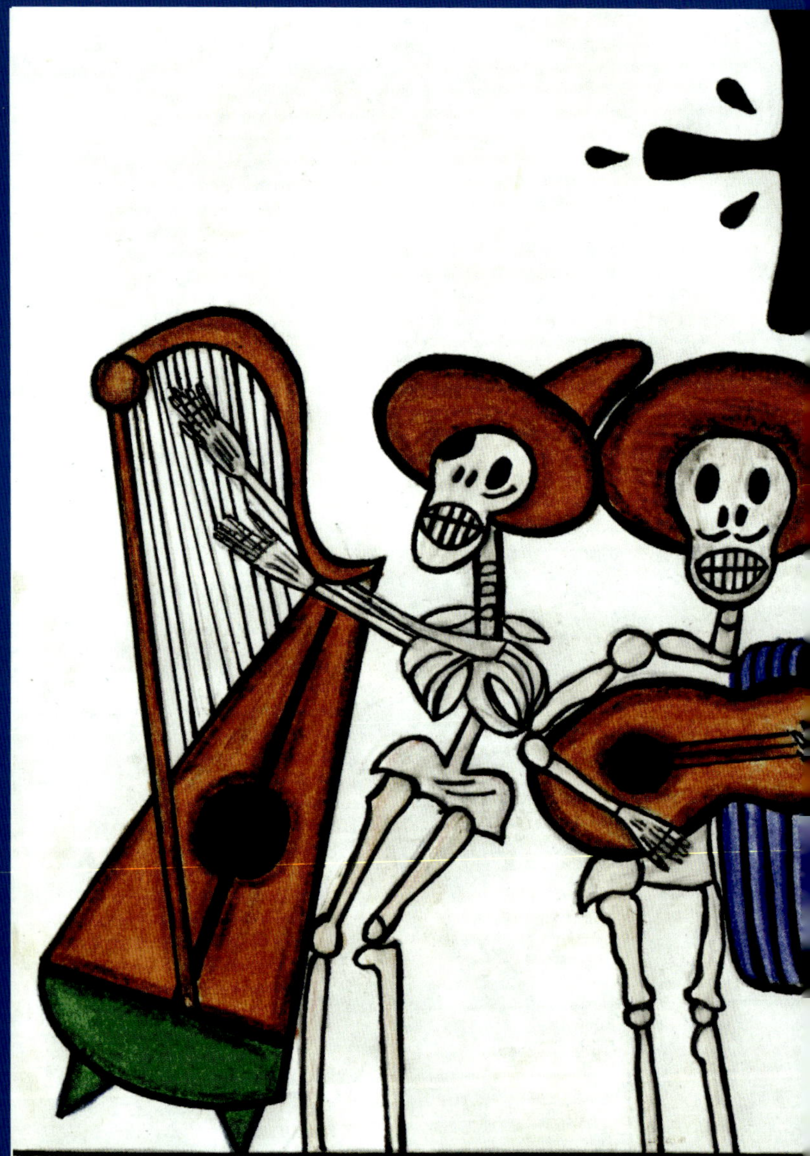

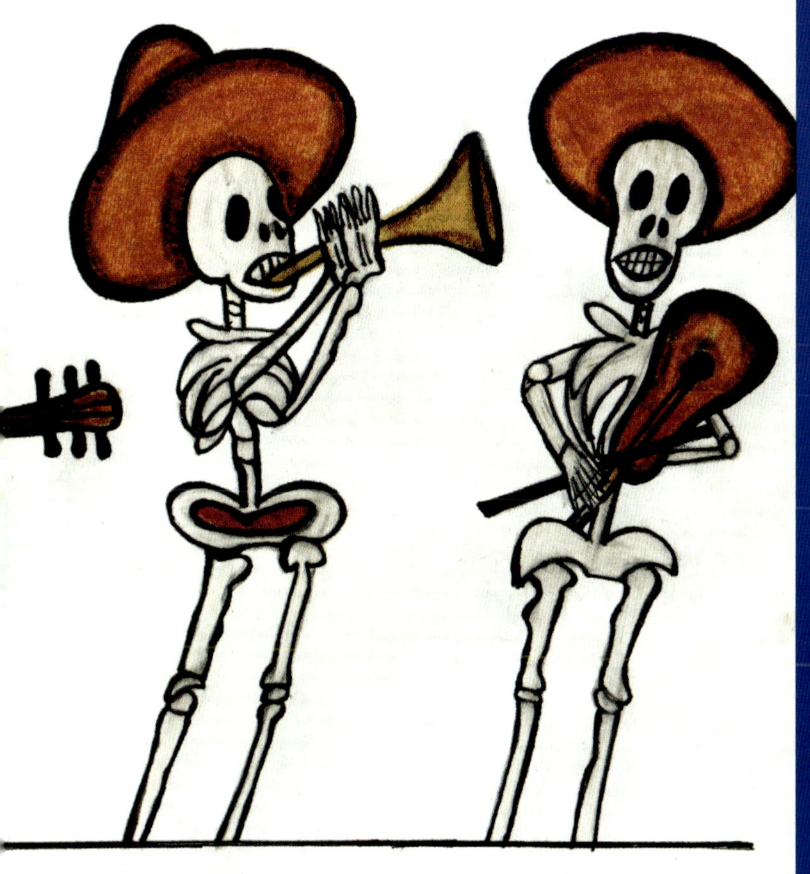

Emilia García *Poncho Calaca Band*

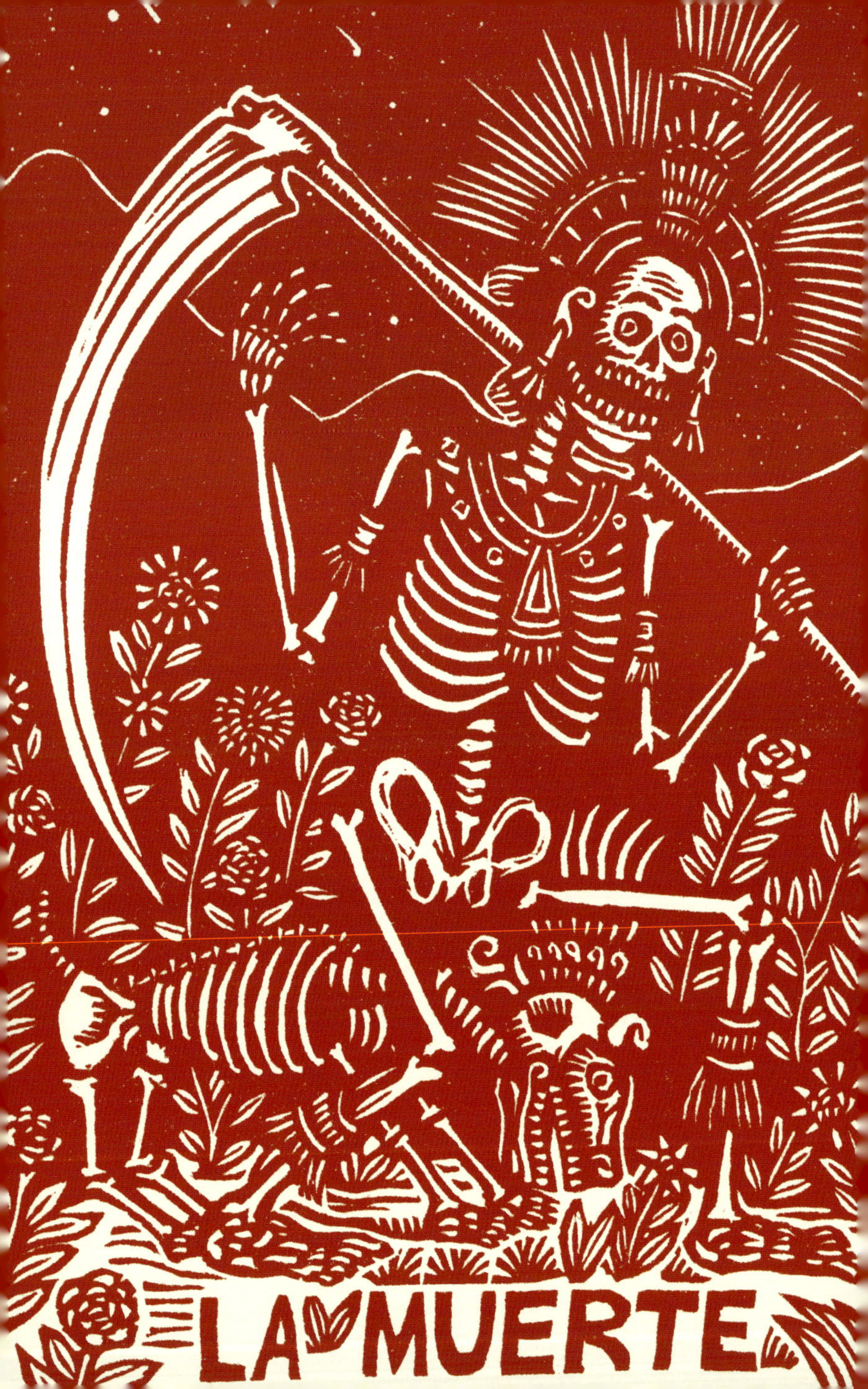
LA MUERTE

◆ Artemio Rodríguez *La Muerte*
◆ Victor Rosas *Untitled*

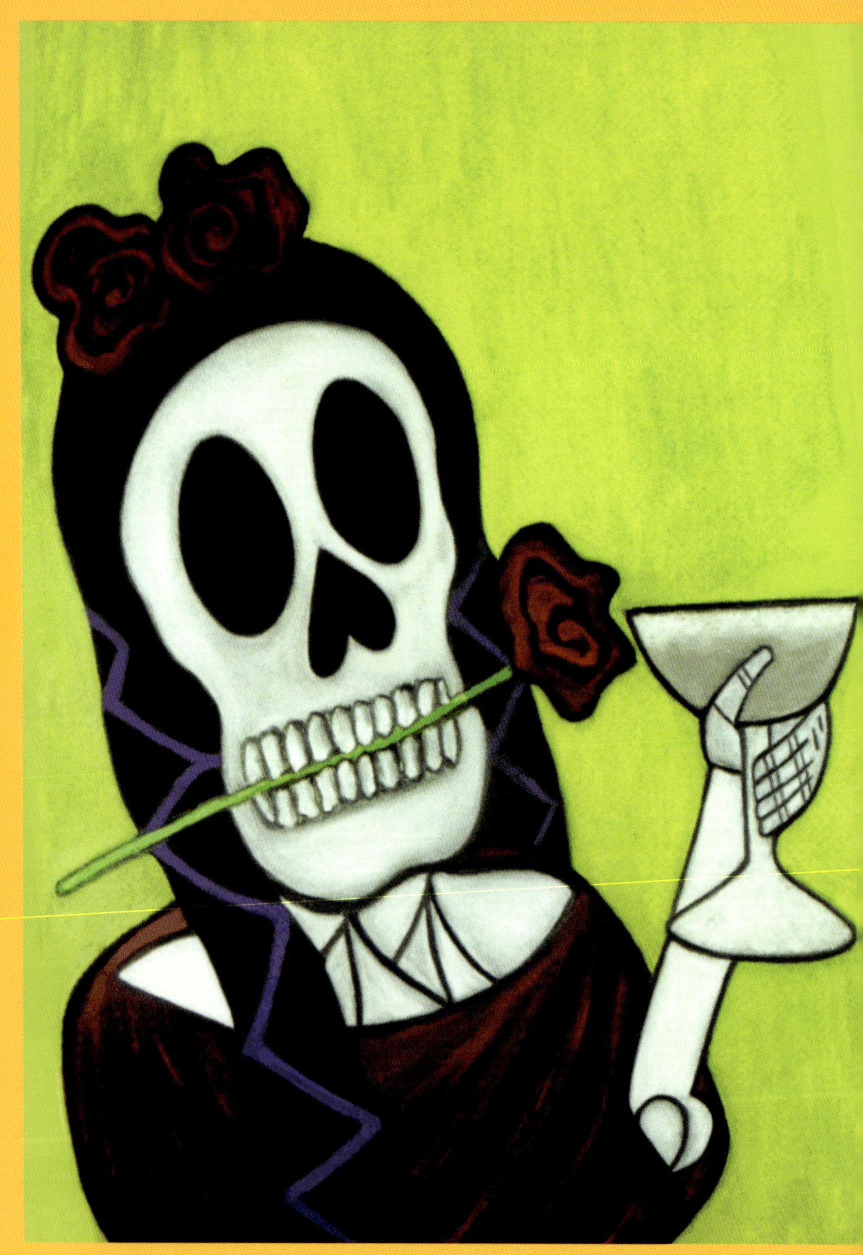

Emilia García *Margarita*

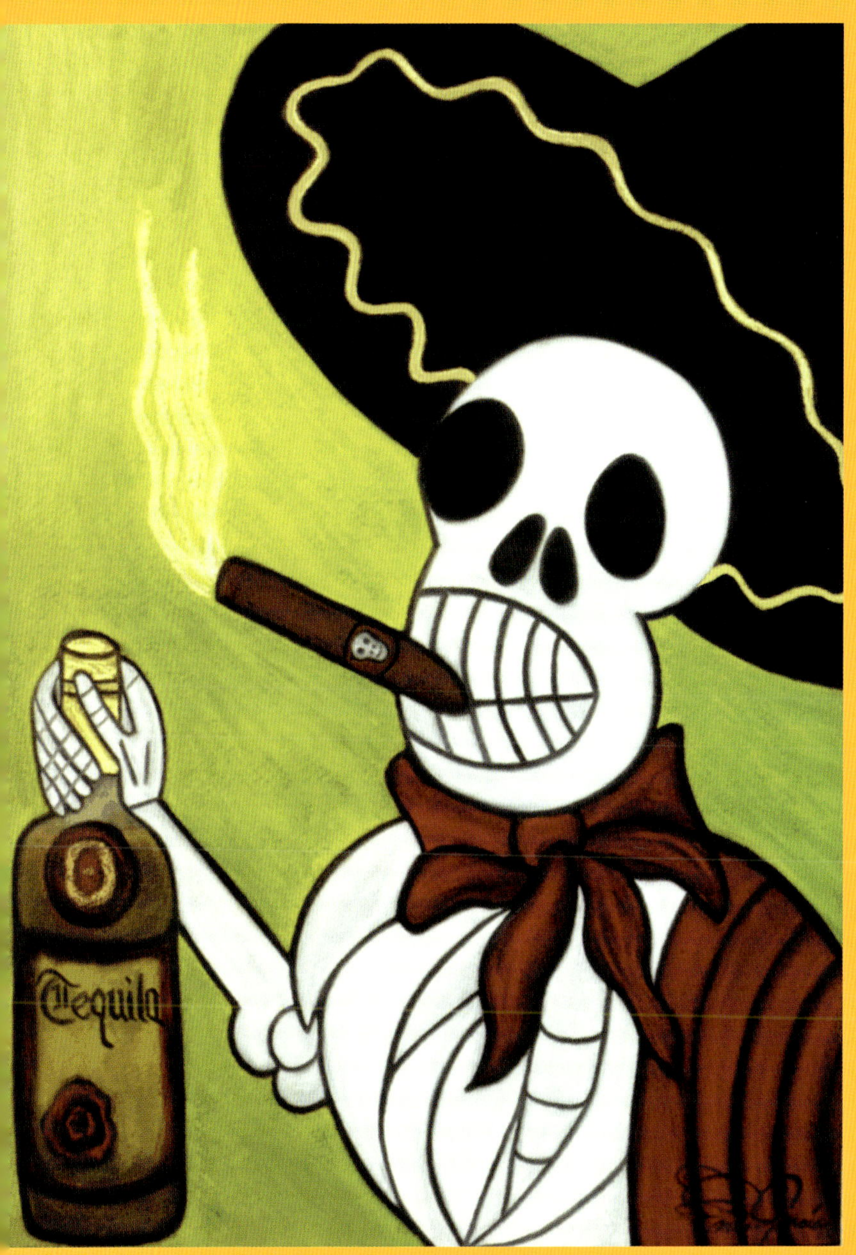

Emilia García *Puro Alegre*

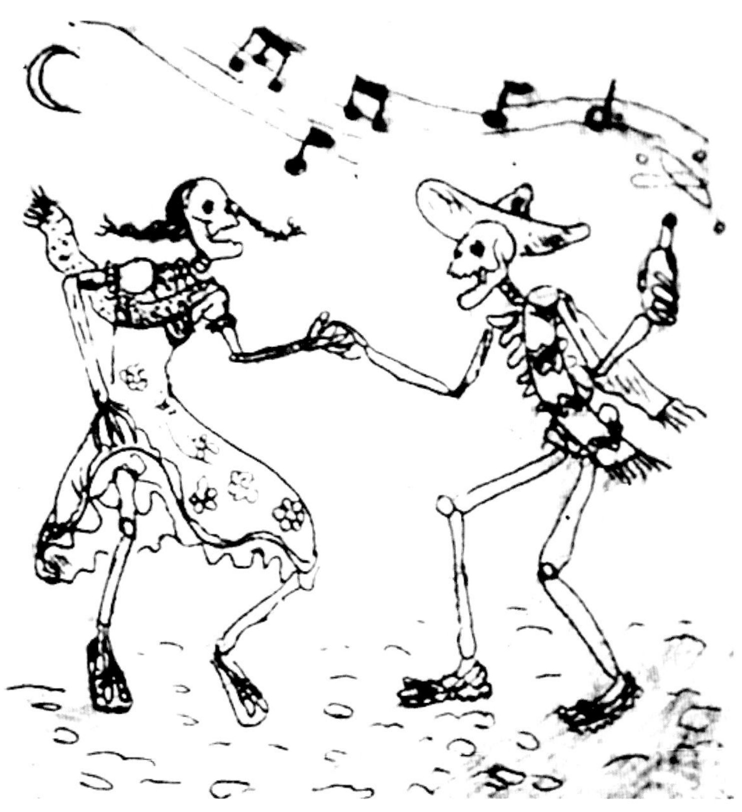

Agustín Barón *El huarachazo*

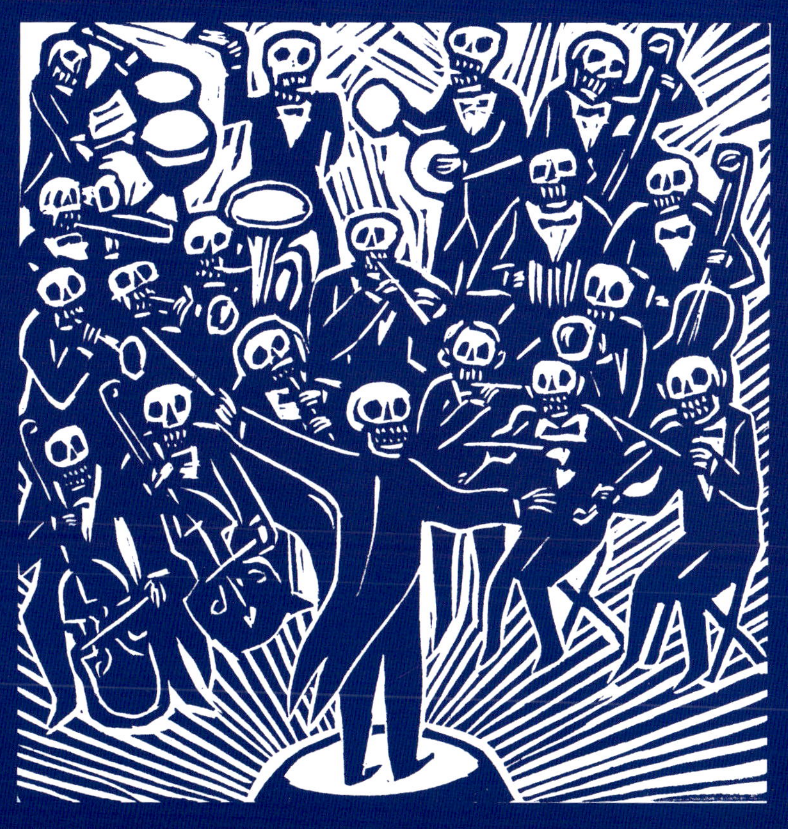

Artemio Rodríguez *Sinfonia Vital*

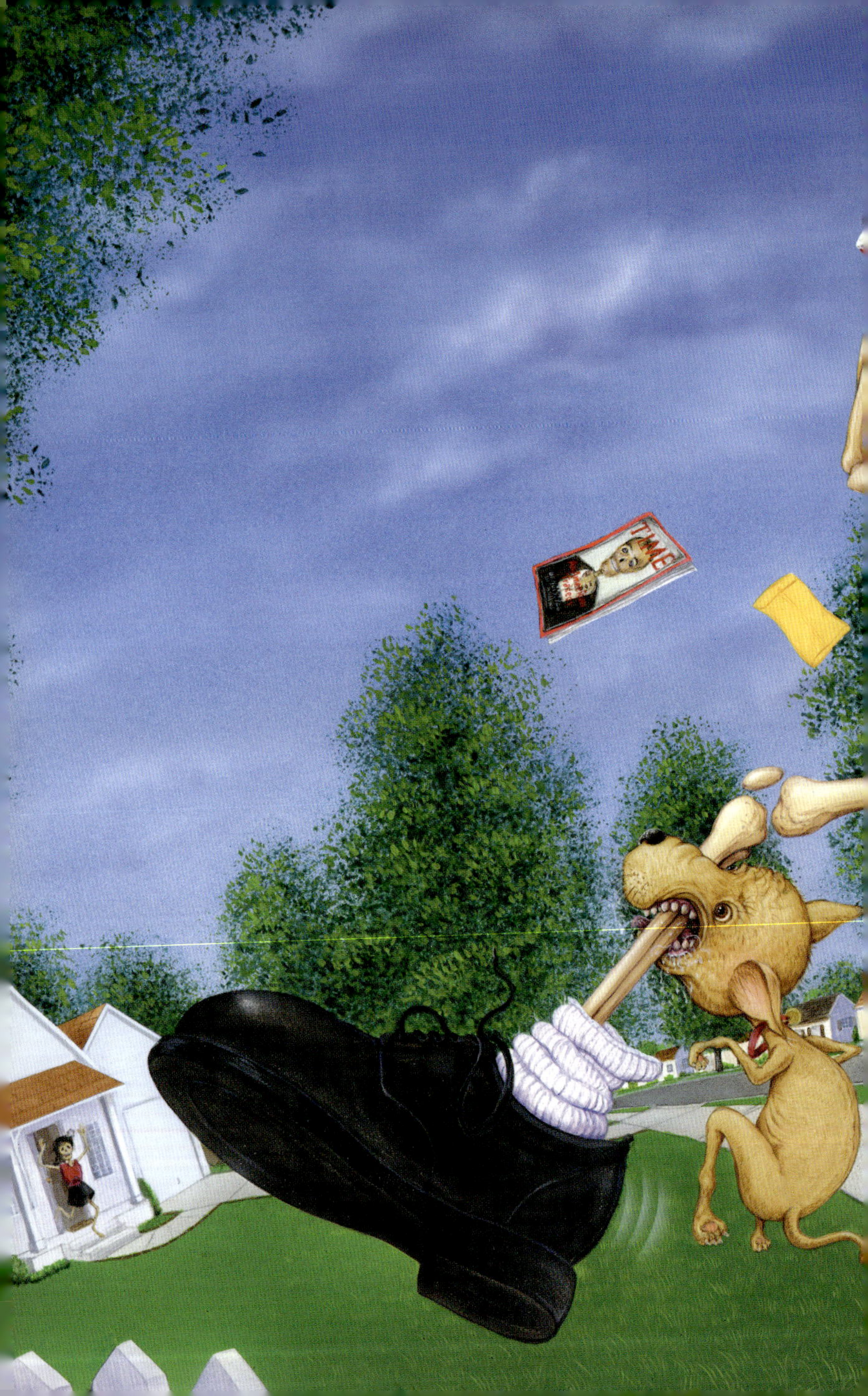
TIME

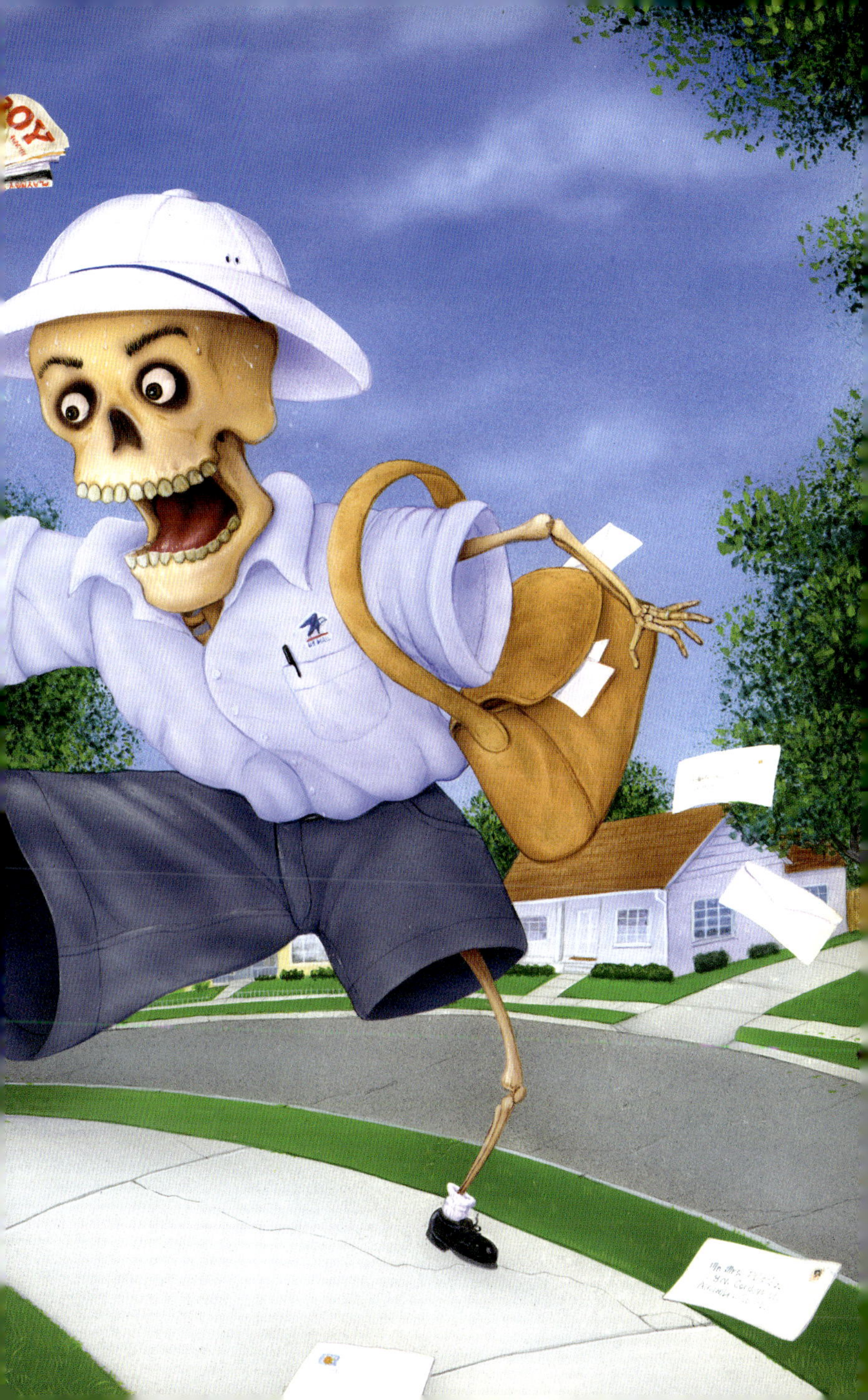

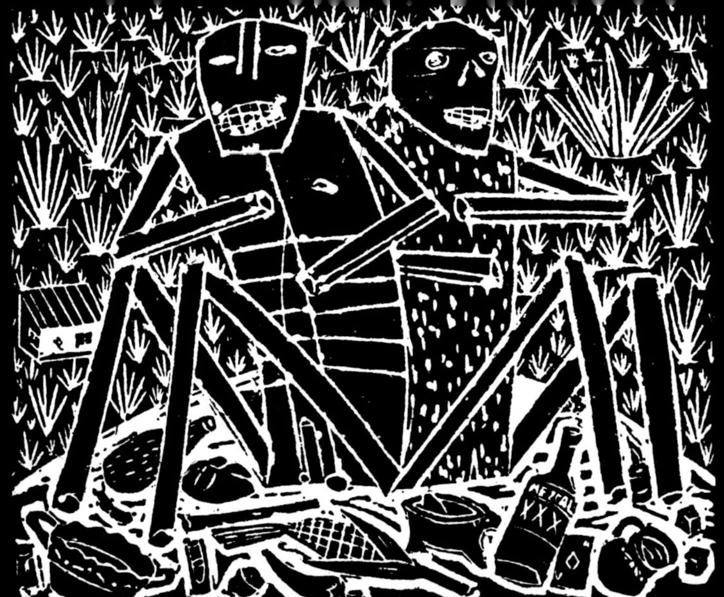

◆◆ Robert Palacios *Bone Appetite*
◆ Joel Rendón *Untitled*
◆ Artemio Rodríguez *Nixtamal*

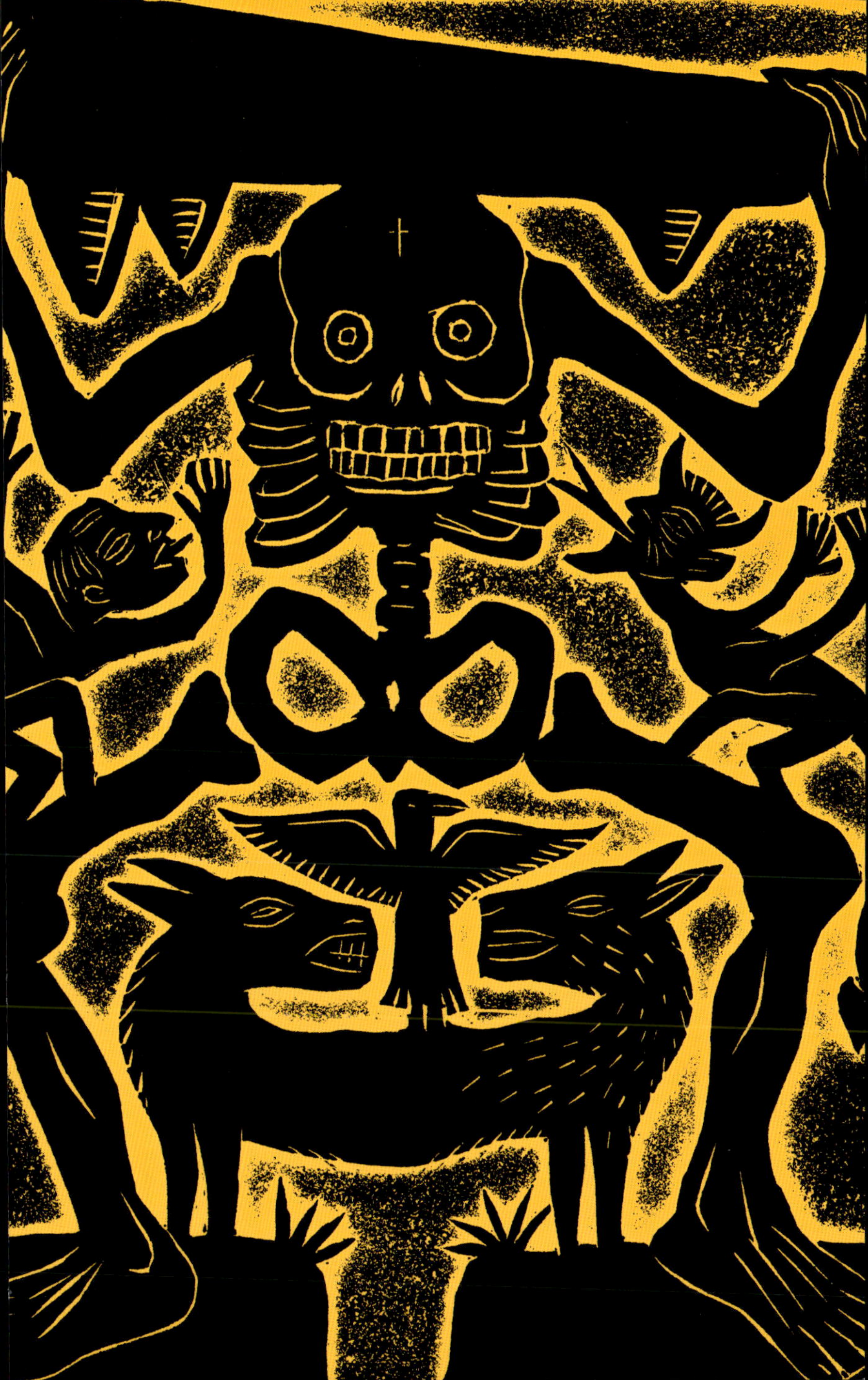

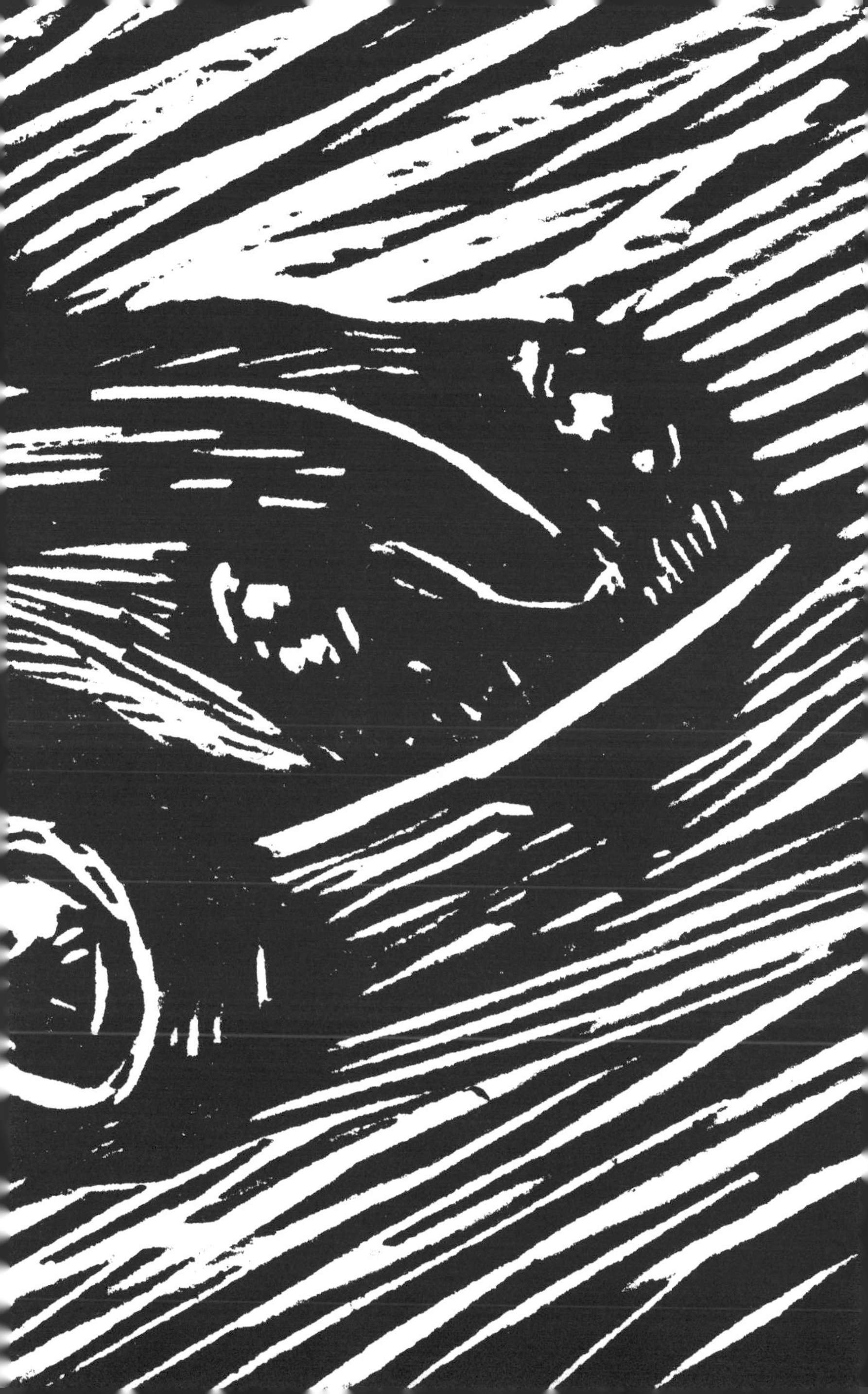

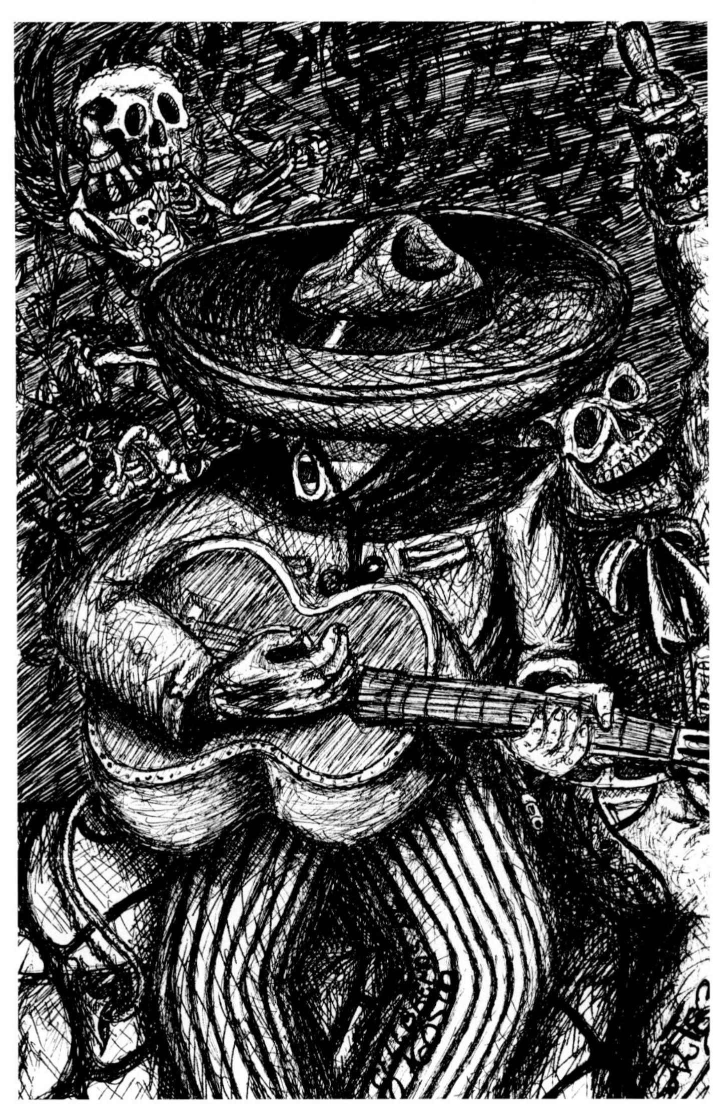

◆◆ Ernie Herrera *VW*
◆ Gabriel Galán *Untitled*
◆ Edgard López *Untitled*

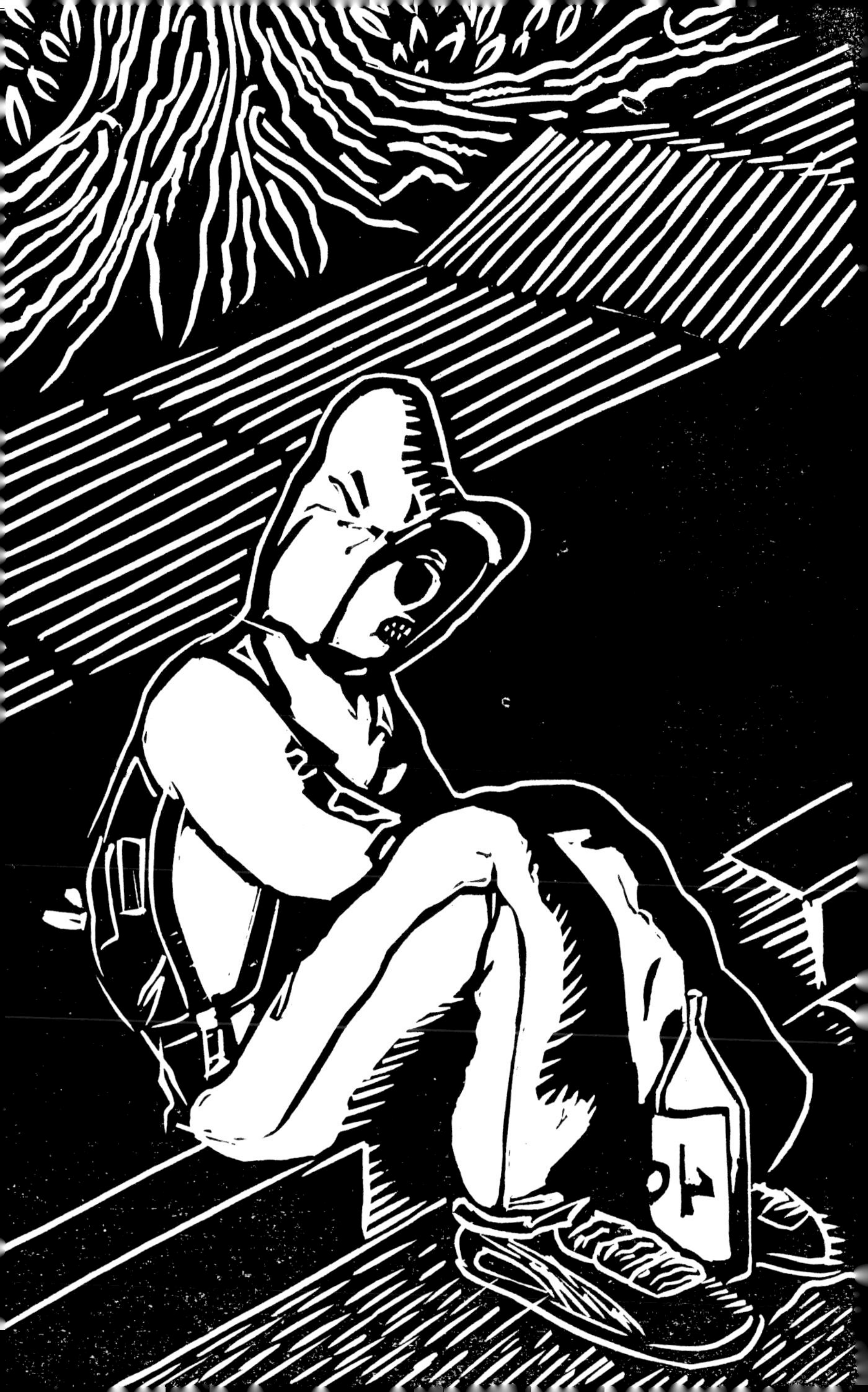

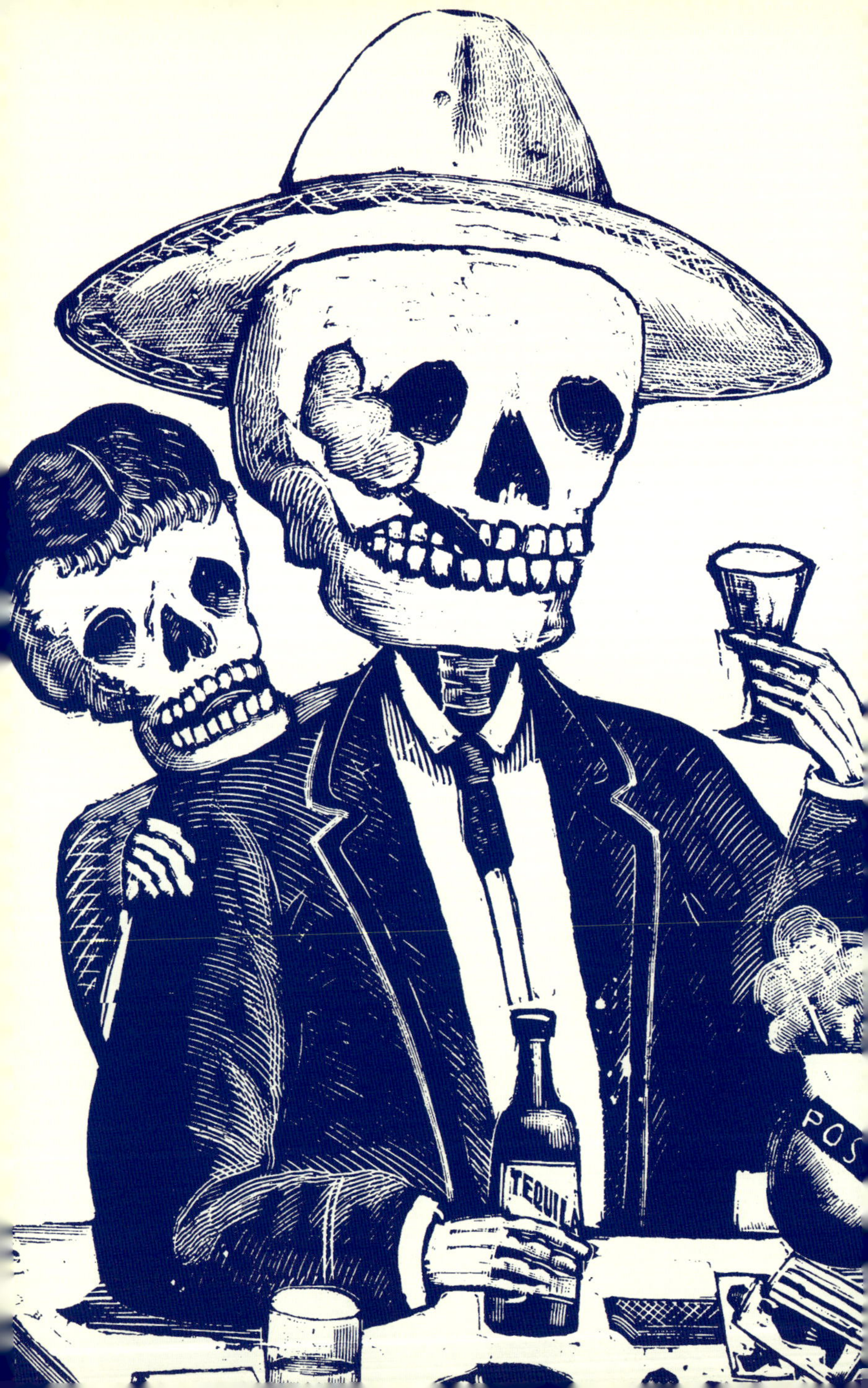
TEQUILA

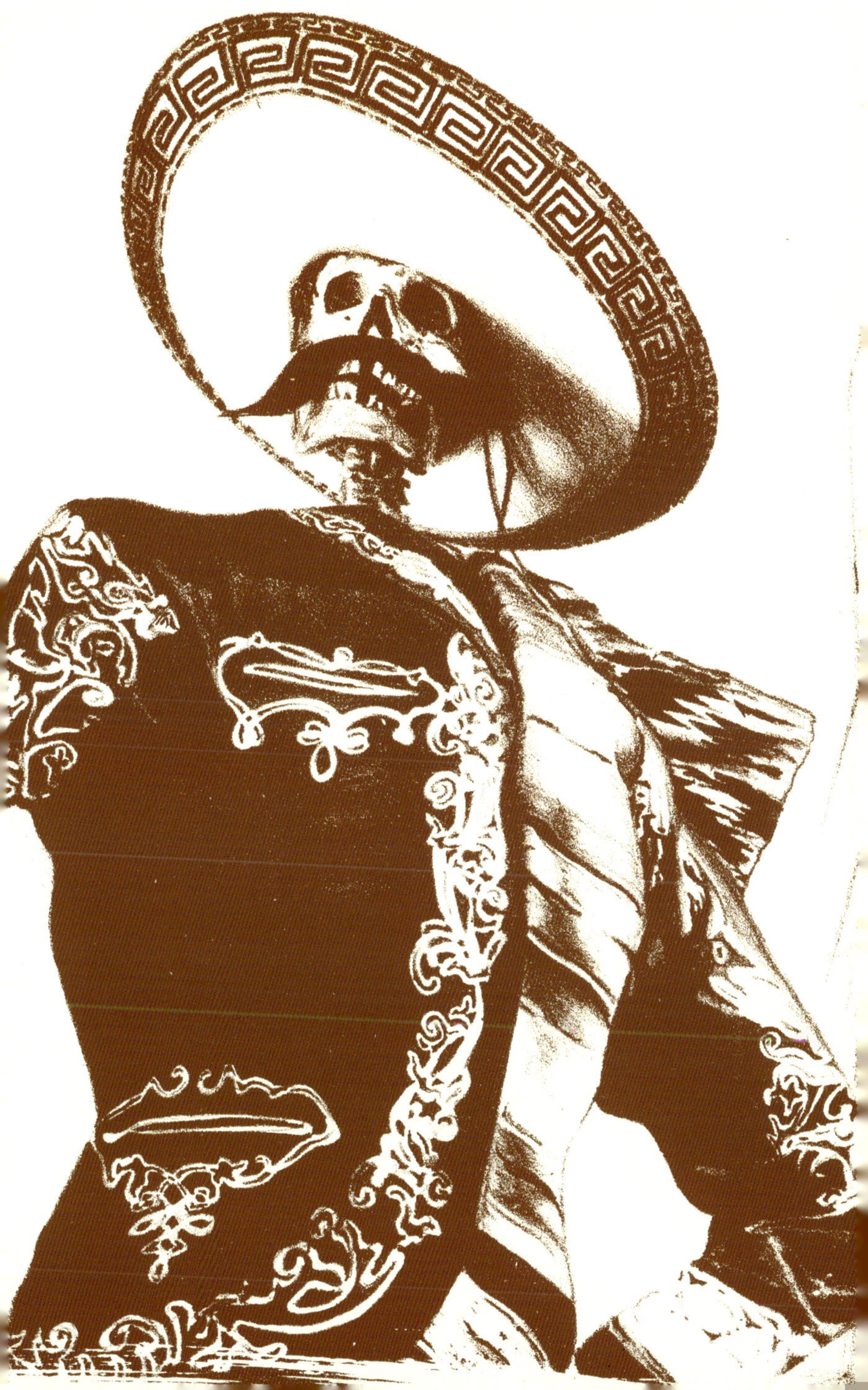

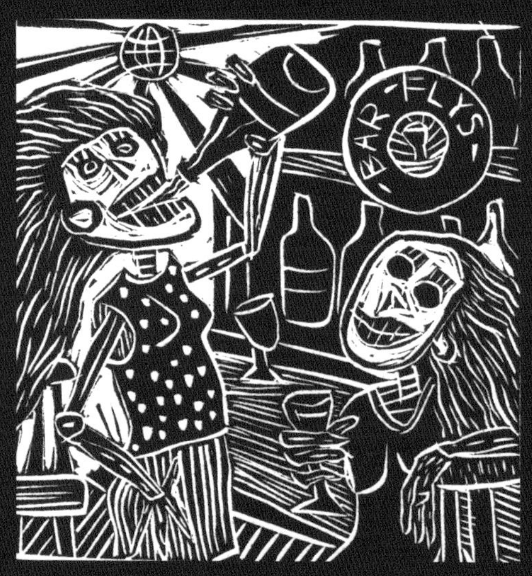

◆◆◆ Manuel Manilla *Calavera Tapatia*
◆◆ Eduardo Gómez *El Mariachi muerto*
◆ Joel Rendón *from Chicago's Life*
◆ Agustín Barón *Los amigos*

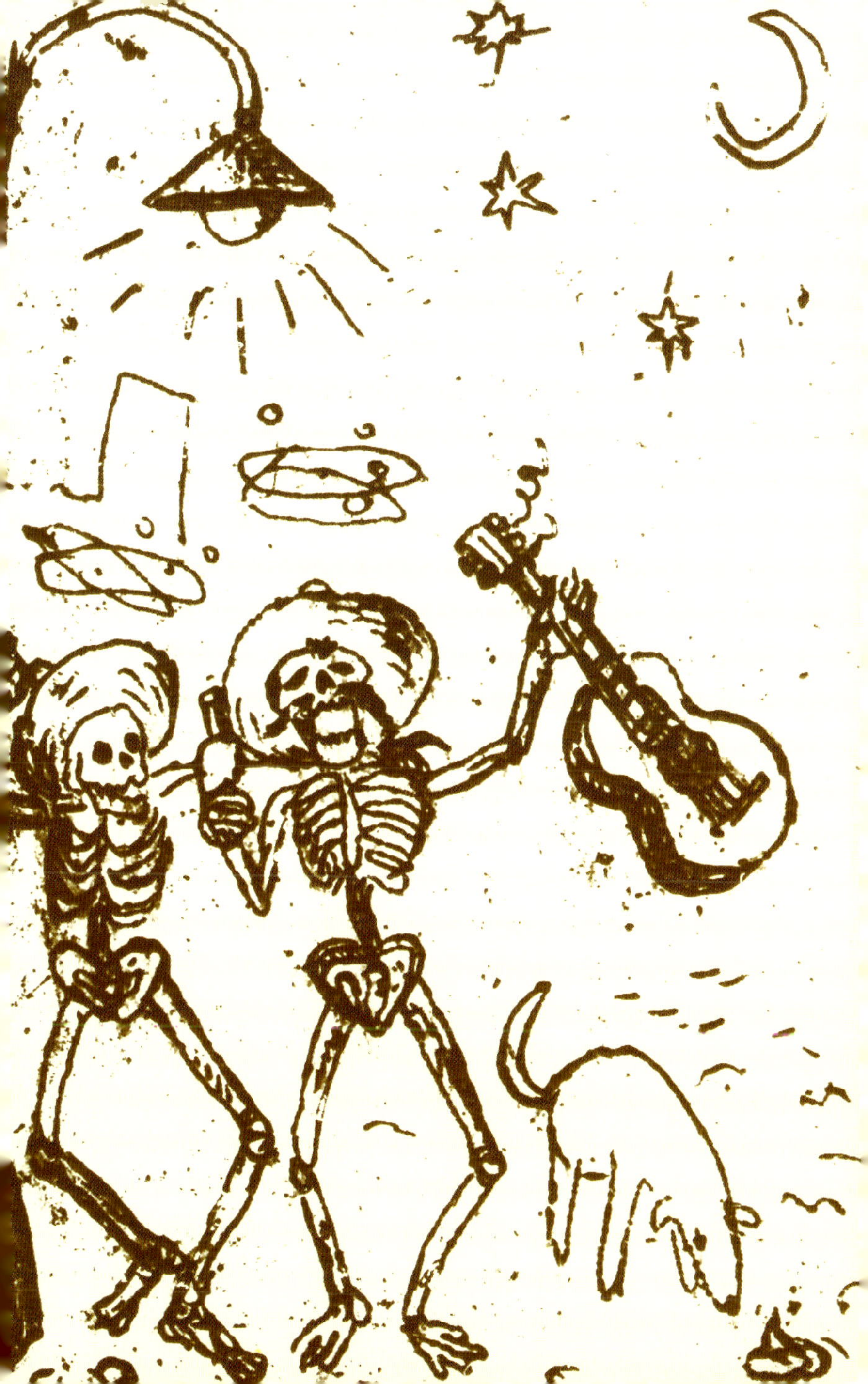

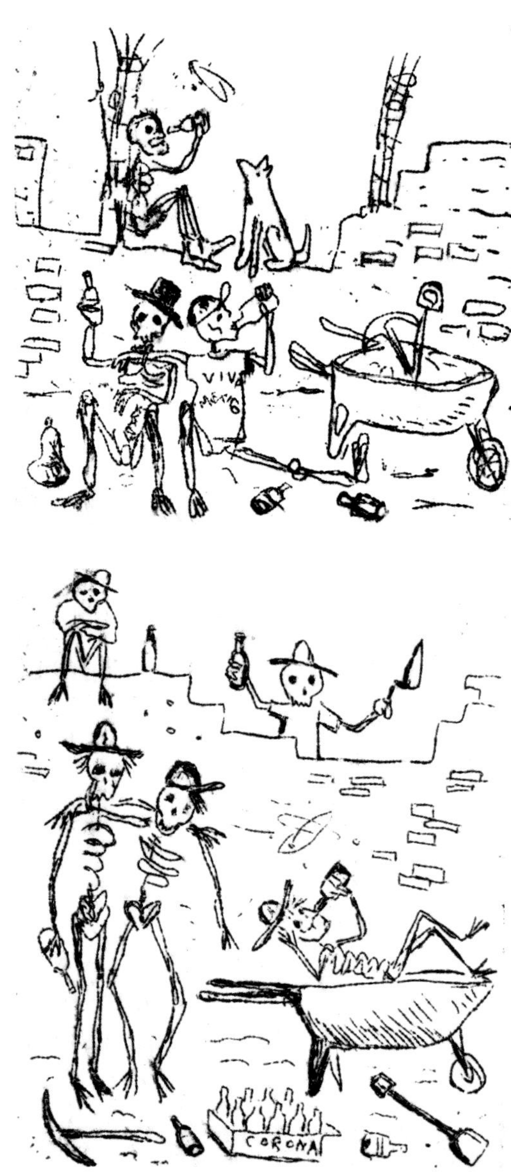

◆ Agustín Barón *from Un día en la vida de los muertos*
◆ Edgard López *Eternity*
◆◆ Artemio Rodríguez *Dead Friends*

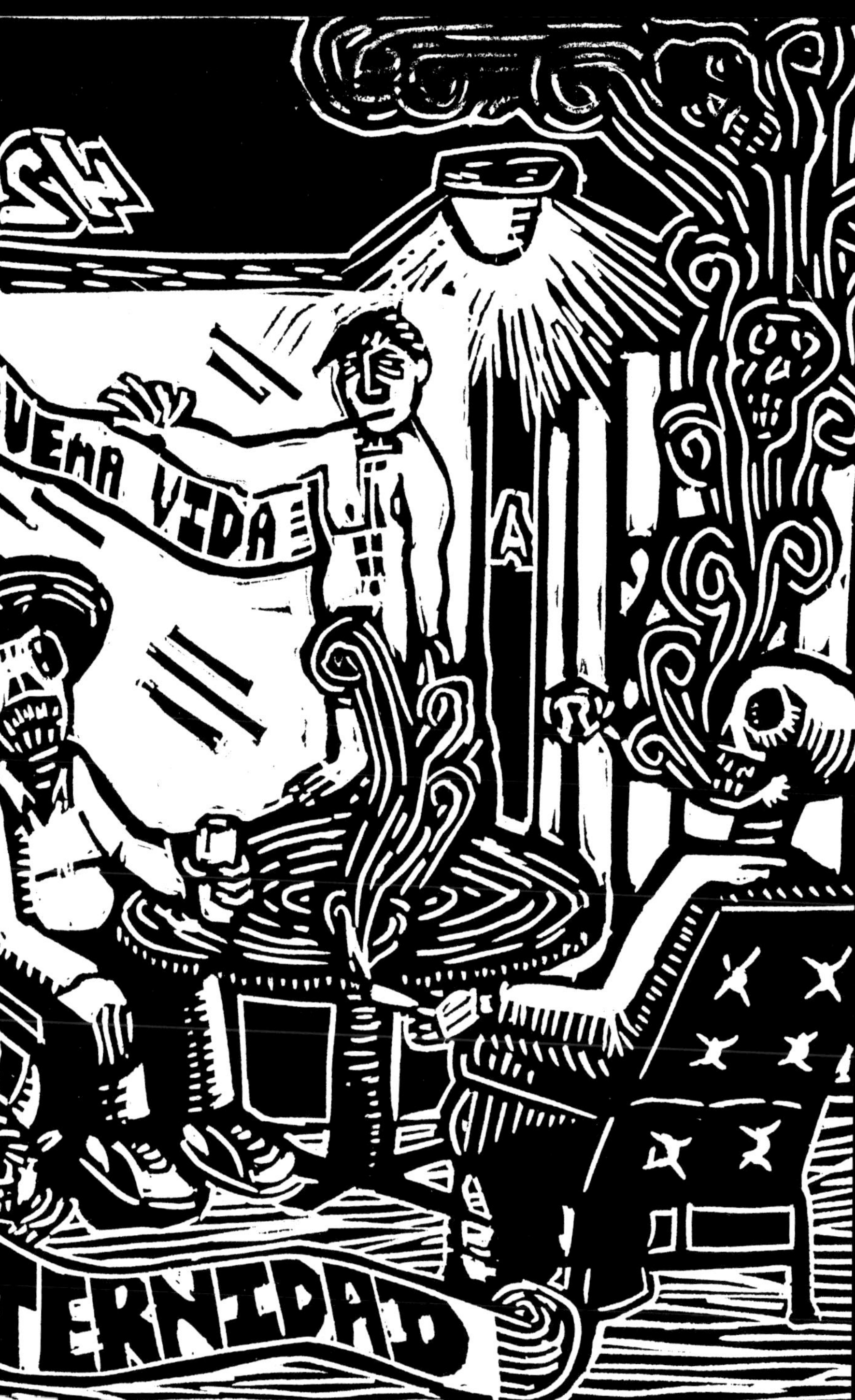
UENA VIDA
A
TERNIDAD

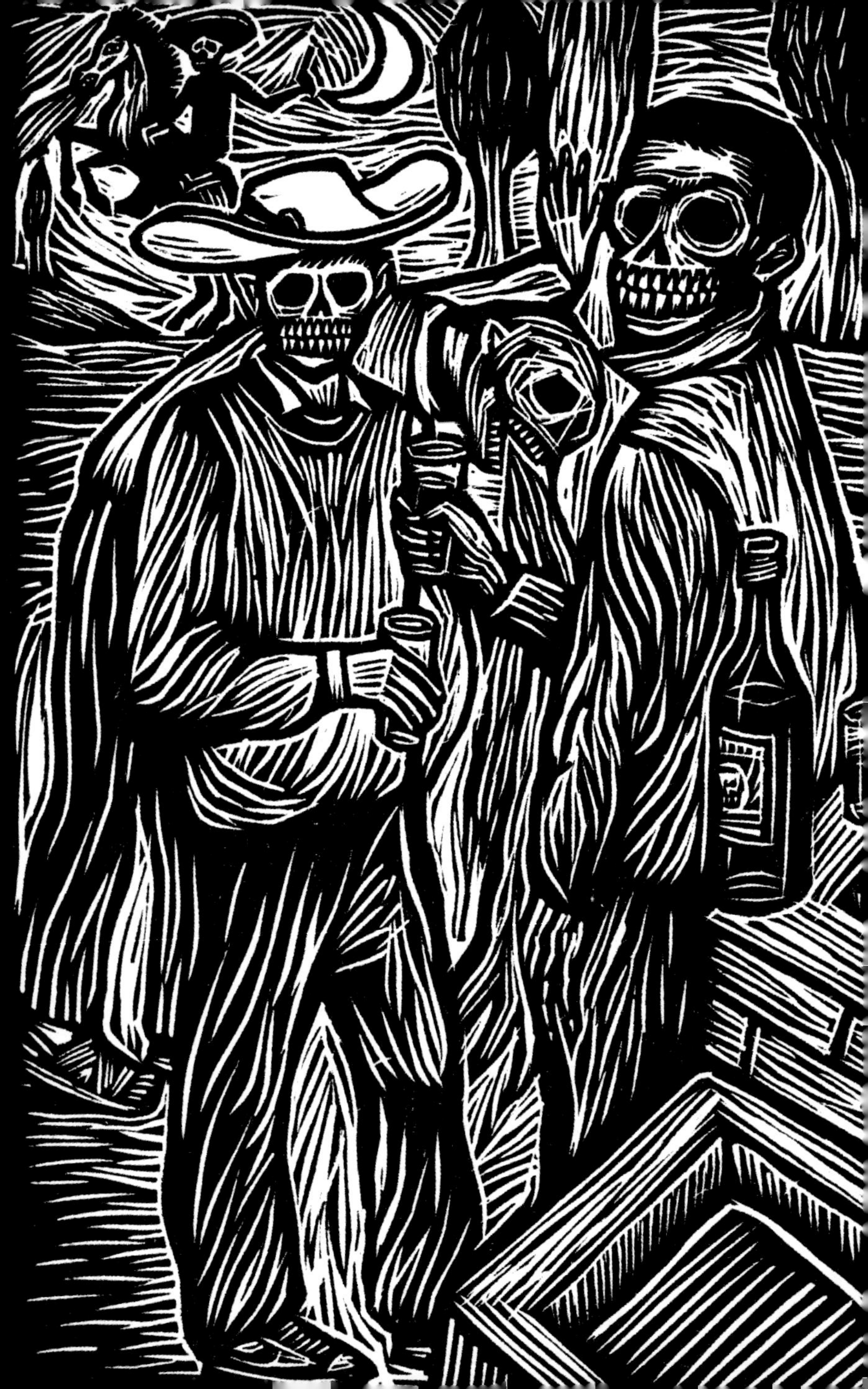

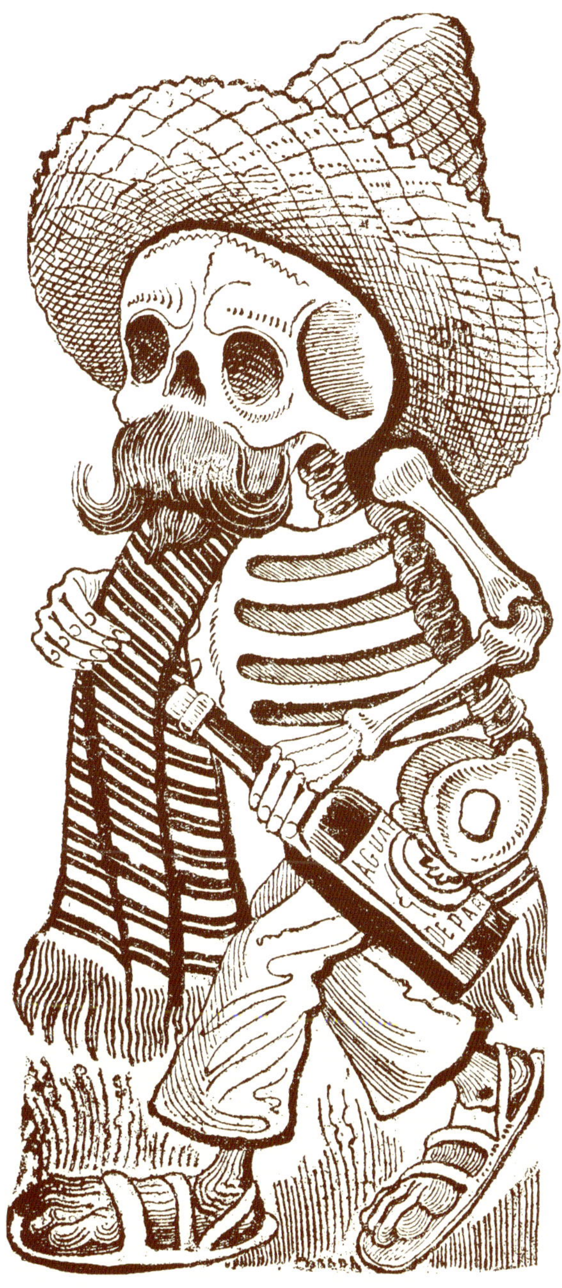

José Guadalupe Posada *Calavera del Montón o Calavera de Madero*

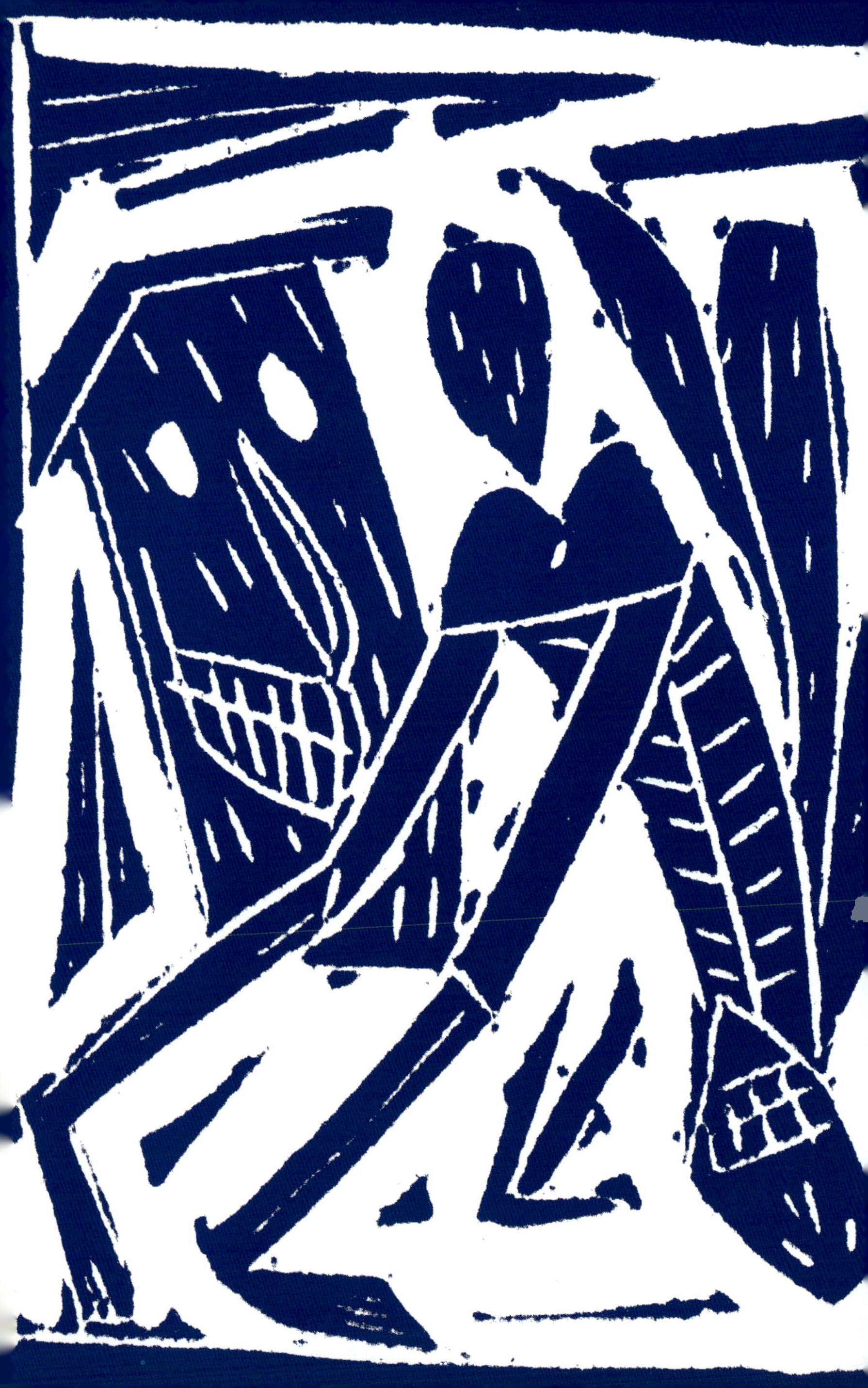

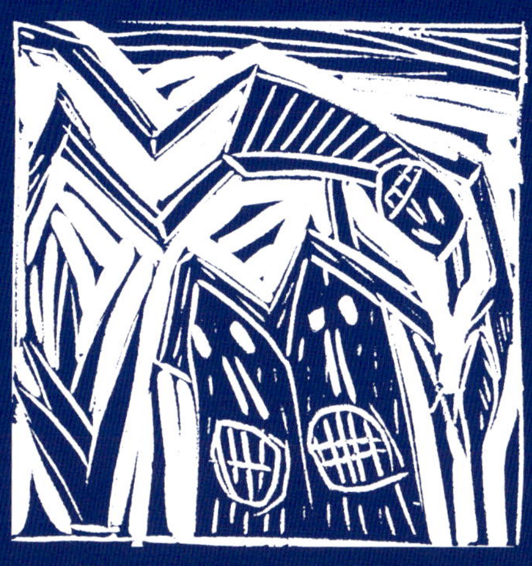

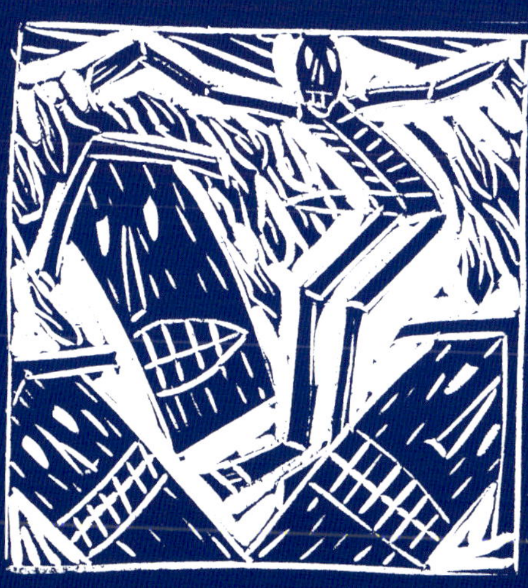

◆◆ Joel Rendón *Pariendo chayotes*
Por encimita
Ahi les voy
◆◆ Artemio Rodríguez *TV Family*

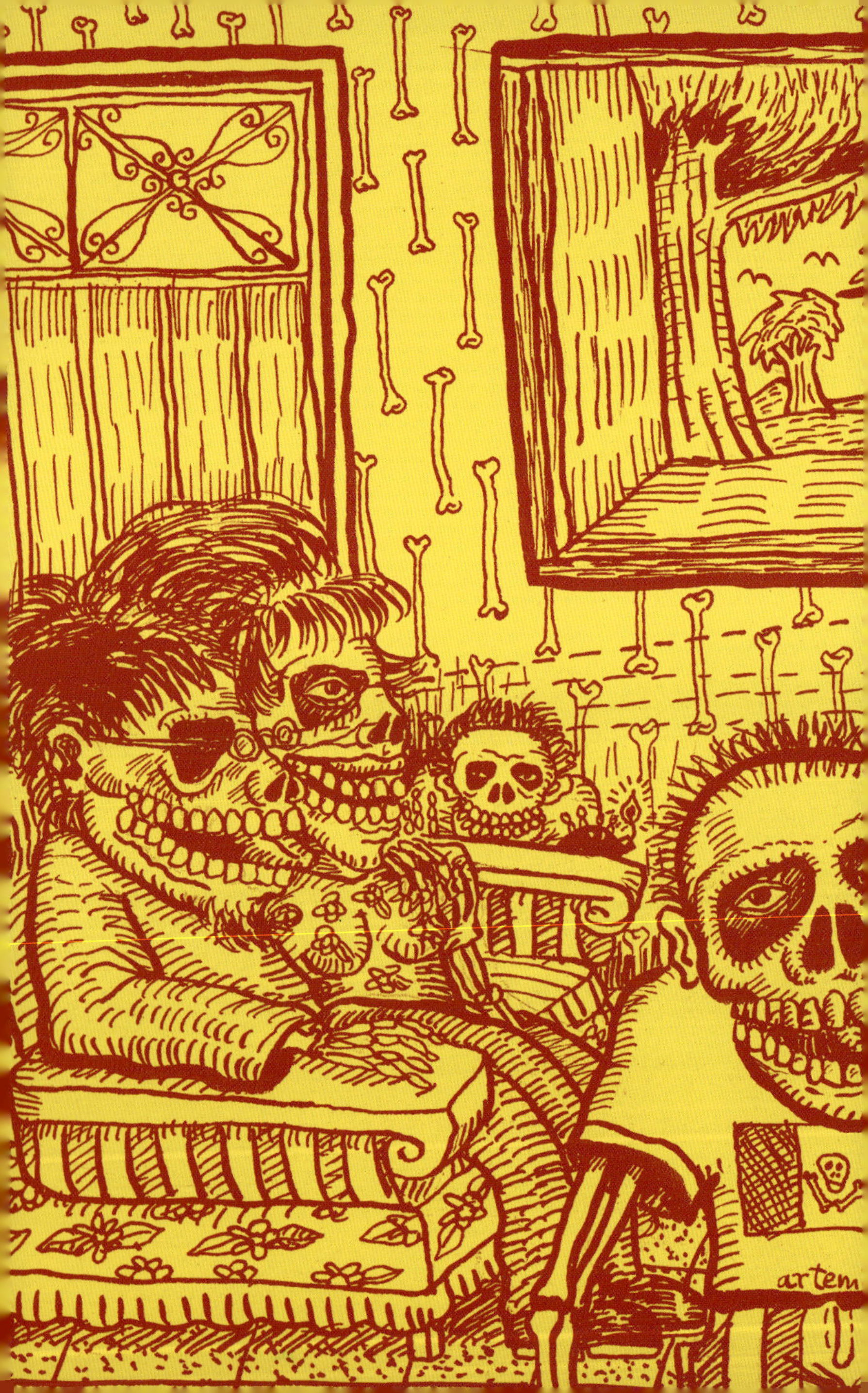
artem

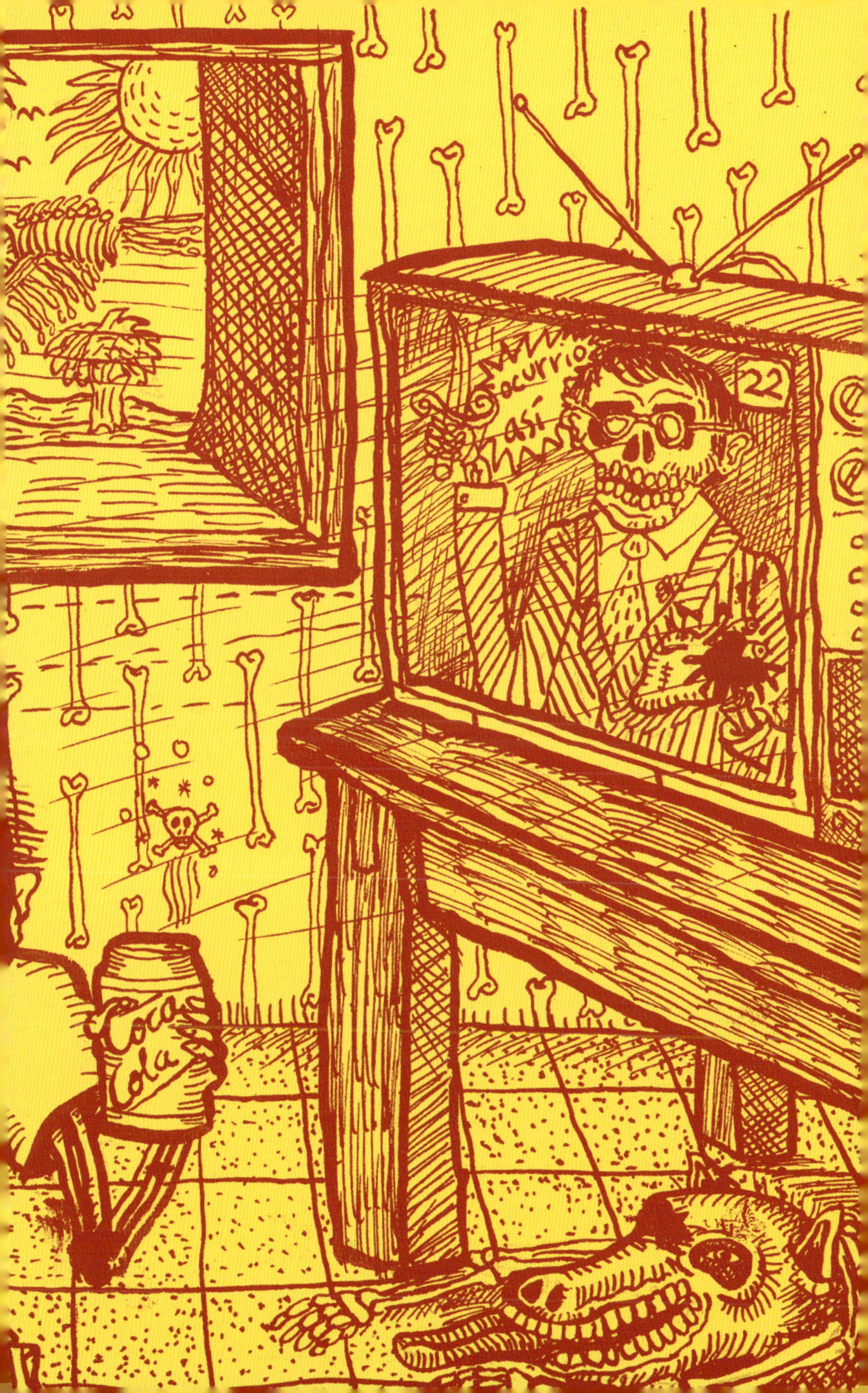
ocurrio
así
22
Coca
Cola

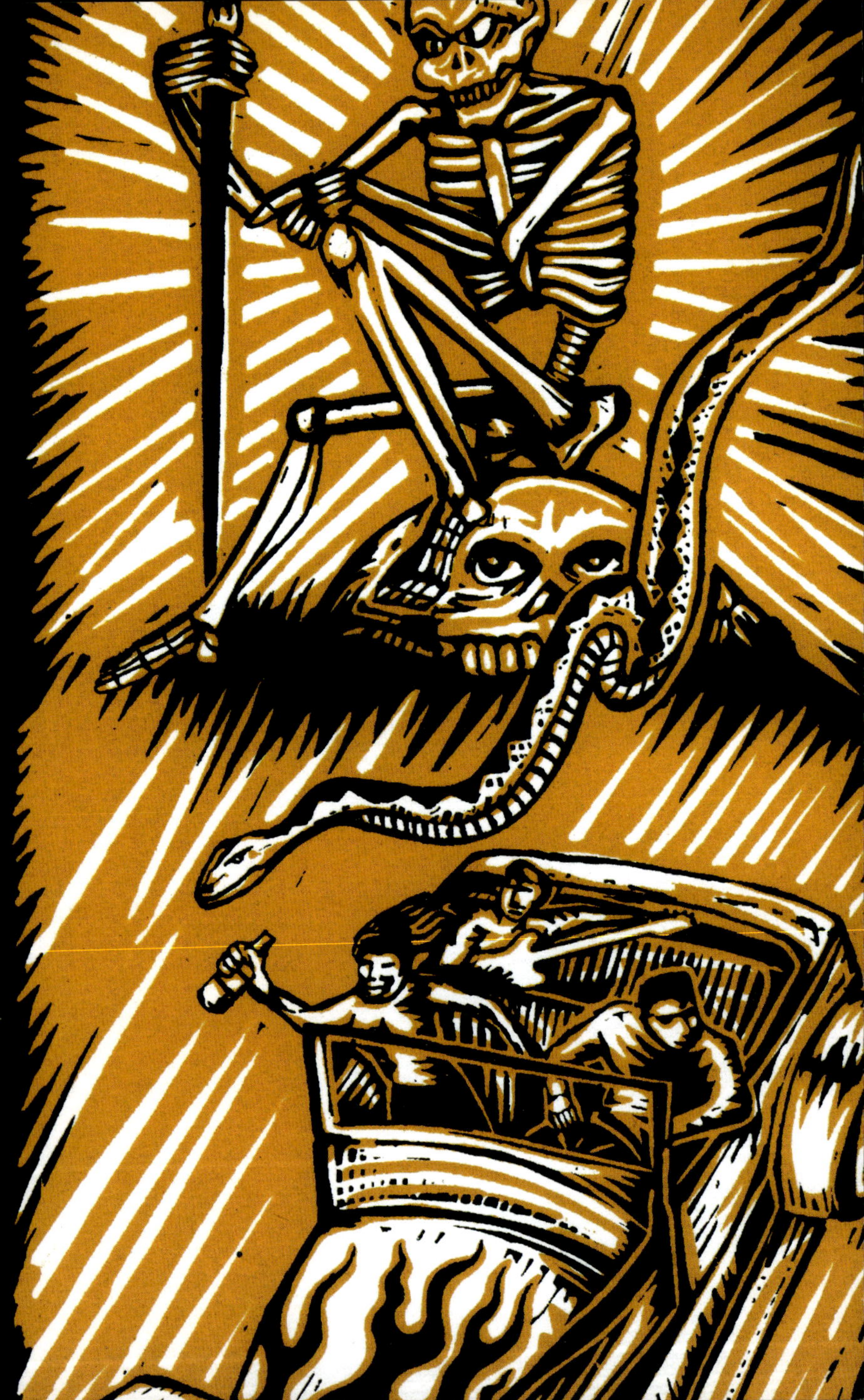

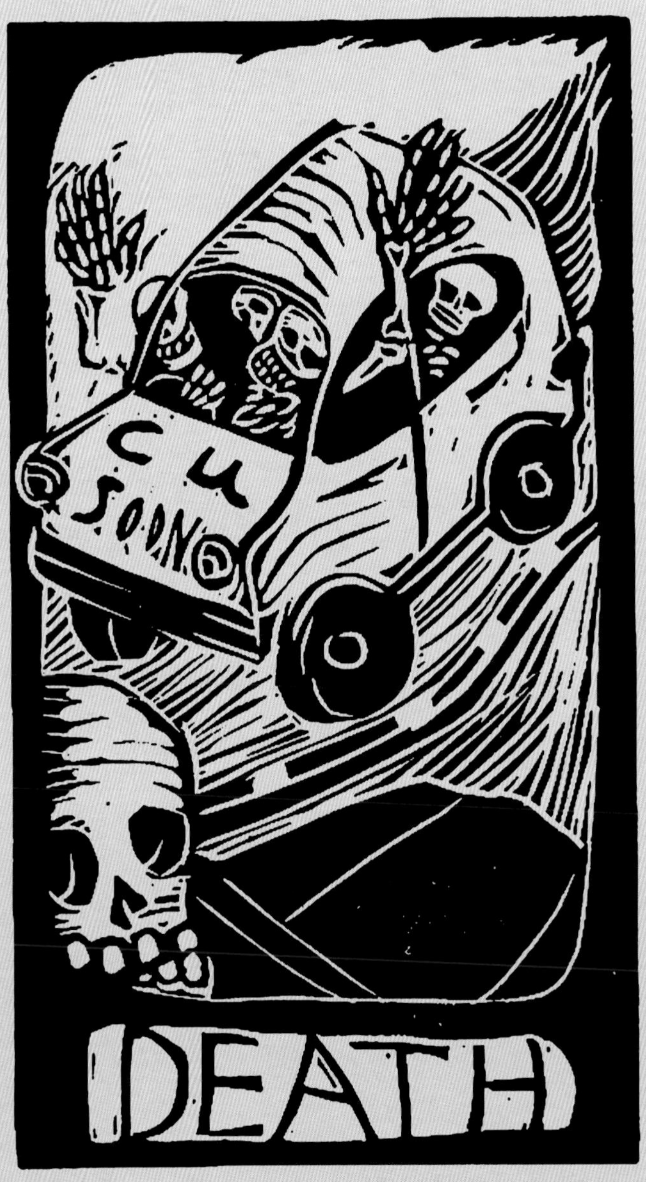

◆Txutxo Perez *El Rey of the Road*
◆Lori Michelon *C U Soon*
◆◆Robert Palacios *I'm Going to Break Your Bones*

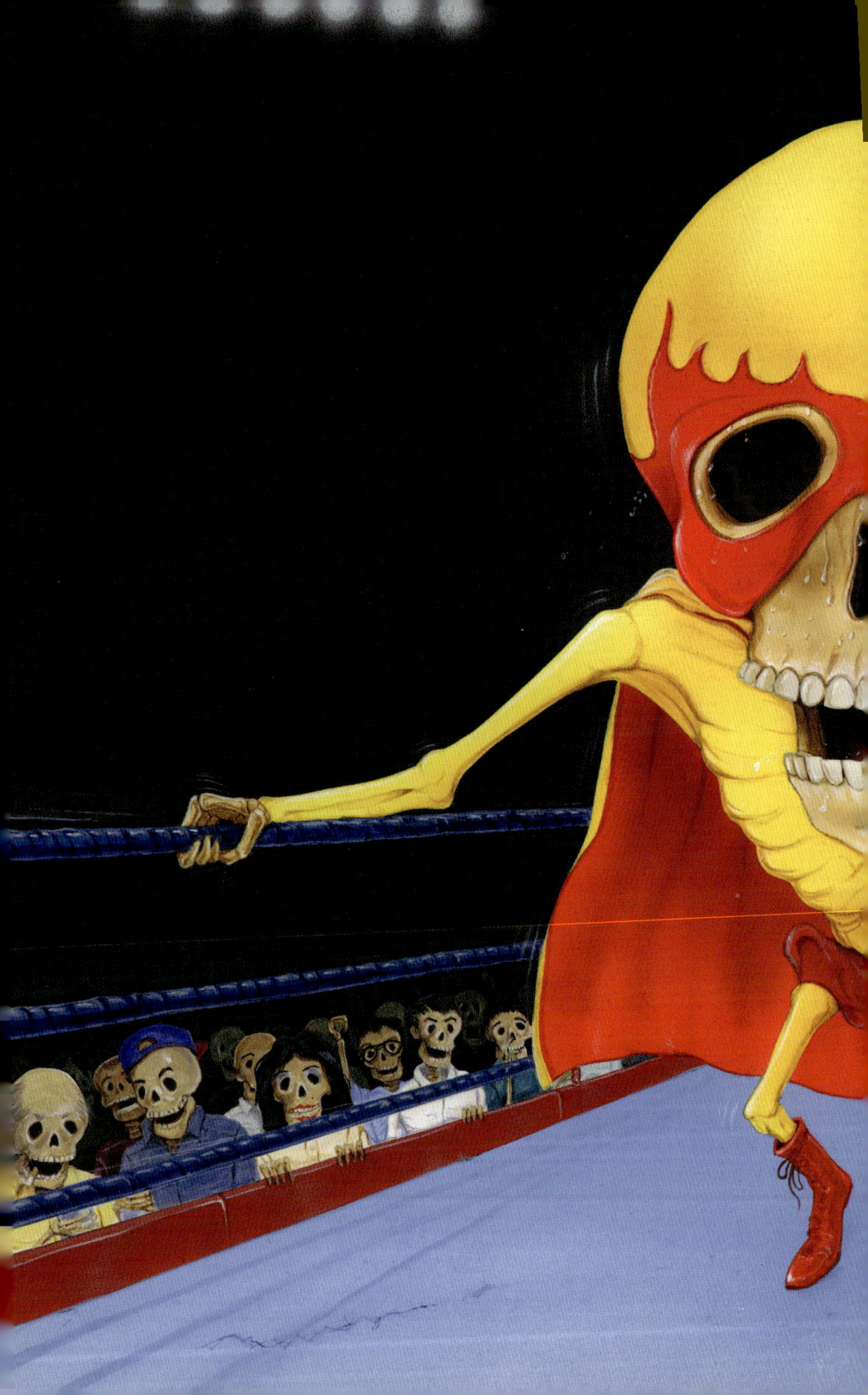

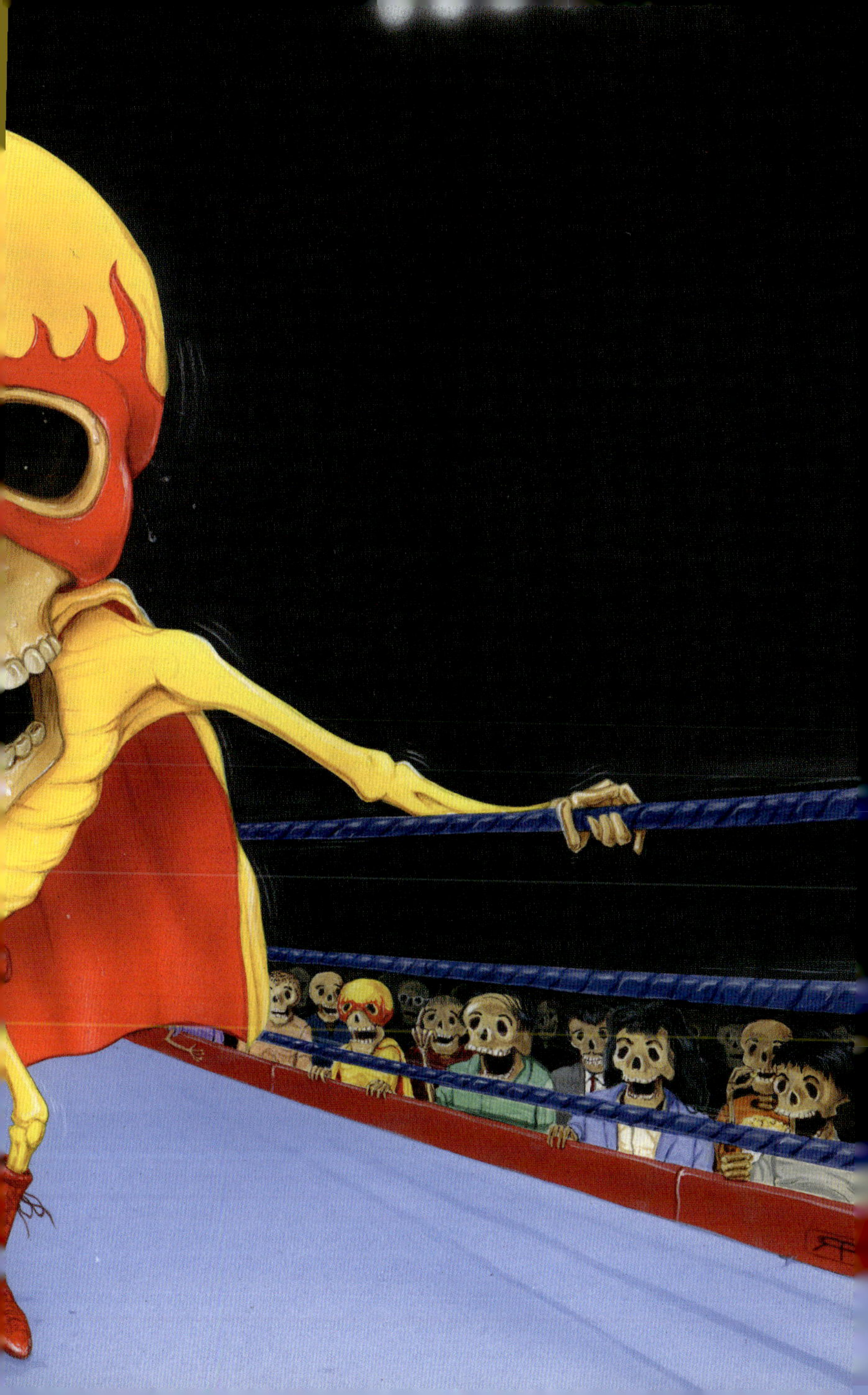

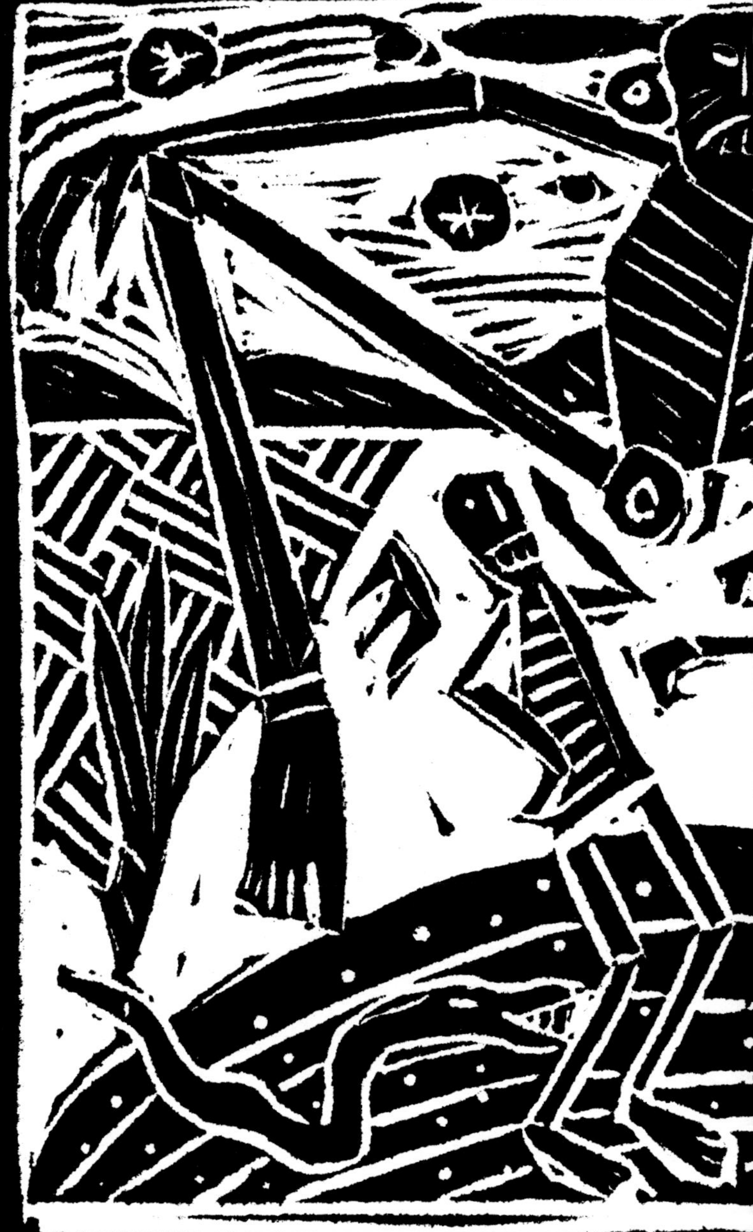

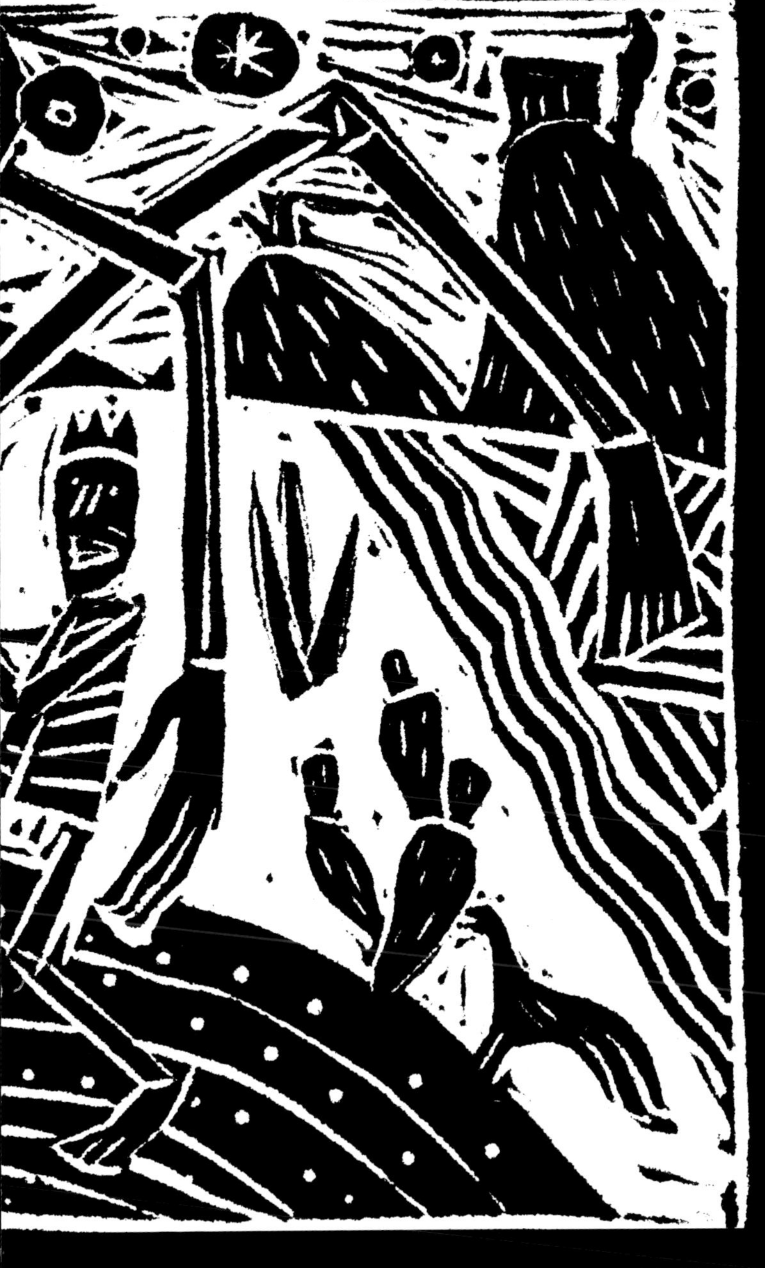

◆ Joel Rendón *Untitled*
◆◆ Daniel González *Muerte en el palenque*

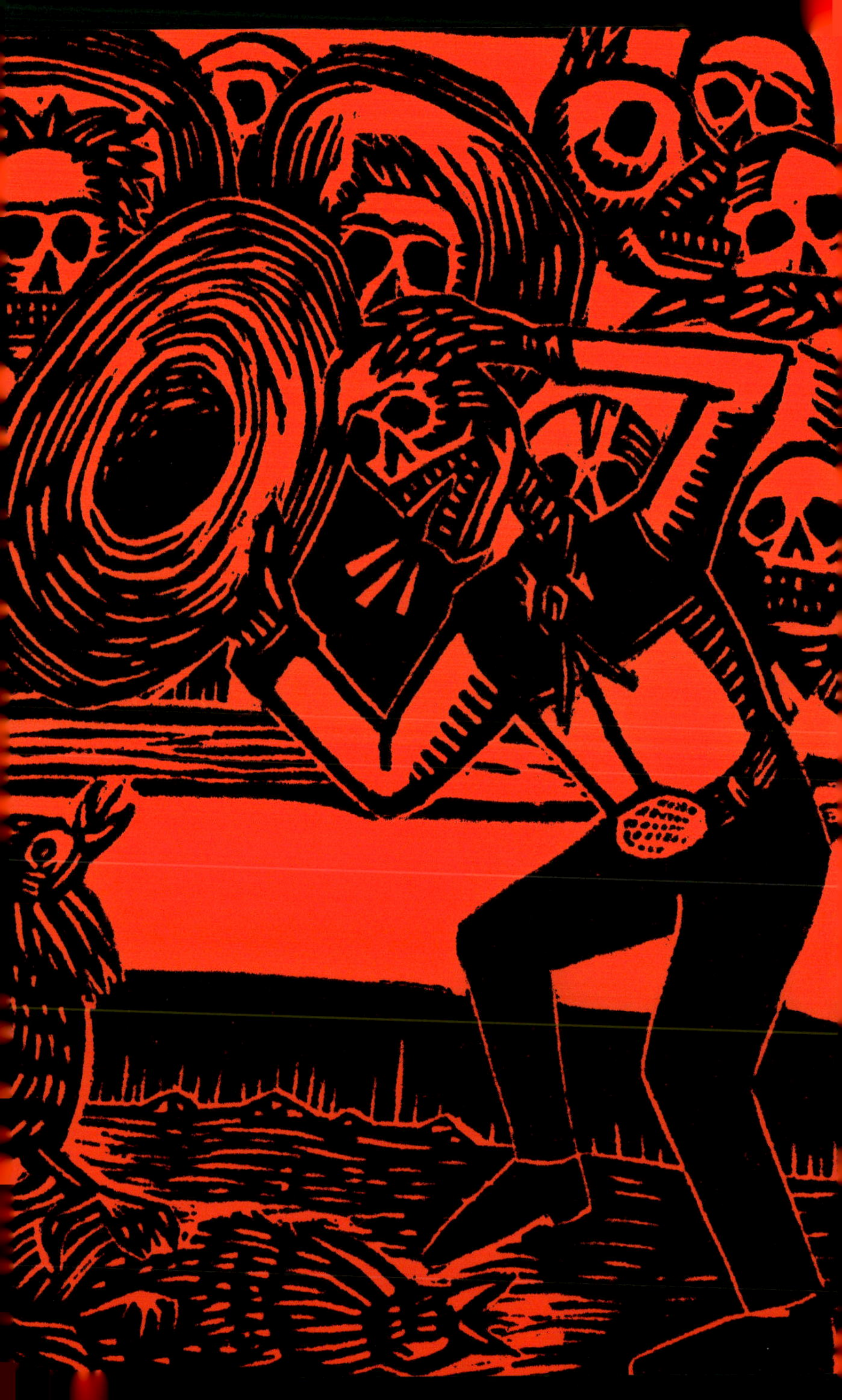

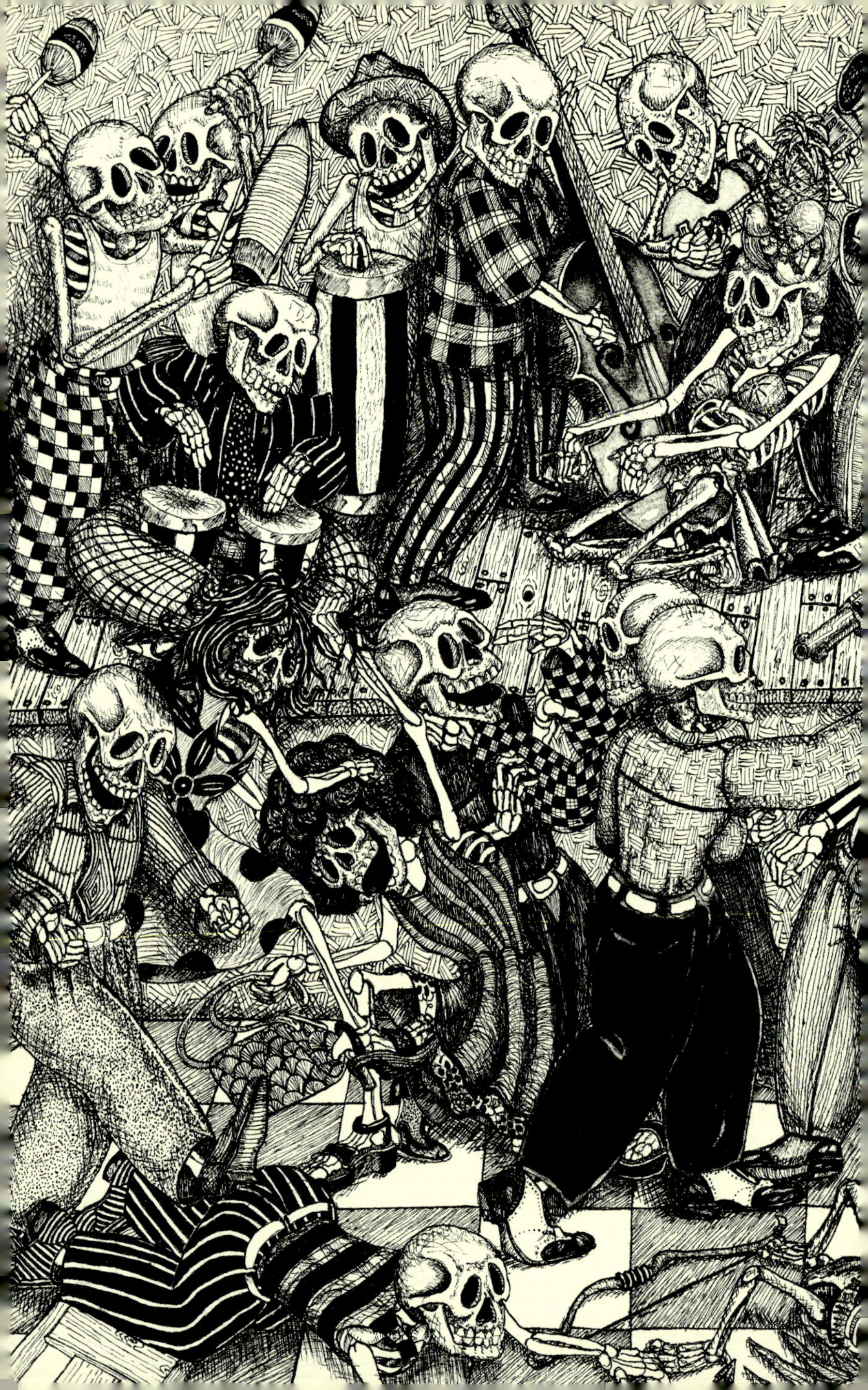

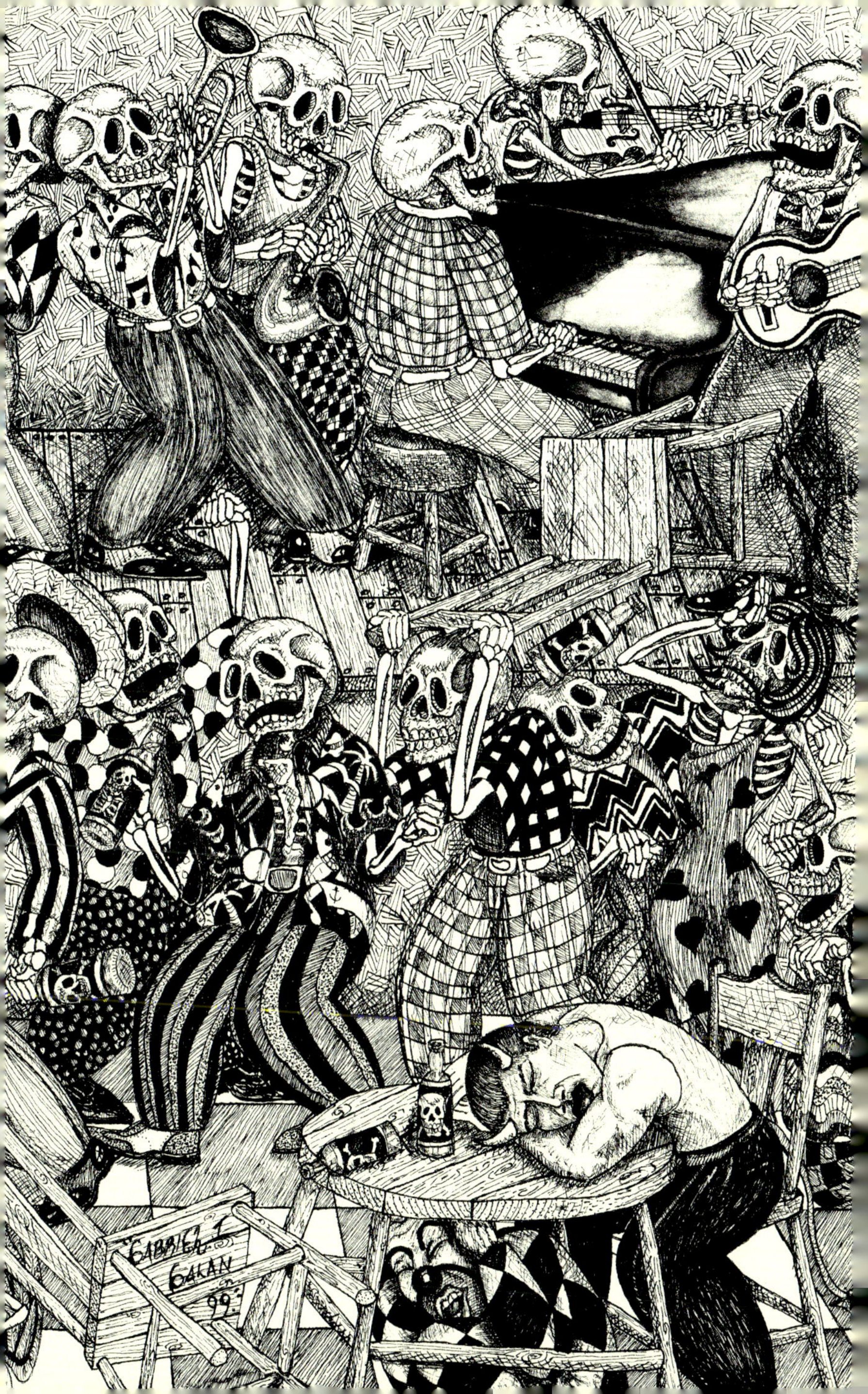
GABRIEL I
GALAN
99

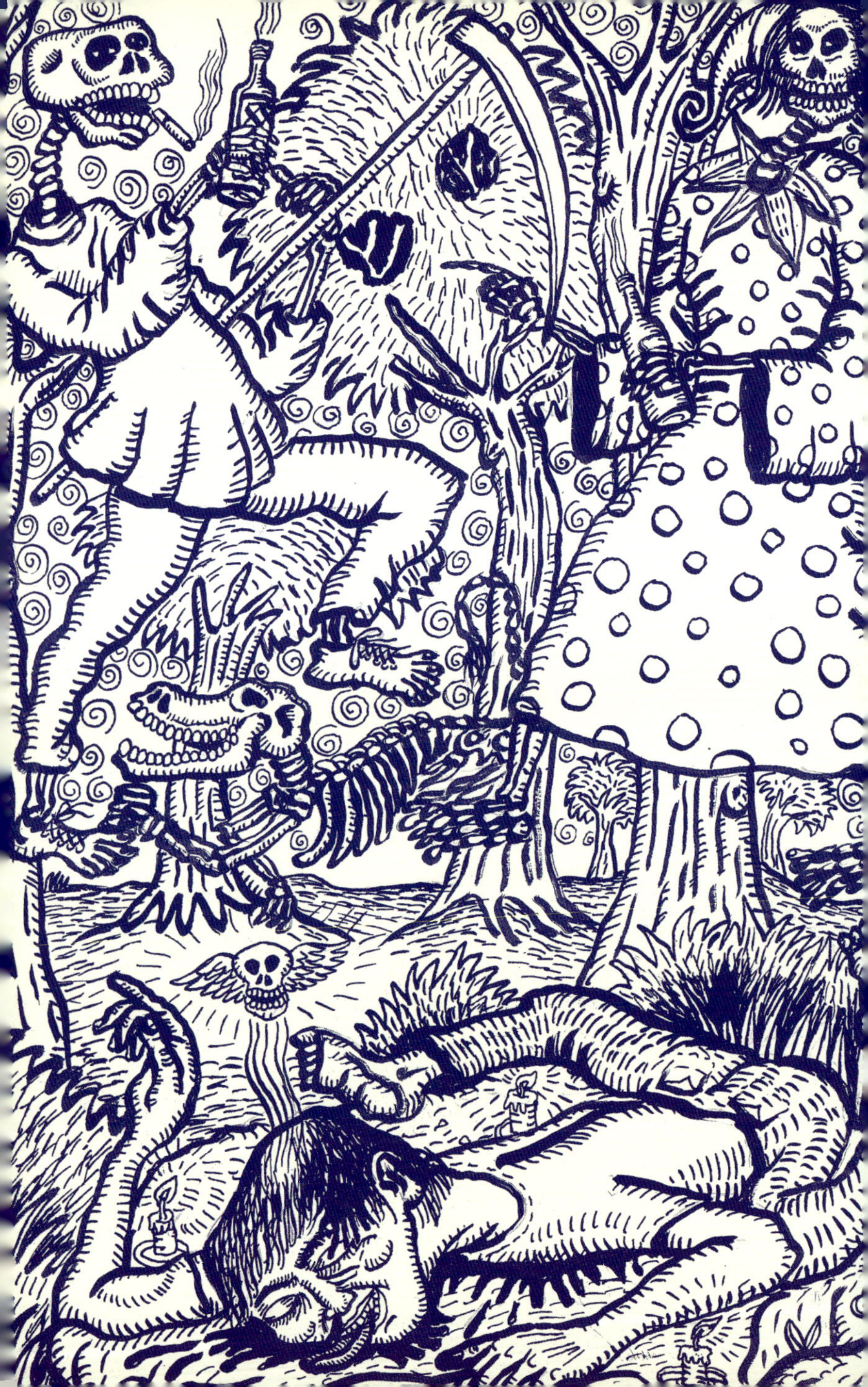

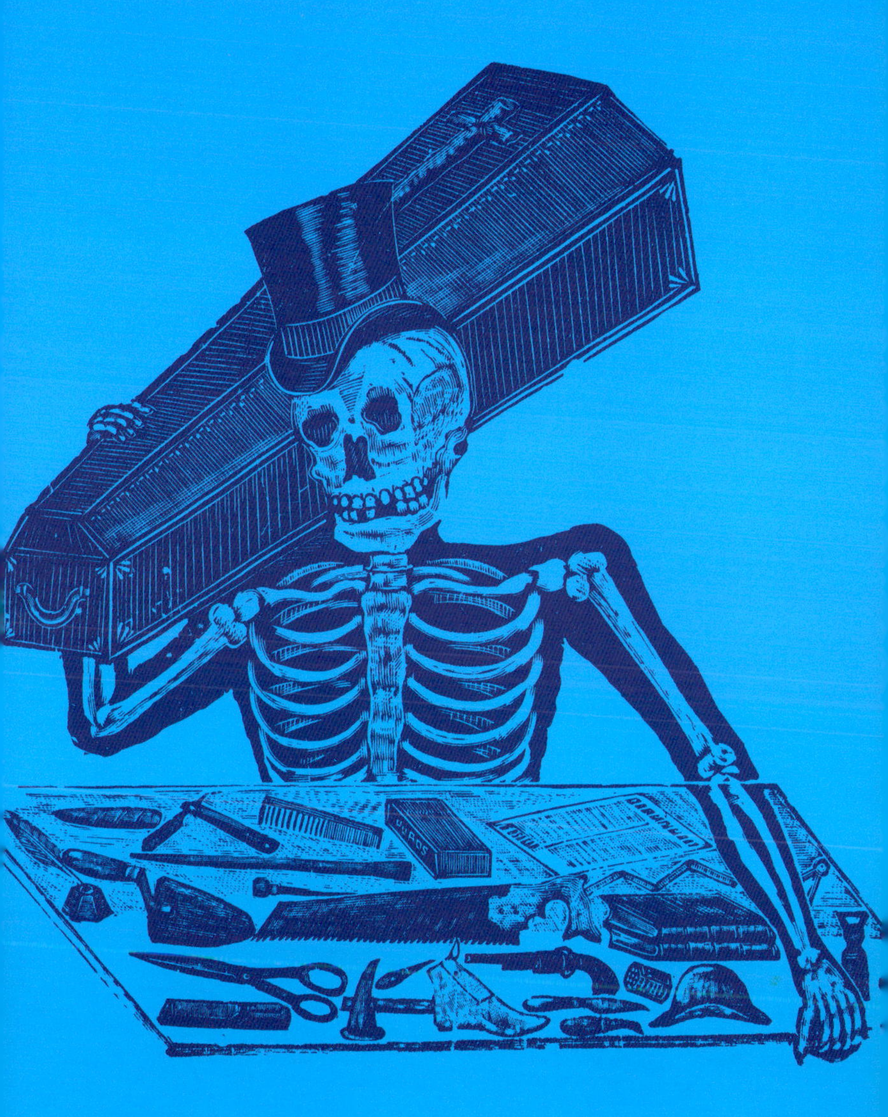

◂◂ Gabriel Galán *La Fiesta*
◂ Artemio Rodríguez *Untitled*
▴ Manuel Manilla *Sin titulo*

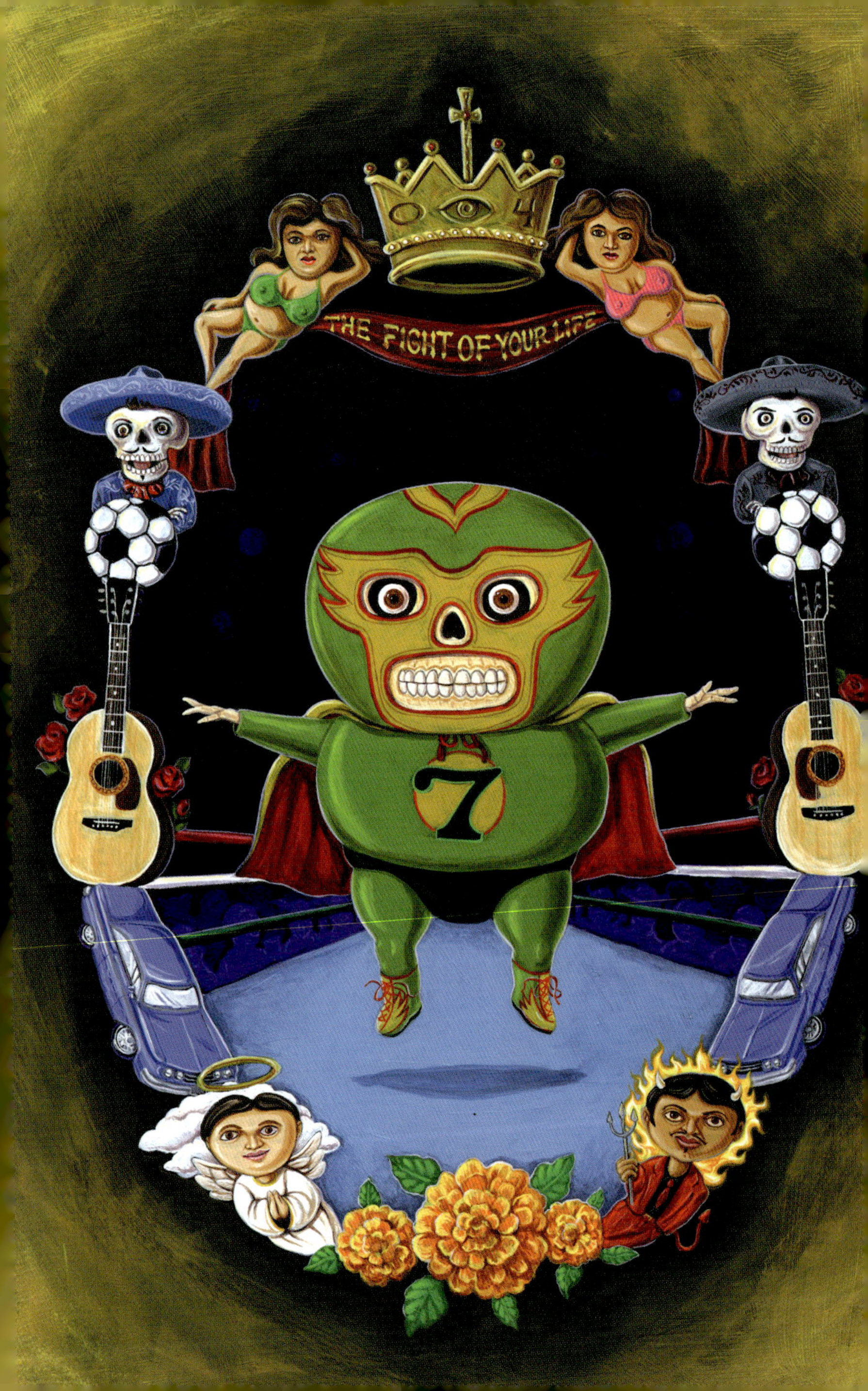
THE FIGHT OF YOUR LIFE
7

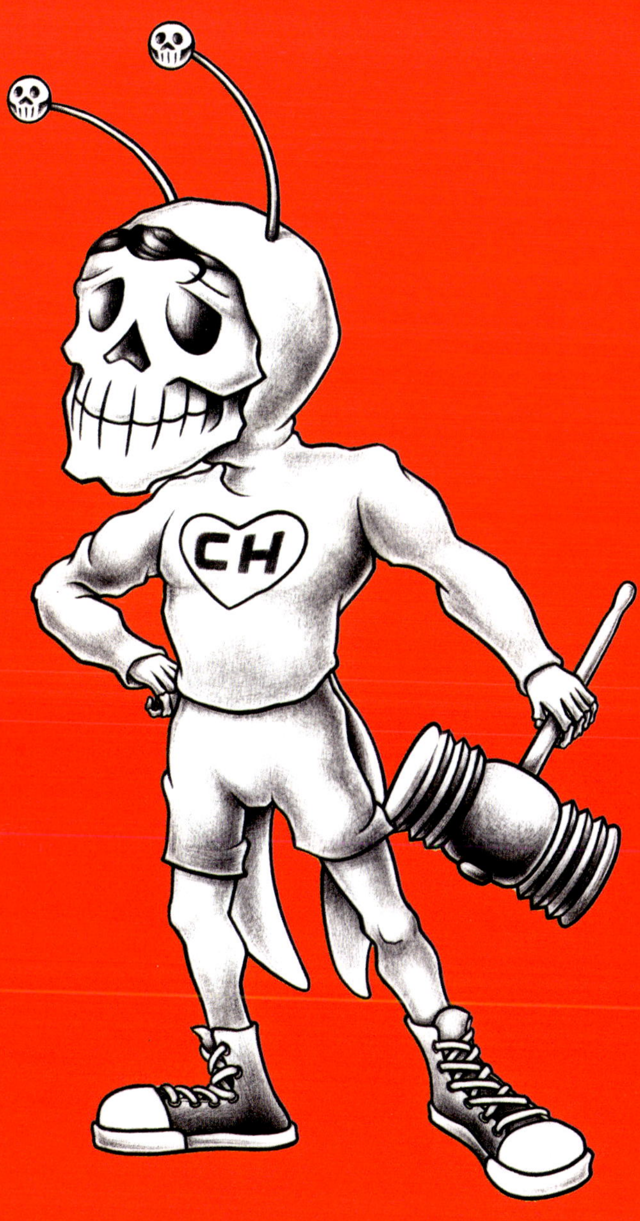

◆ Robert Palacios *The Fight of Your Life*
◆ Mario Votán *Chapulín Colorado*

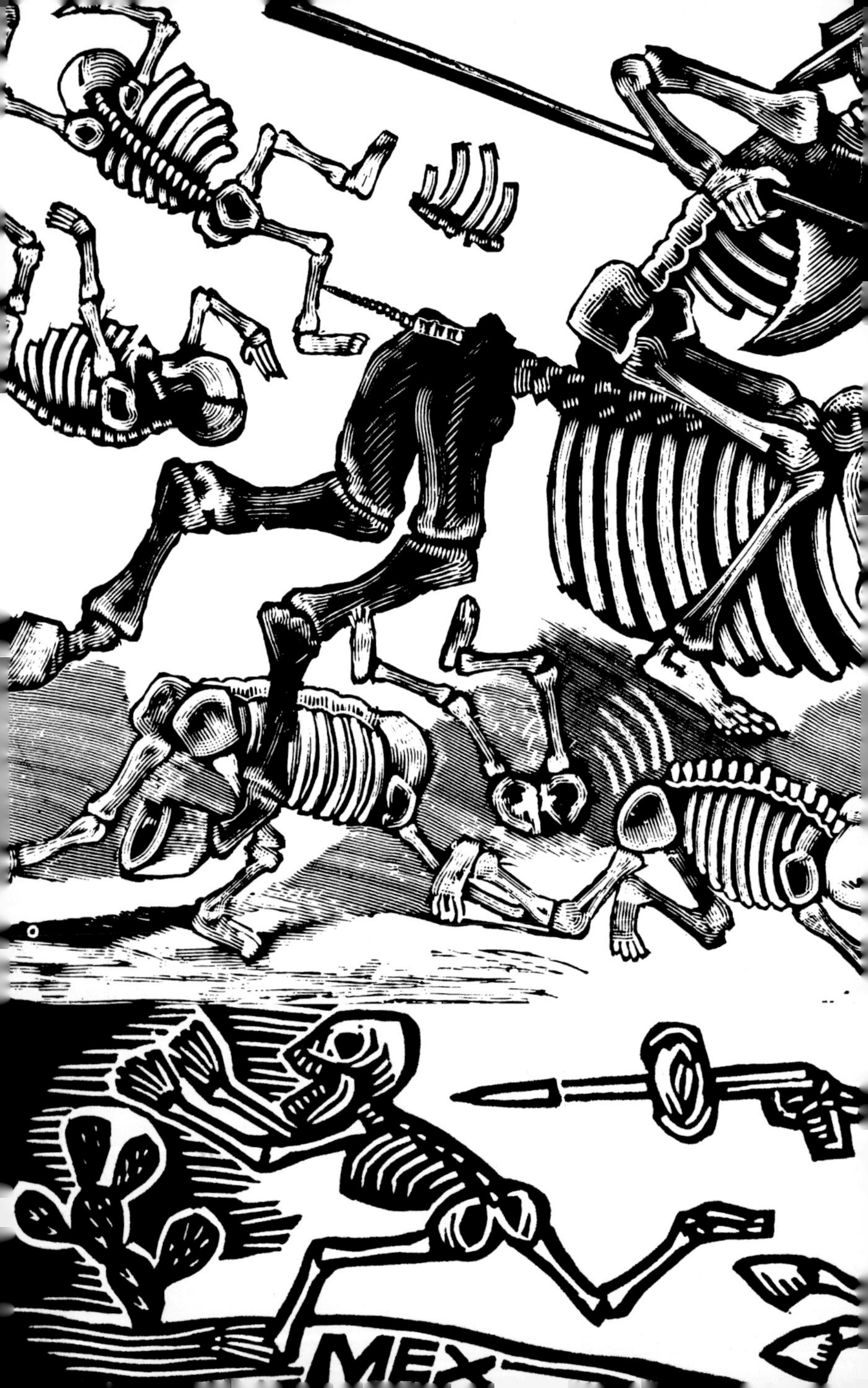
MEX

USA

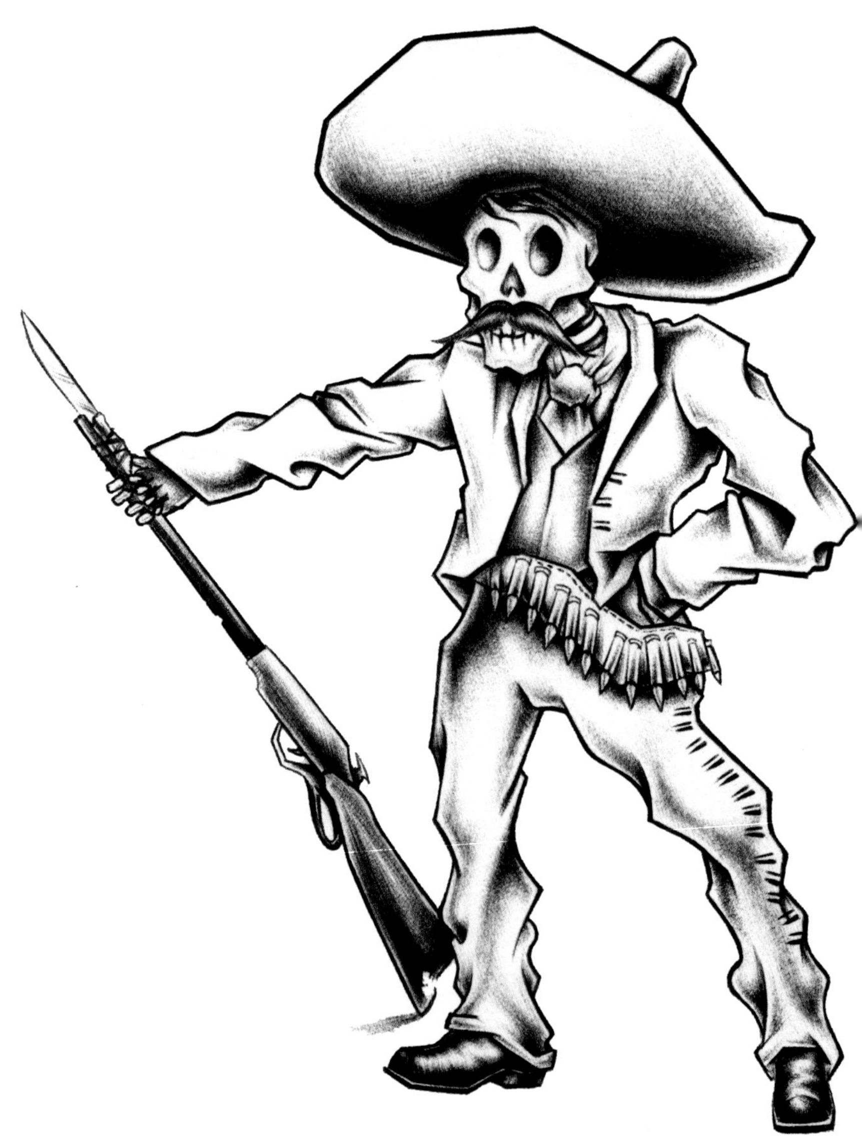

✦✦ José Guadalupe Posada *Calavera de Don Quijote*
✦✦ Artemio Rodríguez *Buenos vecinos*
✦ Mario Votán *¡Viva Zapata!*

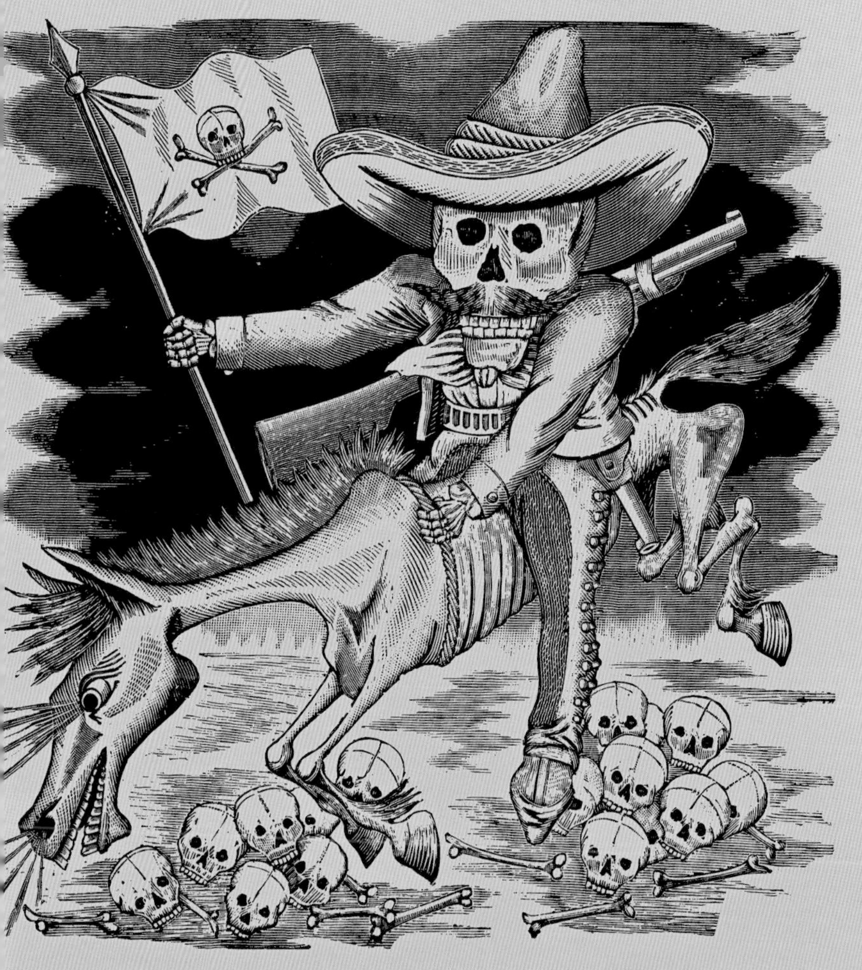

Anonimo *Calavera Zapatista*

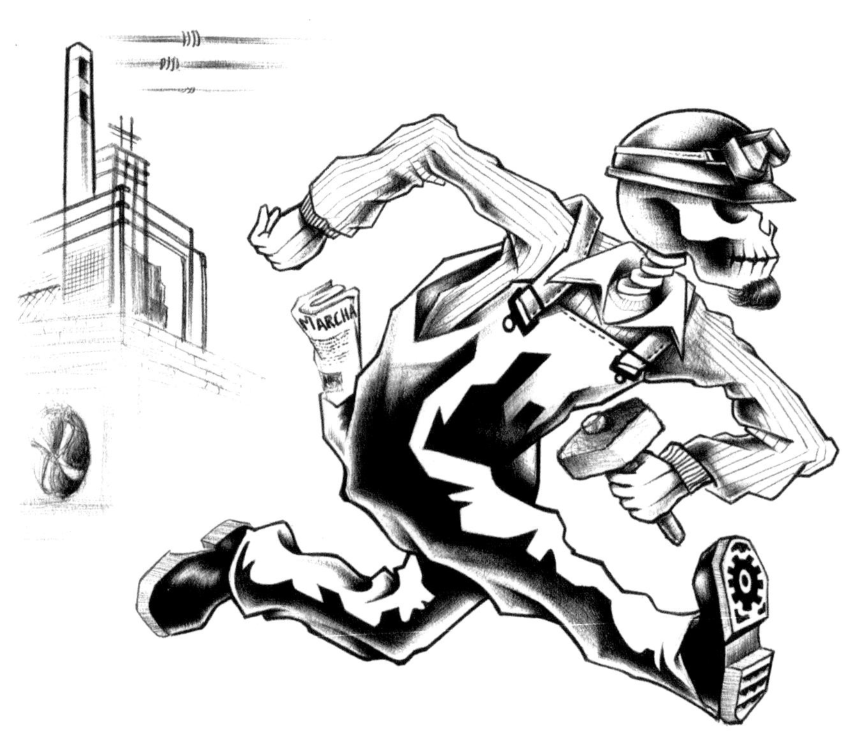

- Mario Votán *Obrero insurgente*
- Anonimo *Calavera Huertista*
- Artemio Rodríguez *Galloping Death*

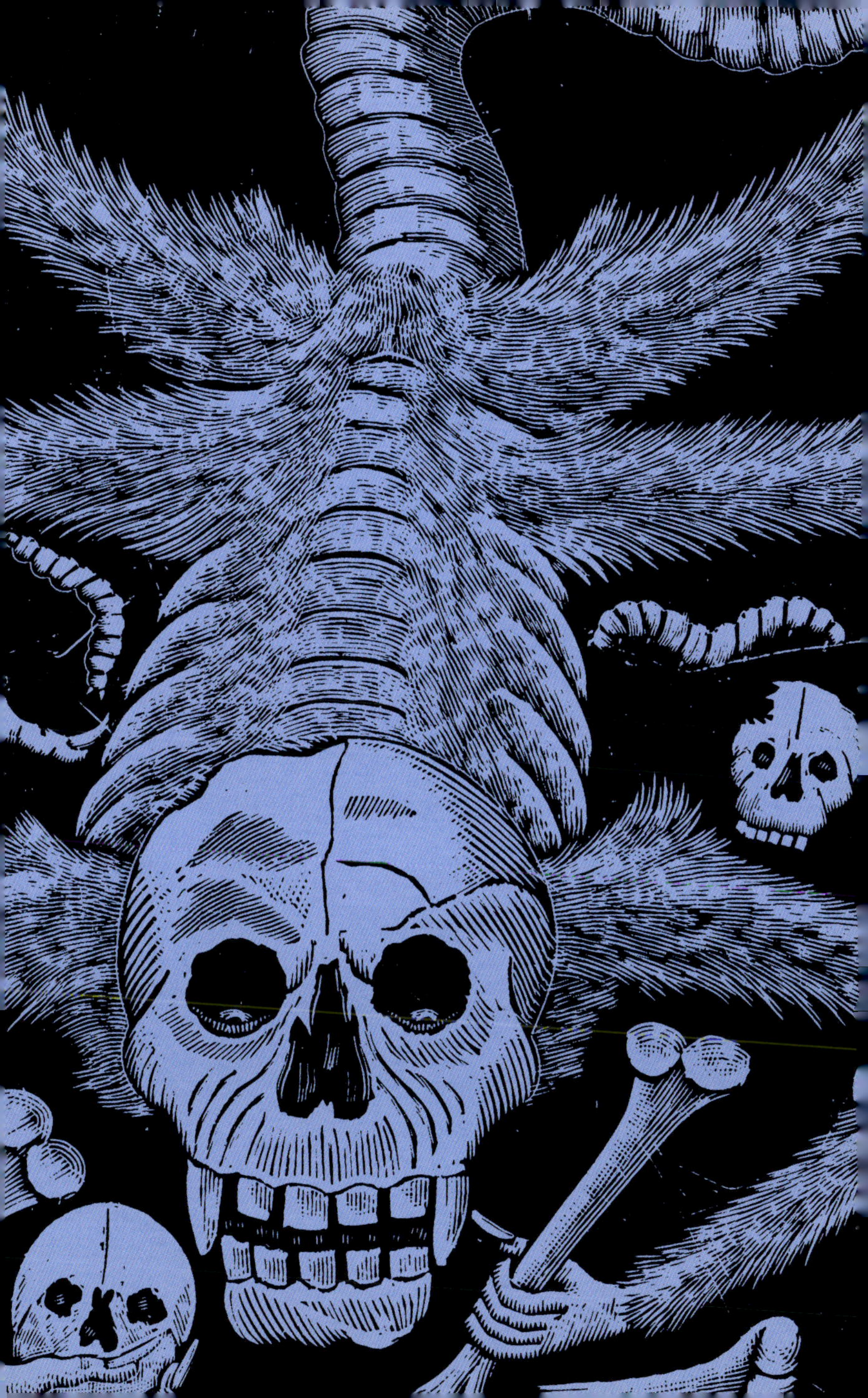

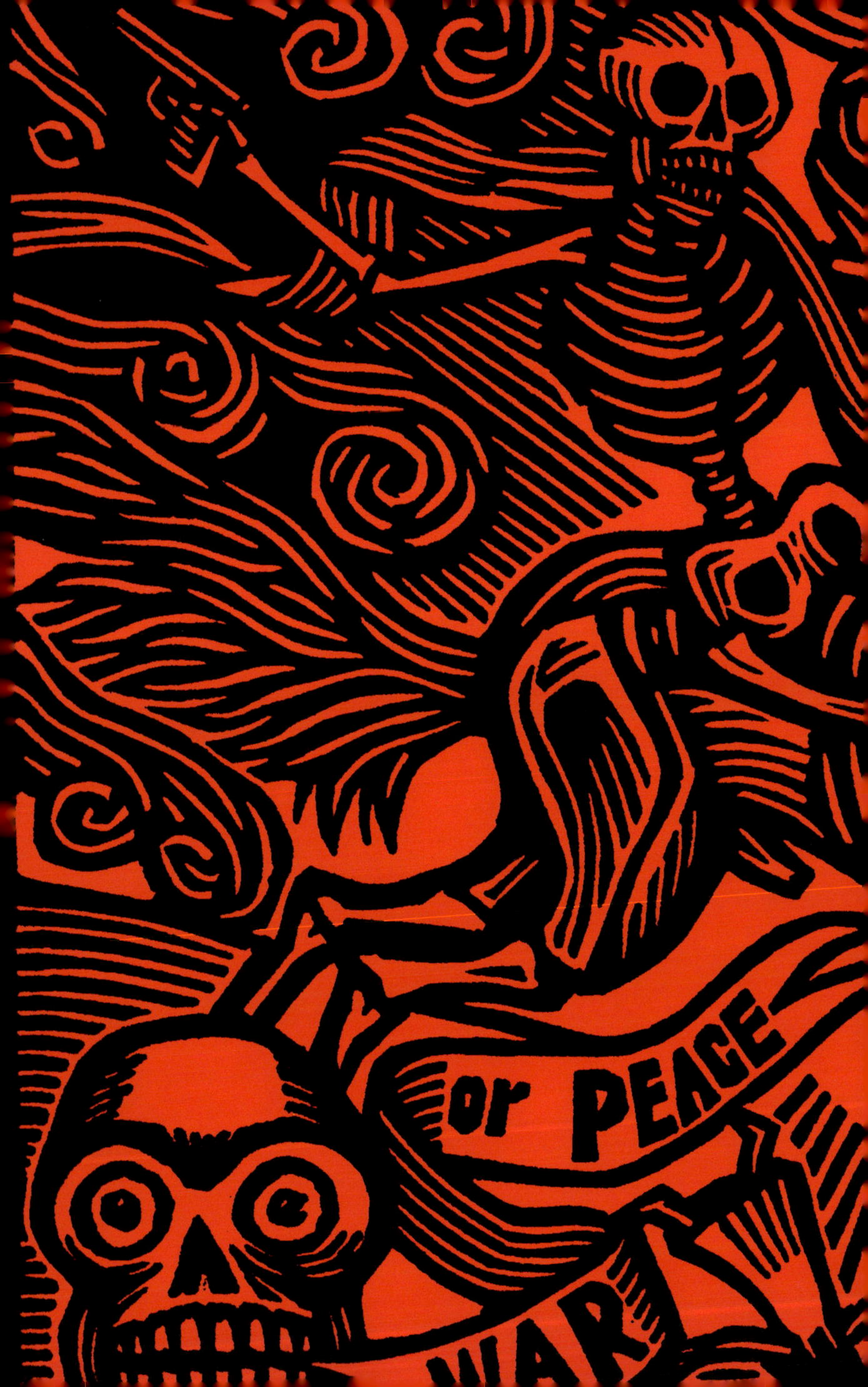
or PEACE
WAR

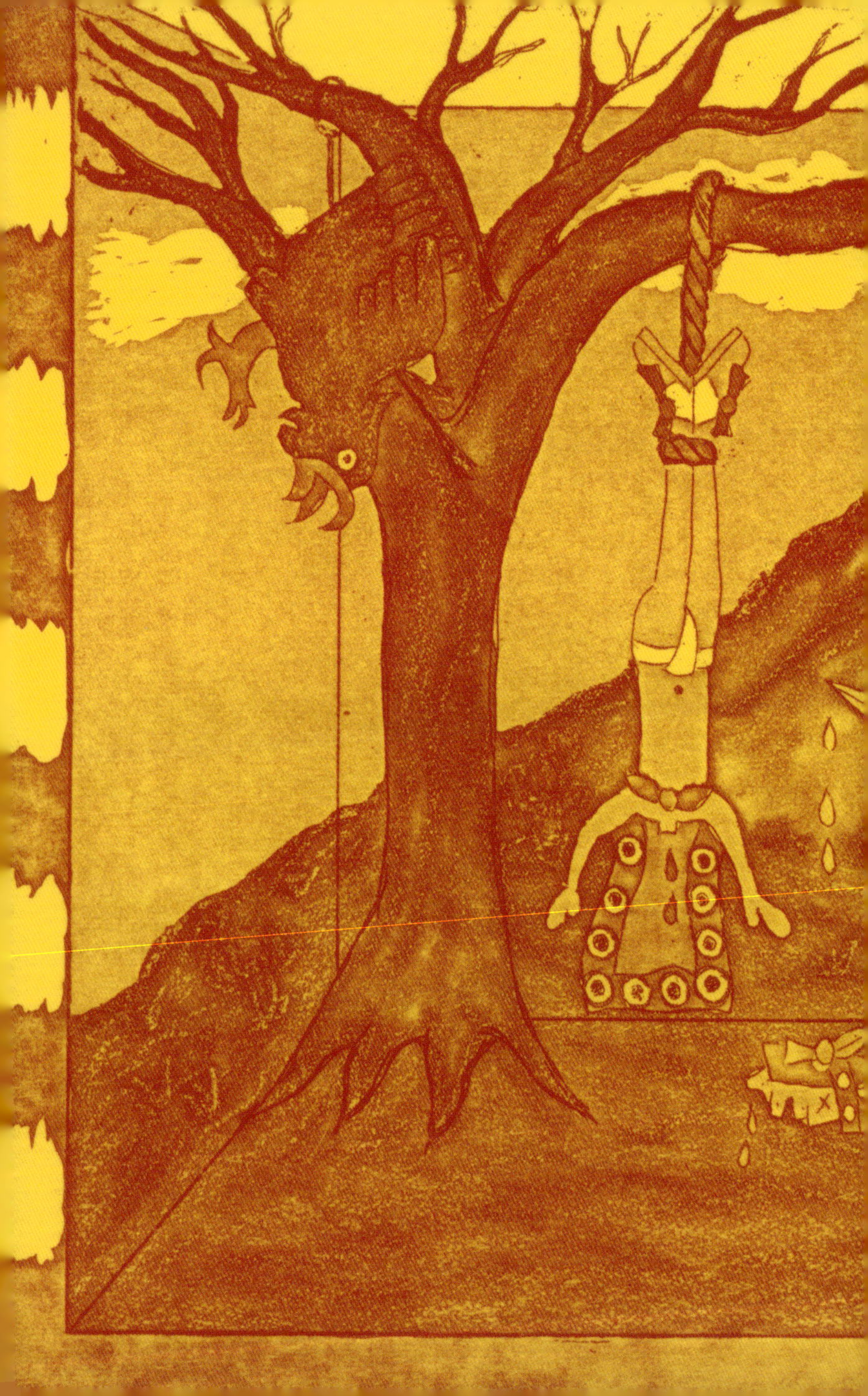

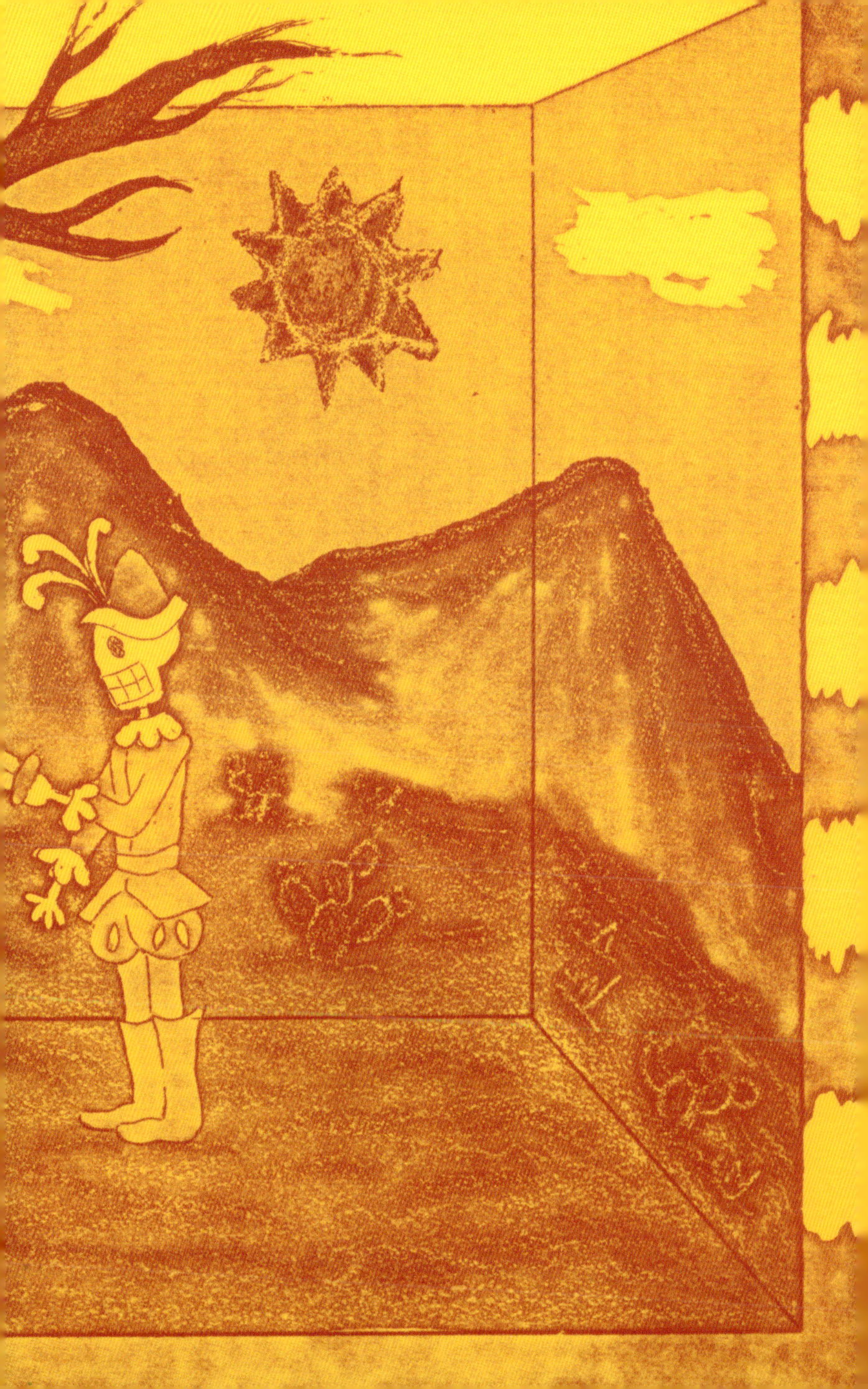

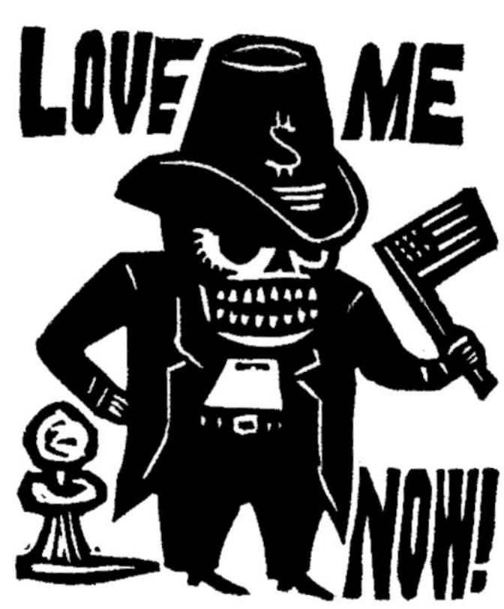

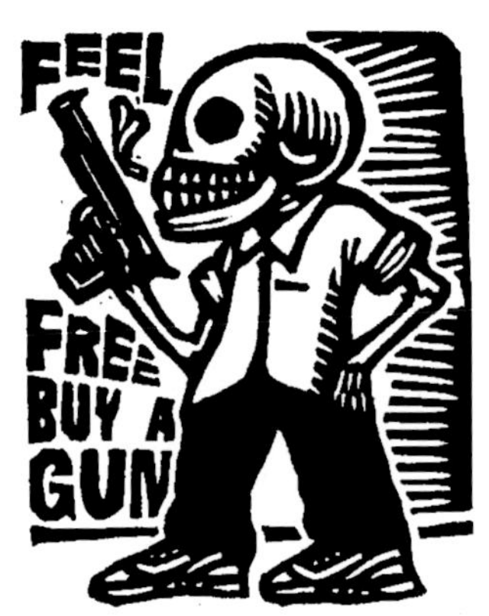

◆◆ Michiko *La caída*
◆ Artemio Rodríguez *Love Me Now, Feel Free Buy a Gun*
◆ Mario Votán *Huey*

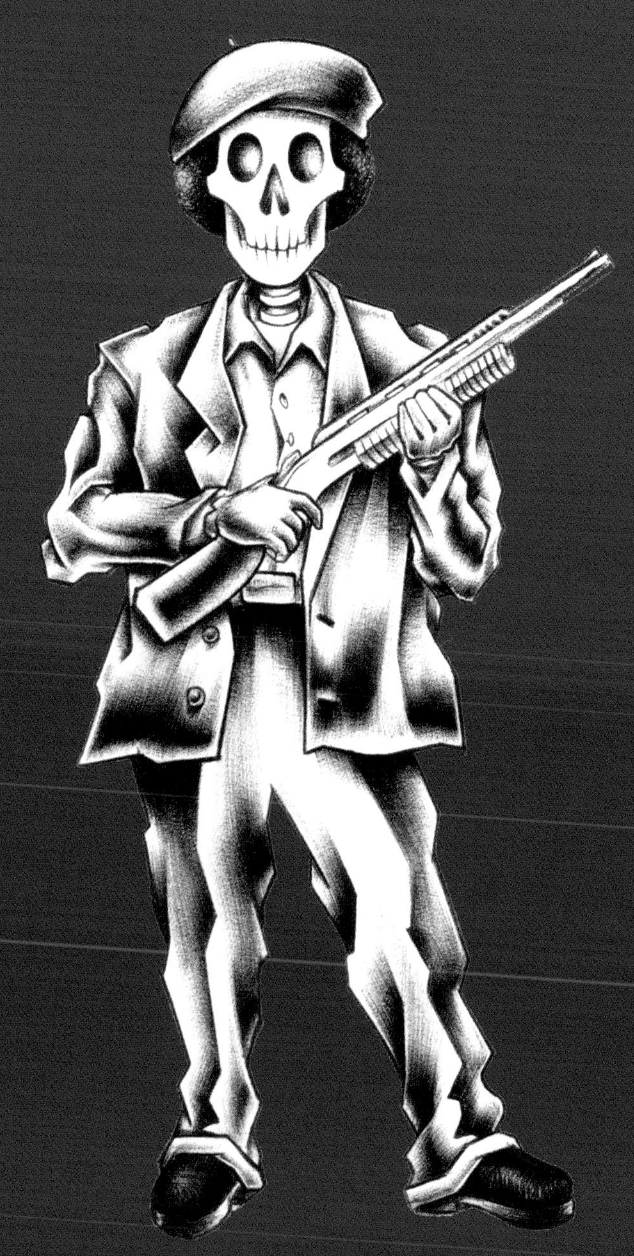

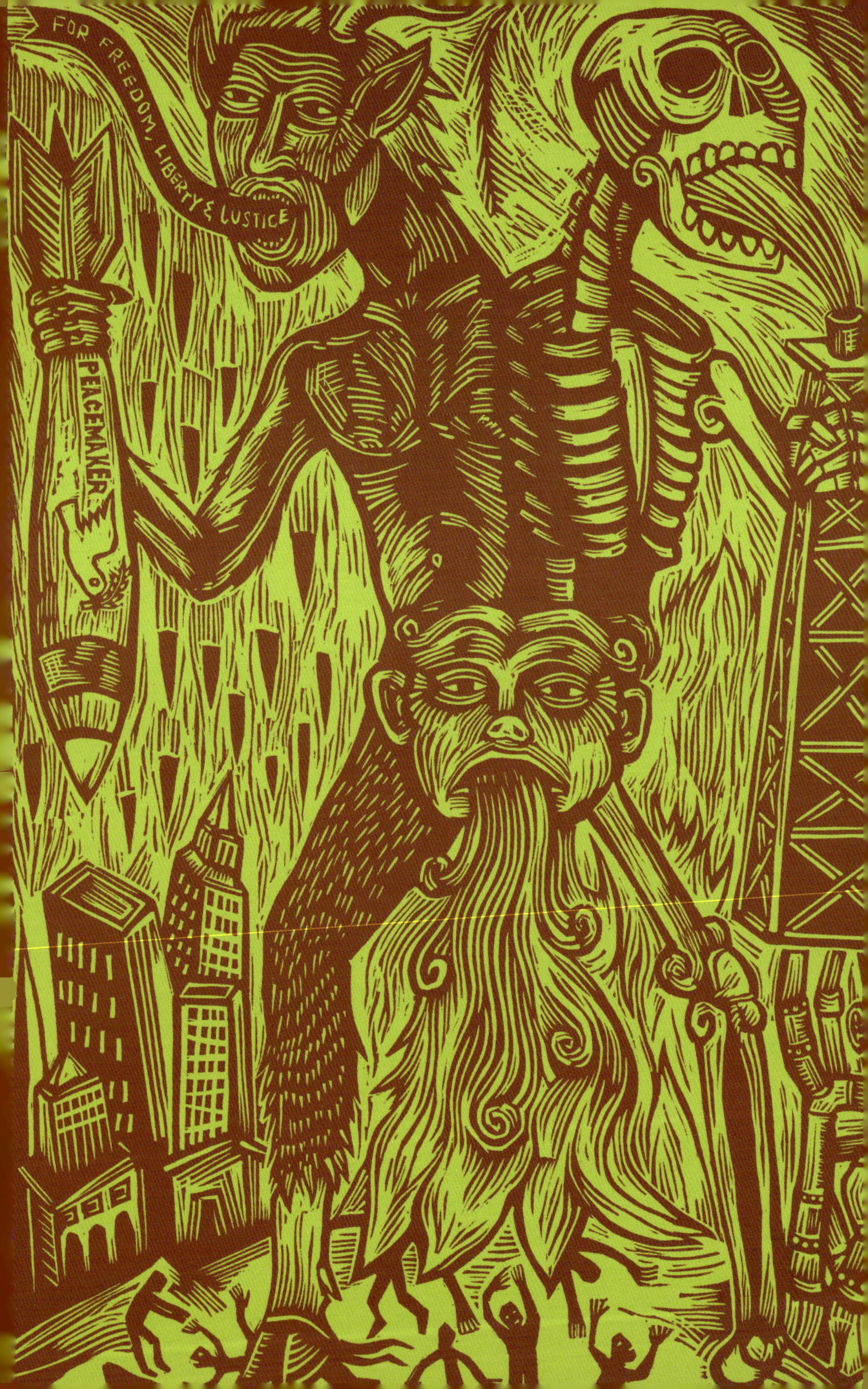
FOR FREEDOM, LIBERTY & LUSTICE
PEACEMAKER

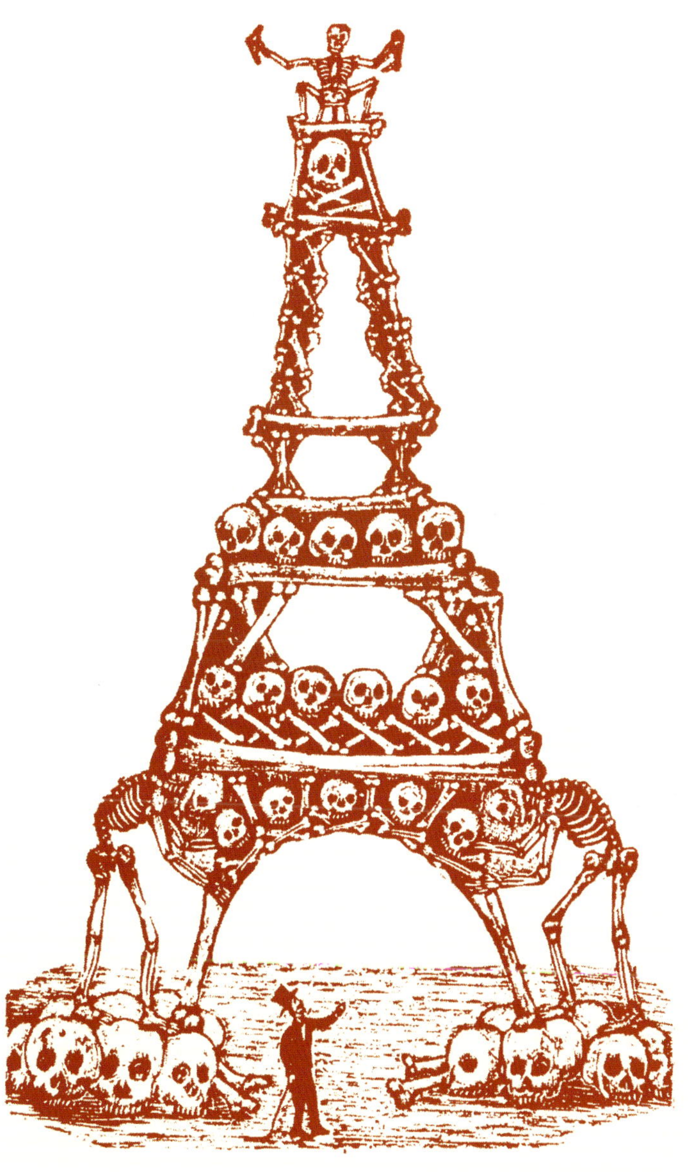

◆ Daniel González *Authority of the Sovereign*
◆ Manuel Manilla *Calavera de la penitenciaria*

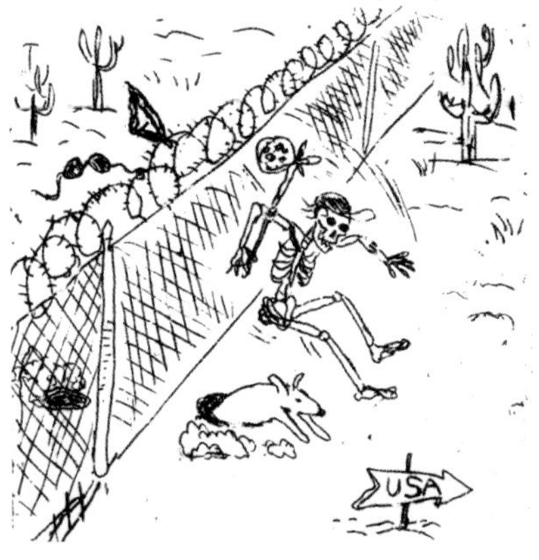

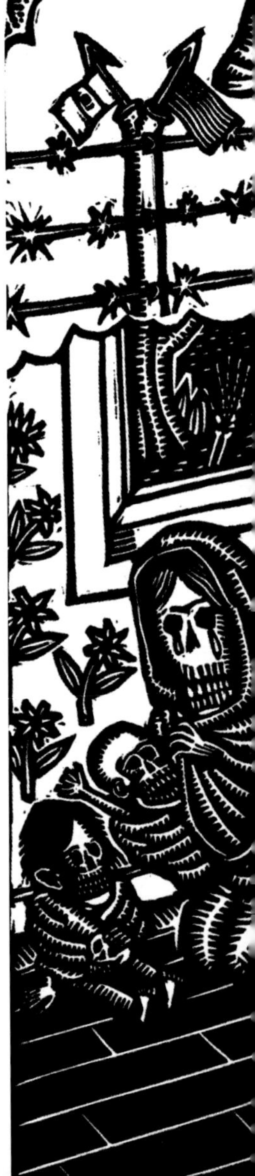

◆ Agustín Barón *from Un día en la vida de los muertos*
◆ Artemio Rodríguez *Somos parte*

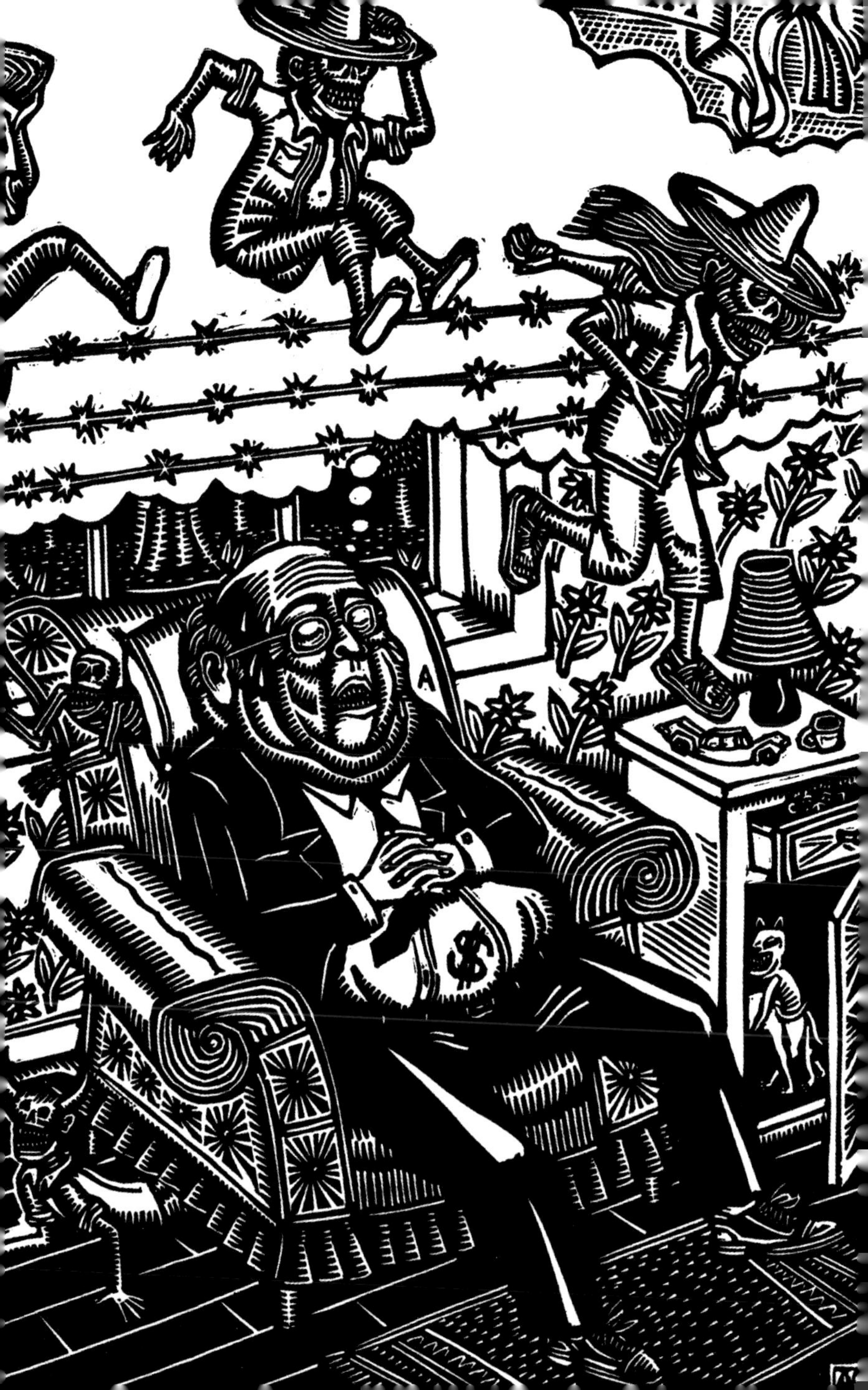

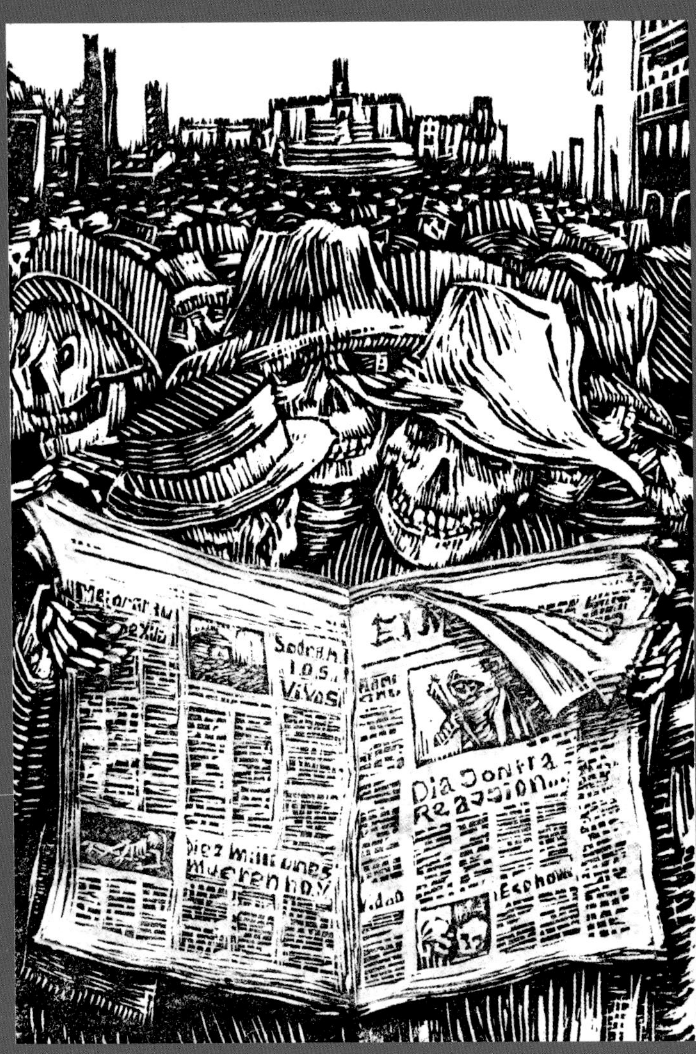

↑ Anna Medina *News Times*
→ Hugo Tecoatl *Sin titulo*

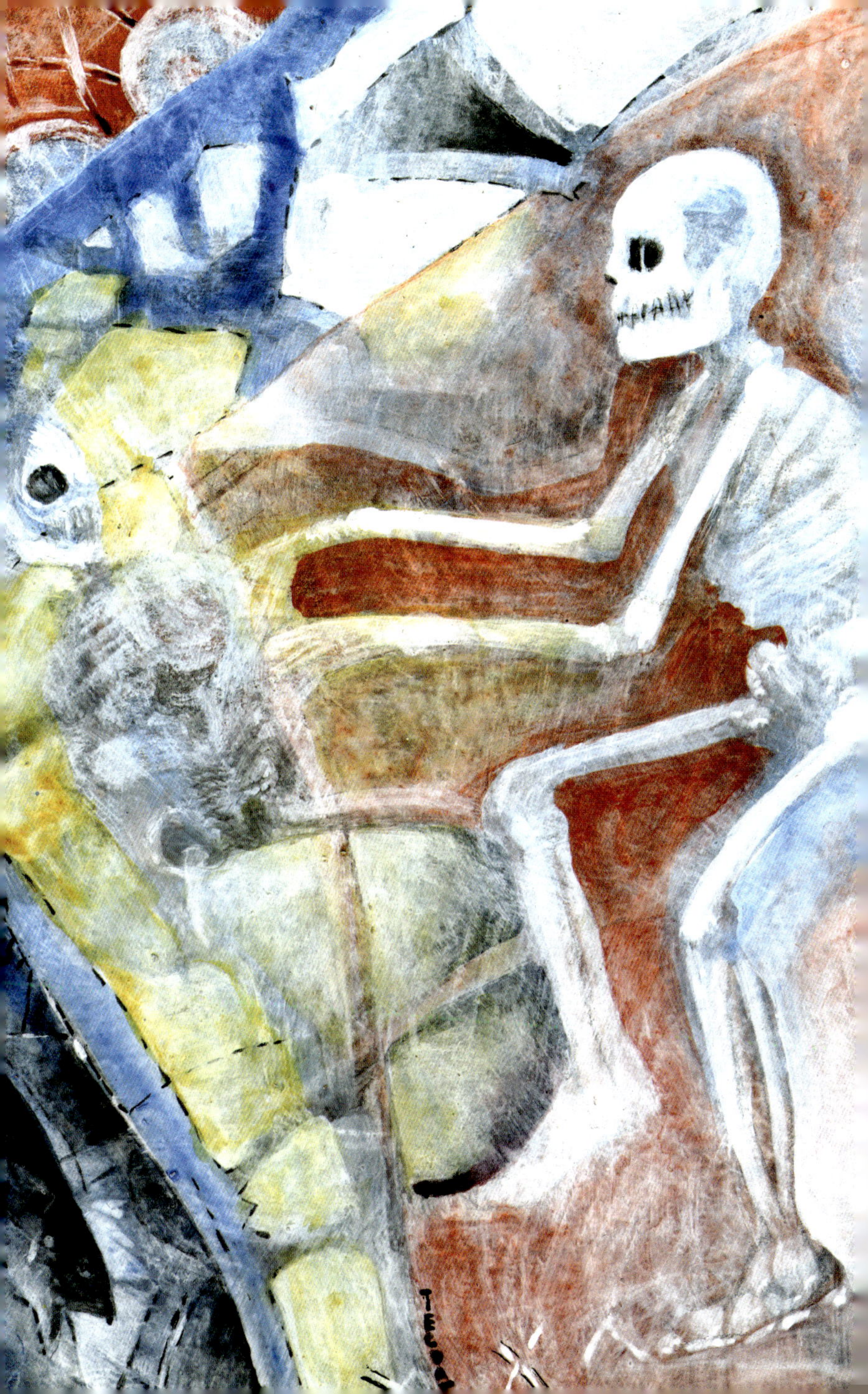

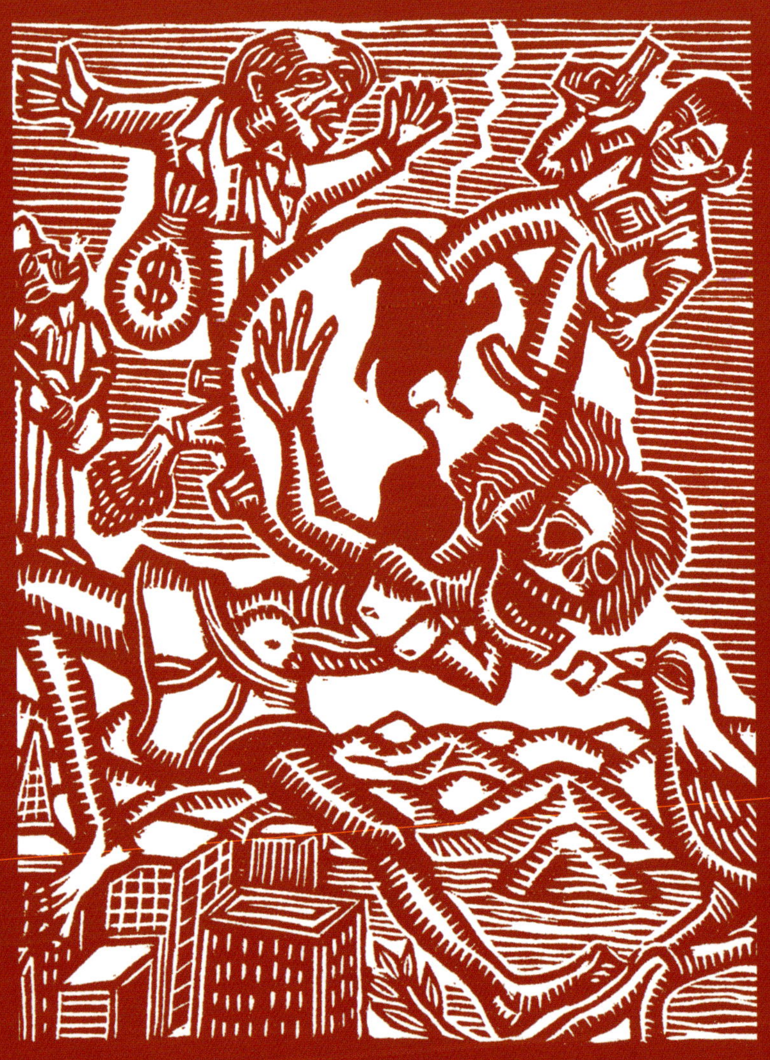

- Artemio Rodríguez *Money and Death*
- Victor Rosas *Canival*

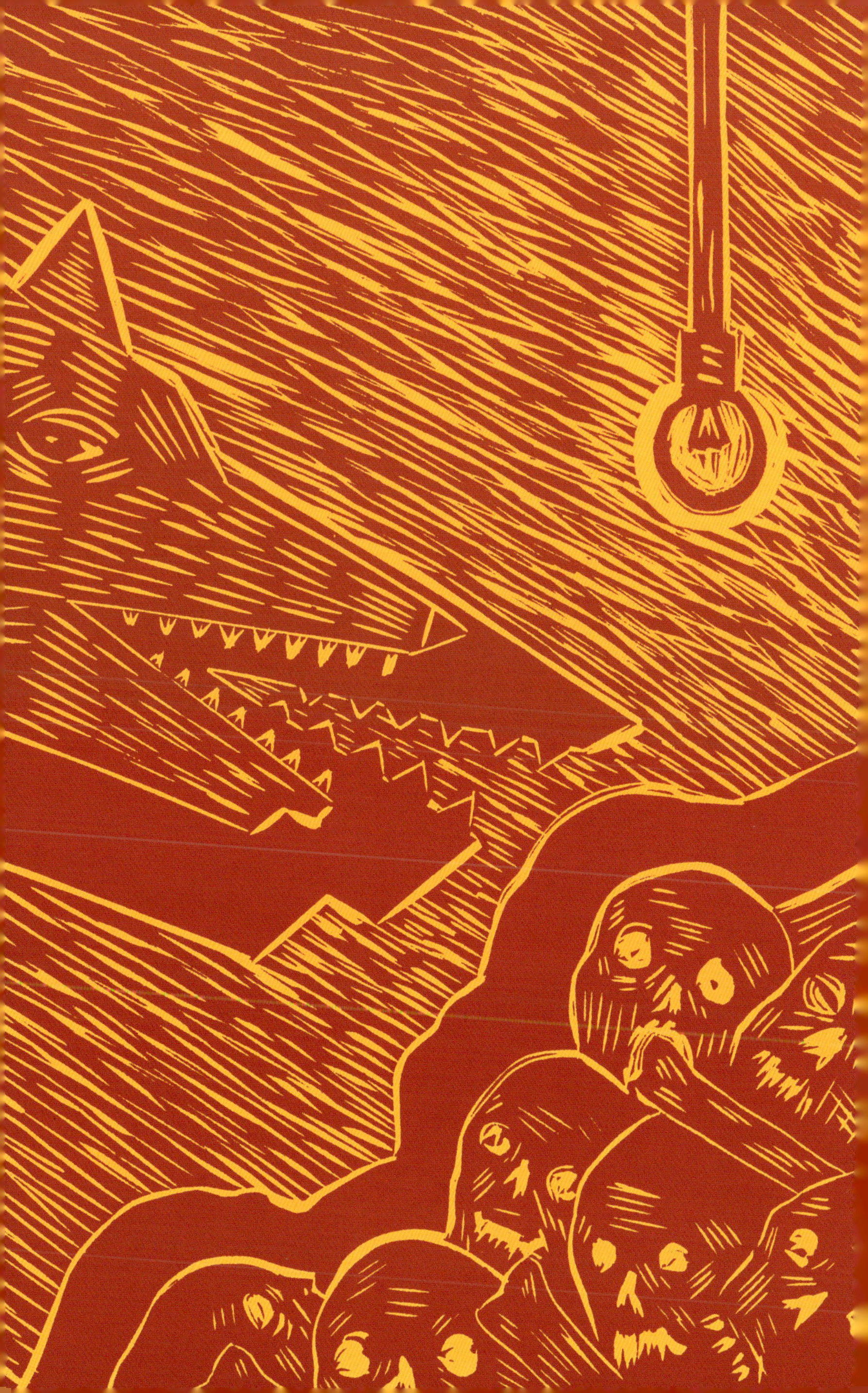

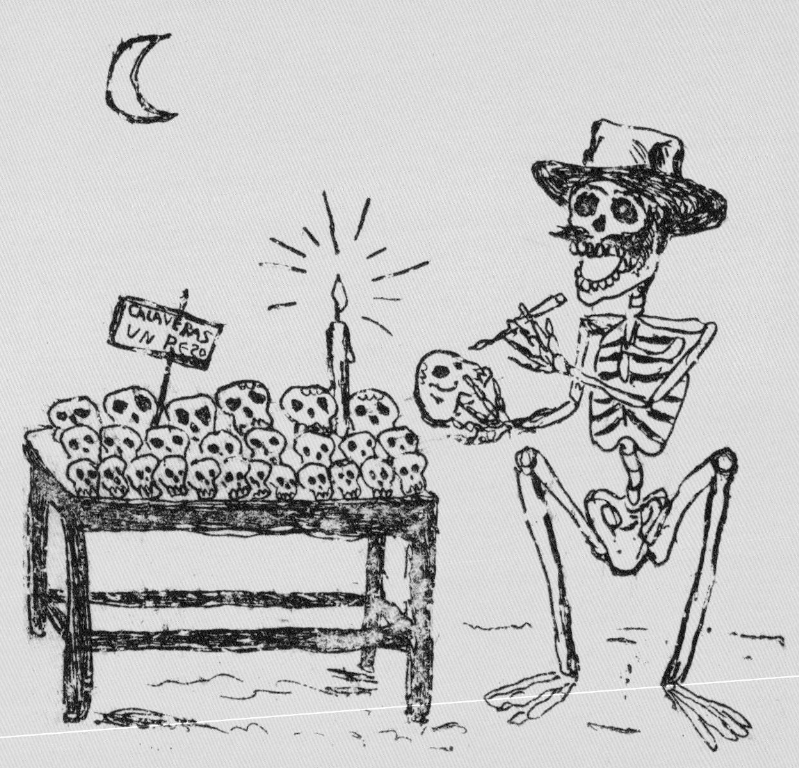

- Agustín Barón *from Un día en la vida de los muertos*
- Alexis Hugo Nutini *Ofrenda a Leora*

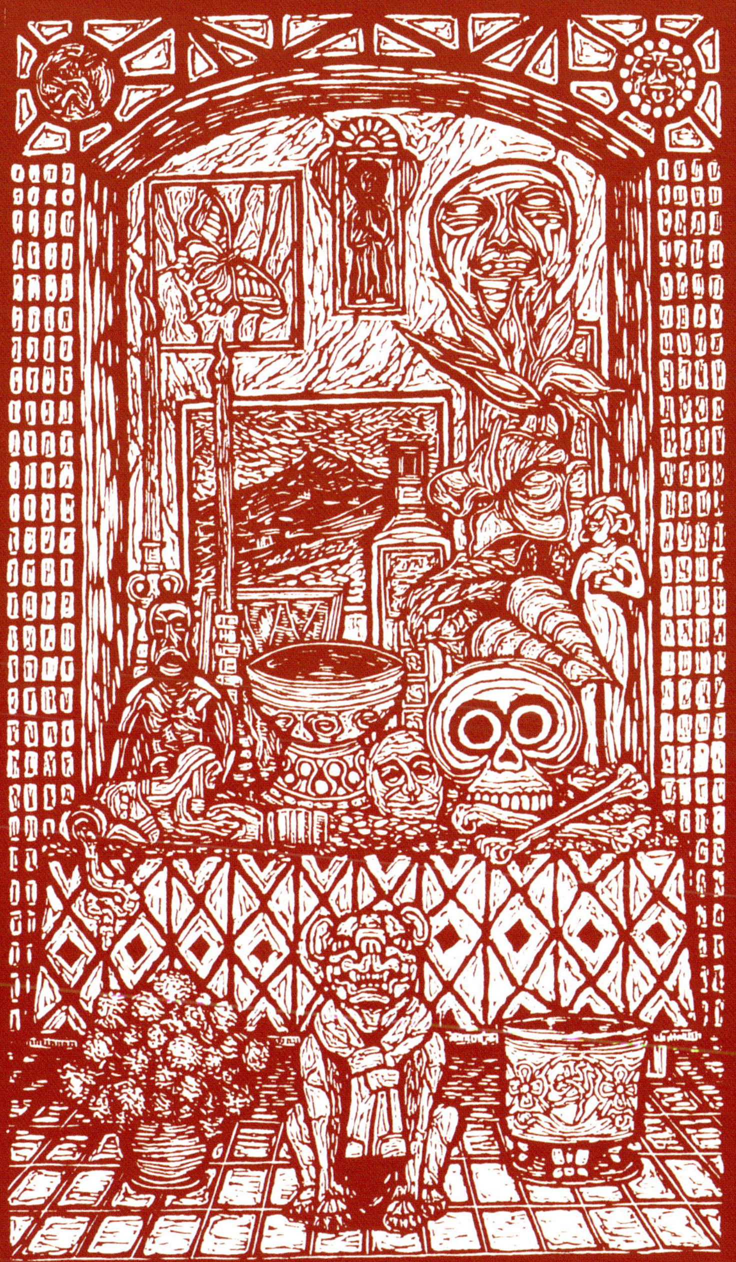

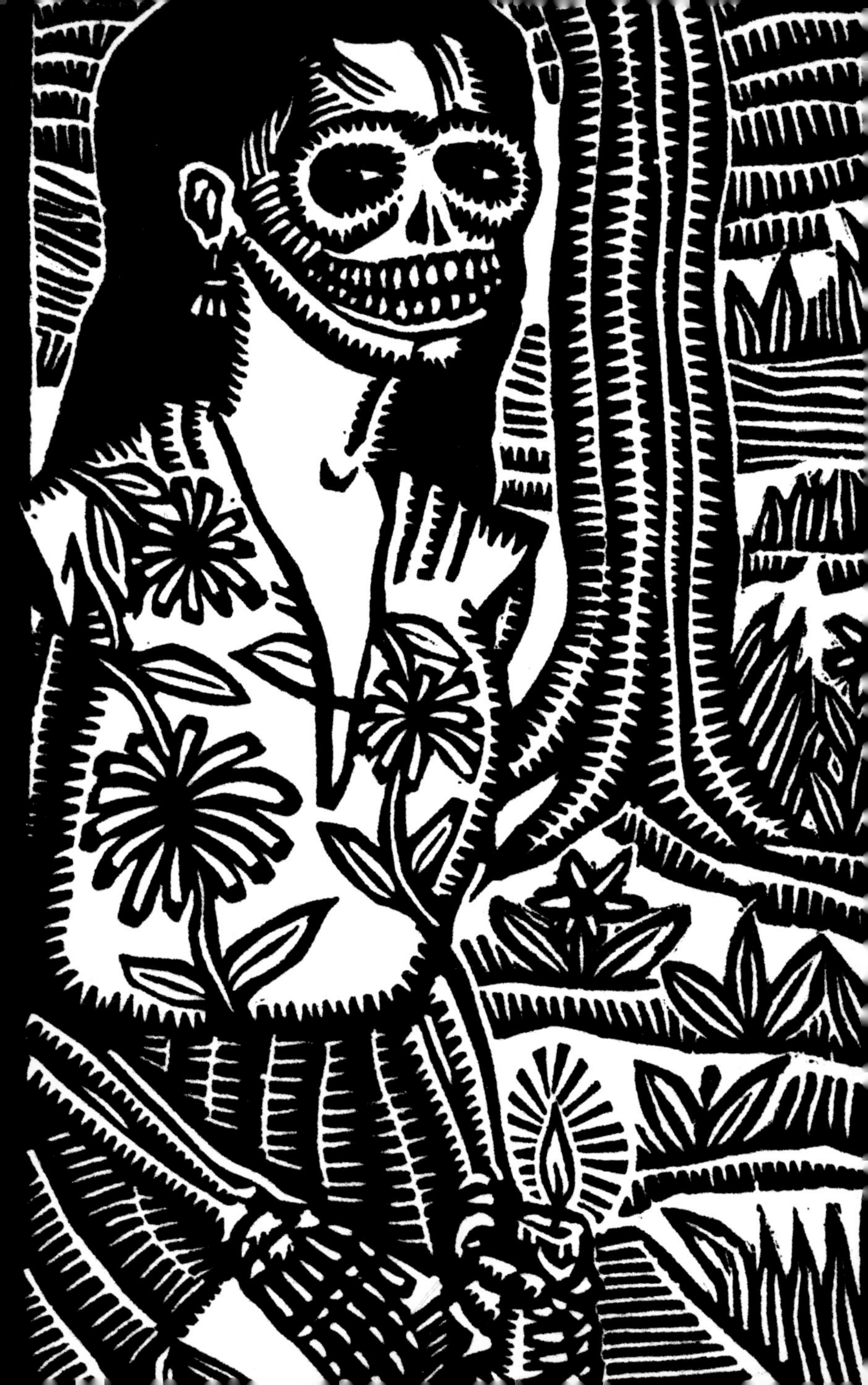

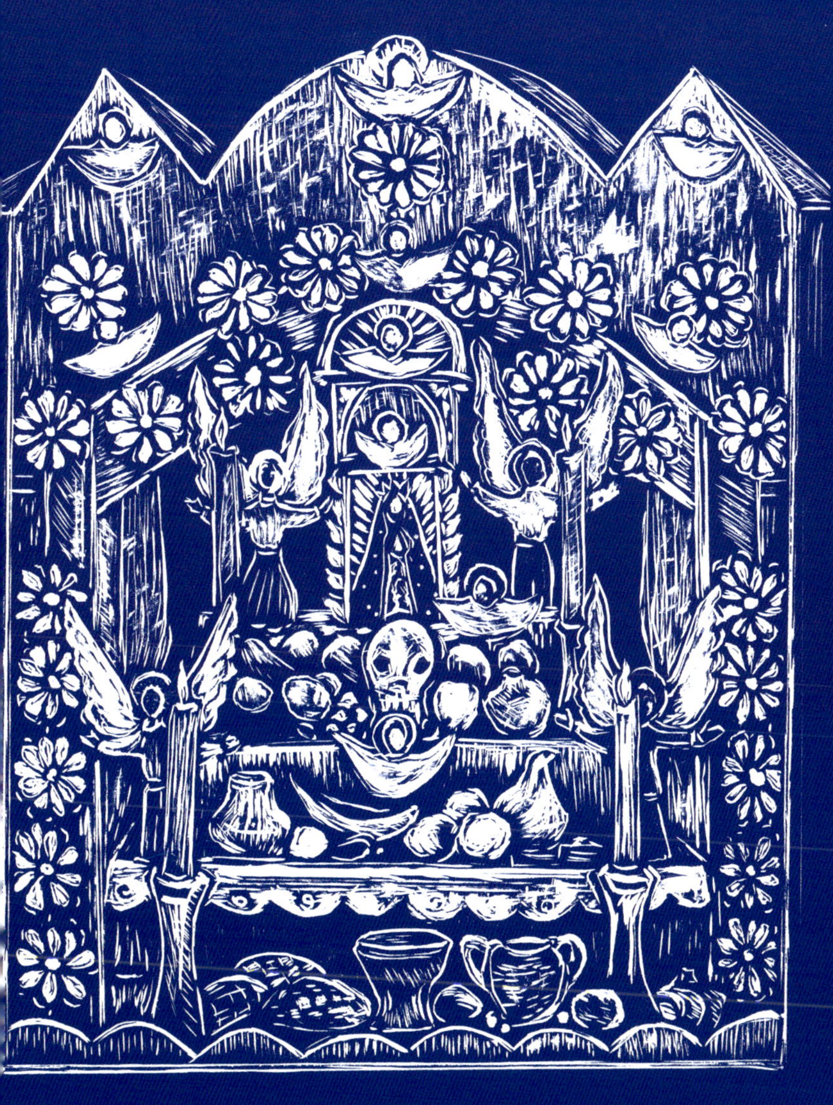

◆ Artemio Rodríguez *from Vive*
◆ Ofelia Esparza *Nicho*

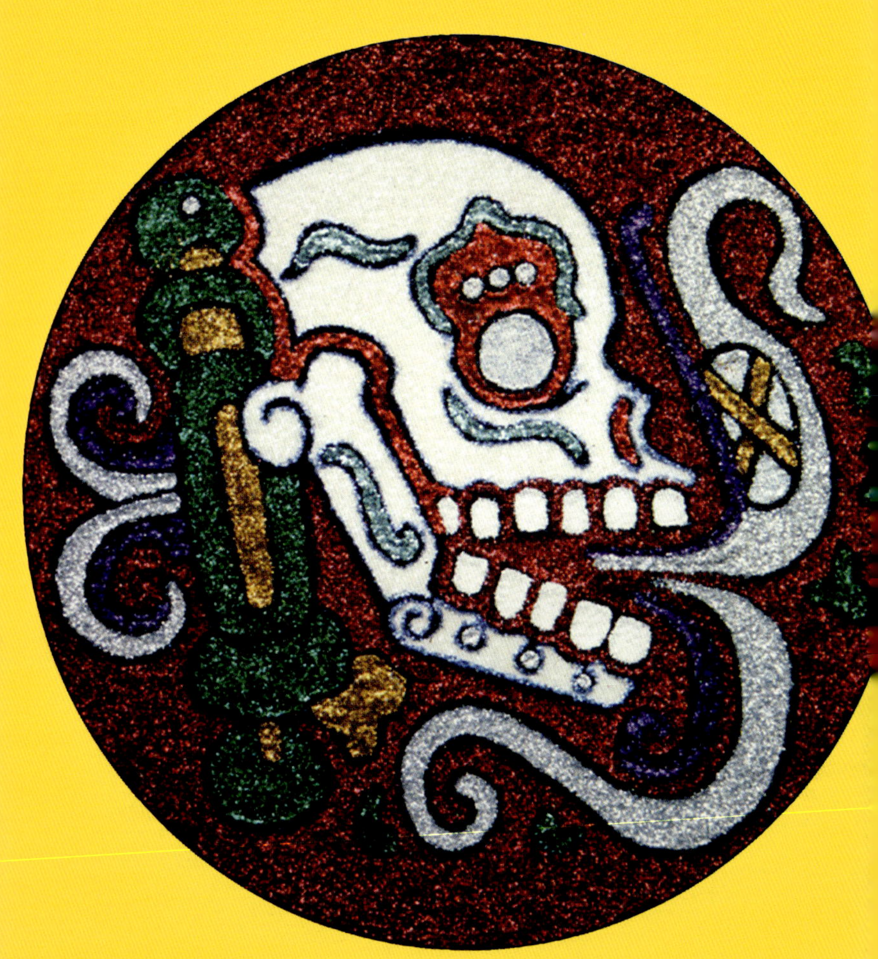

Tlizsa Jaurique *Tezcatlipoca*

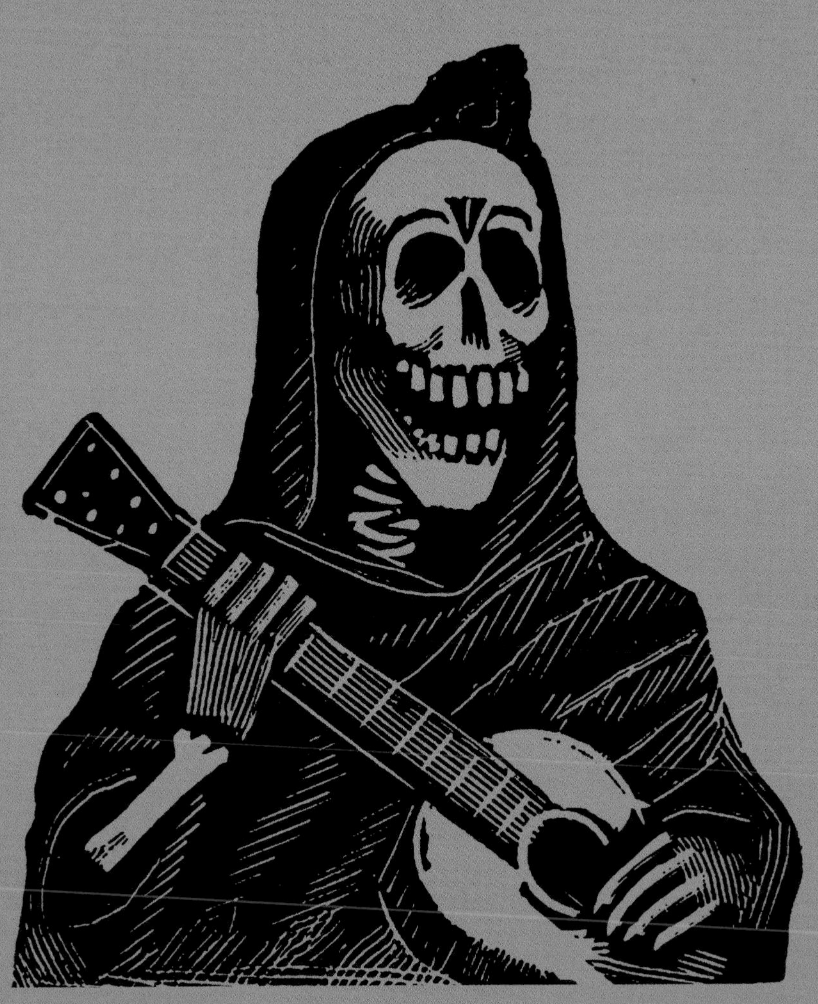

José Guadalupe Posada *Del gran panteón amoroso*

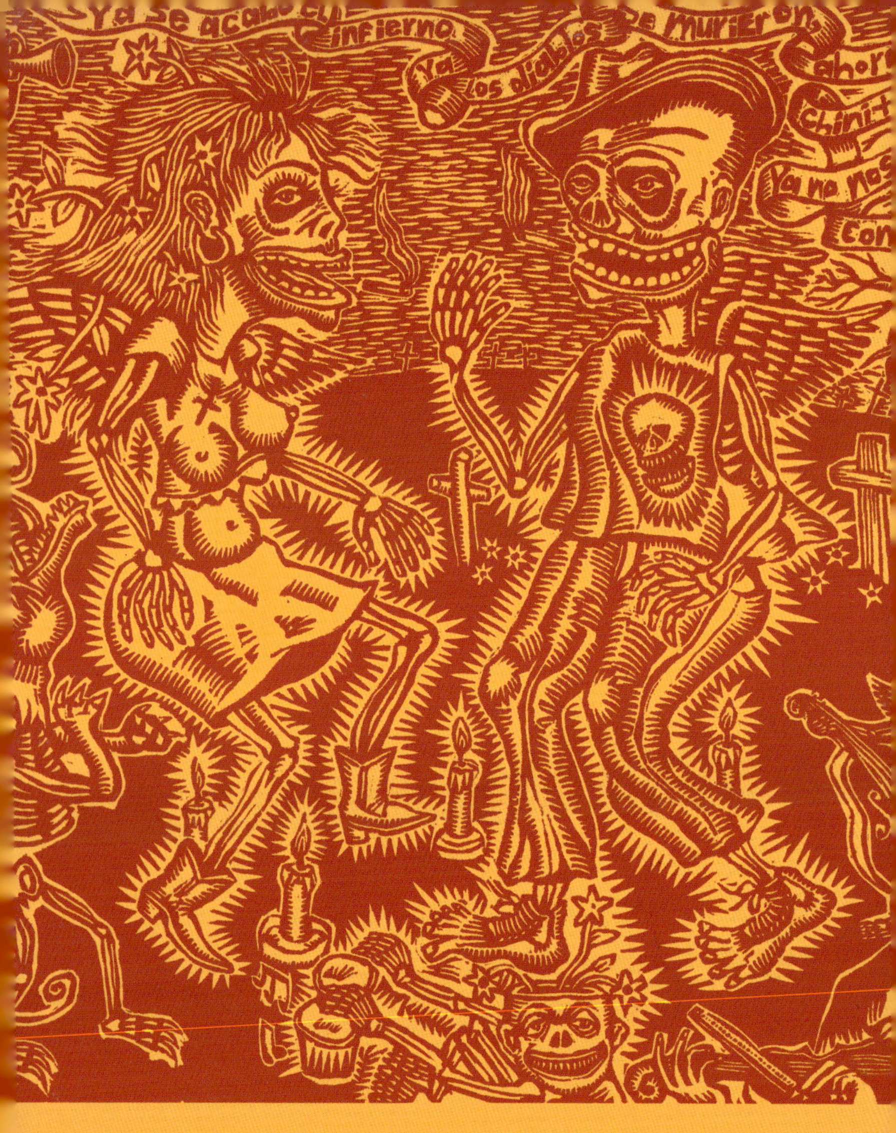

Artemio Rodríguez *La quebradita*

THE END

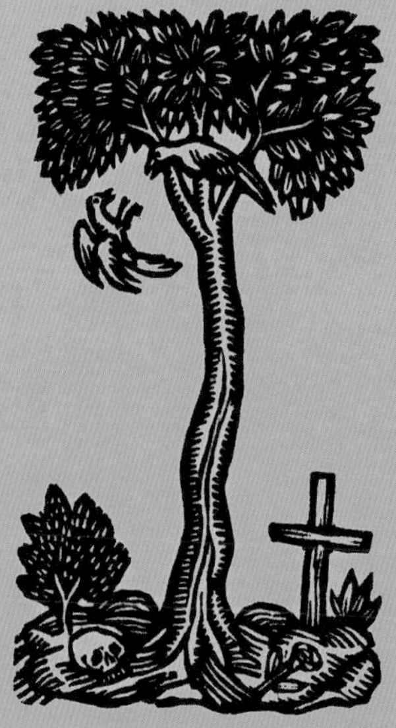

FIN

Artemio Rodríguez *from Vive*

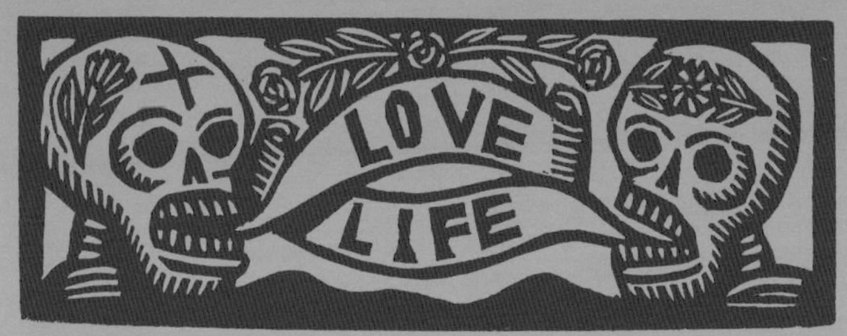

Artemio Rodríguez *Love life*